Major Criminological Theories:
Concepts and Measurement

Liqun Cao

Foreword by Francis T. Cullen

WADSWORTH

™

THOMSON LEARNING

Wadsworth/Thomson Learning
10 Davis Drive
Belmont, CA 94002-3098
USA

For information about our products, contact us:
Thomson Learning Academic Resource Center
1-800-423-0563
http://www.wadsworth.com

International Headquarters
Thomson Learning
International Division
290 Harbor Drive, 2nd Floor
Stamford, CT 06902-7477
USA

UK/Europe/Middle East/South Africa
Thomson Learning
Berkshire House
168-173 High Holborn
London WCIV 7AA

Asia
Thomson Learning
60 Albert Street, #15-01
Albert Complex
Singapore 189969

Canada
Nelson Thomson Learning
1120 Birchmount Road
Toronto, Ontario MIK 5G4
Canada
United Kingdom

ISBN 0-534-19631-4

The Adaptable Courseware Program consists of products and additions to existing Wadsworth Group prod
that are produced from camera-ready copy. Peer review, class testing, and accuracy are primarily the
responsibility of the author(s).

This book is dedicated to

Paula Dubeck and Francis T. Cullen,

and to

Department of Sociology and Division of Criminal Justice,

for their intellectual nurture during my wondering years

at the University of Cincinnati and

for their friendship afterwards.

Contents

Tables

Figures

Foreword

Francis T. Cullen
University of Cincinnati

Theory lies at the core of criminology. What counts as a criminological theory will differ according to what standards one uses, but in general the term refers to a set of interrelated propositions that explain why crime is more likely to occur in certain individuals or in certain areas and not others. Theory is important, therefore, because it predicts which factors are, and are not, implicated in the causation of crime. Similar to looking into a powerful telescope, a theory helps us to see parts of reality that heretofore were obscured from view. As the world is suddenly illuminated, we can understand in fresh ways why crime occurs. We also can begin to create policies and practices that might target for reform these criminogenic features of our world.

About two decades ago, commentators were decrying the lack of innovative thinking about crime. The criminological imagination was said to be in the doldrums. Over the intervening years, however, scholars have invented new theories and have breathed life into perspectives that had been relegated to the criminological dustbin. At present, the field has an array of theories that hope to capture our attention and allegiance. A special contribution of Professor Cao s volume is that he provides succinct but insightful accounts of the major criminological theories prevailing today.

This richness in criminological theorizing is both a blessing to be cherished and a burden to be shouldered. The wealth of theorizing is to be welcomed because it means that we have multiple visions on what might lead to criminal involvement. We are not rigidly confined to a single paradigm that closes off other, potentially more enlightening, ways of envisioning the complex reality underlying criminality. However, the burden of being presented with so many visions of reality of so many major theories is that they are not all equally illuminating. Some are likely to be substantially correct; some are likely to have value up to a point; and some are likely to be misguided.

How, then, are we to decide which vision or theory to embrace? Oftentimes, students of crime endorse a theory because it resonates with some preexisting belief that they adopted or experience that they have endured. A theory just seems correct. It strikes the person as merely a matter of commonsense that one theoretical perspective is correct while another lacks merit. The difficulty, however, is that one person s commonsense is another person s nonsense. Thus, someone raised in an inner-city slum where gangs are rampant might pledge allegiance to a theory that attributes crime to exposure to delinquent peers. In contrast, someone raised in a family where a parent was in law enforcement and where individual responsibility was stressed might see crime as a choice made by people who think that crime pays and that punishment can be avoided.

When such a clash of commonsense occurs, the challenge is to de cipher which theory of the reality of crime should be endorsed or, in the least, given more weight. Many textbooks on criminological theory will bring readers to this point, and then tell them that scientific research studies should be relied upon to decide the empirical status of competing perspectives. The genius of Professor Cao s *Major Criminological Theories* is that it relays the rest of the story. It not only introduces readers to the scientific method but also and more noteworthy shows specifically how key concepts in each theoretical tradition are measured. Students thus are given the rare opportunity to glimpse the inner workings of science to see how scholars have innovatively developed ways of assessing the central components of competing theories.

Through this strategy, Professor Cao teaches valuable lessons about both the content and science of criminological theory. For enterprising students whether alone or in collaboration he provides methodological information that might be used to design their own studies! For all of us, he reminds us that in learning about criminological theory, it is not enough to know the theories. Instead, to be culturally literate in criminology it is equally important to be well-versed in the ways in which scholars have, with diligence and considerable intellect, devised methods to put our theories including those we like and dislike to empirical test.

Indeed, I have been taught much by studying this fascinating book. In a way, I am envious that you are just embarking on your own excursion through *Major Criminological Theories*. It will be an exciting adventure in which Professor Cao, much as a tour guide, leads you across the complicated but compelling landscape of theoretical criminology. By the trip s end, you will know the ins and outs the concepts and measurement of criminological theory. You will have learned much and be prepared to move onward in your quest to uncover more about the origins of crime.

Preface

The primary goal of *Major Criminological Theories: Concepts and Measurement* is to advance criminology as a science. Although the audience may be criminologists and criminal justice educators in general, the book is written mainly for upper-level undergraduate and graduate students. It lists the achievements in measures of the major criminological theories and presents criticisms of some current practices in research. It can be used either as a principal or as a supplemental text to other texts or anthologies in courses on theories of crime and delinquency. There is no similar criminology text on the market. This is one of a kind.

While it is written for students, I have no doubt that it will also benefit any researchers who are engaging in criminological/criminal justice studies. It is argued that efforts towards standardization are part of the process of scientific theory building because they force scholars to constantly refine their theoretical perspectives and measuring instruments and because they force researchers to choose more comparable measures. This observation is certainly worthwhile for all criminologists to be aware of in their research. The citations of the theoretical and research literature and the list of references are extensive and will prove useful to professionals in general to build or enhance their research projects. The notes in each chapter are intended for interested readers who want to investigate a certain topic further.

The book intends to increase students appreciation of and to sharpen criminologists vision of the key concepts in criminological theories and their measures. It is not an attempt at a new theoretical development, such as through theory competition, theory elaboration and theory integration, or theoretical verification through empirical analysis, or any other ways of creating a new variation of a theory; rather it is an attempt at strengthening the very foundations in doing criminological research right. It provides a guideline for students of criminology or criminal justice to engage in their own research. There are two unique features of this book: (1) deduction of a theory is used, and (2) a summary of the theoretical operationalizations is emphasized.

The book is the culmination of more than a decade of research and teaching of criminology. It combines criminological theories with a concern for measurement of abstract concepts. The bifurcation of theory and methodology is too common in the curriculum of criminology/criminal justice. The division into separate spheres misrepresents the nature of scientific inquiry. Theorizing and empirical research are reciprocal and interrelated parts of scientific theory building. This book thus attempts to reflect this reciprocal process in the study of crime. It intends to transcend the limitations of previous textbooks of criminology. By rejecting both romantic testing of theory at will and rigorously sterilizing a classic statement, it contributes to the construction of a more scientific approach to criminology. It allows for a more penetrating analysis of existing problems of scientific criminology and of the ways to address these problems.

Two events provided the inspiration for writing this book. First, in the spring of 1997, Jay Weinstein, then chair of the departmental personnel committee, advised me in private after the committee s recommendation to accord me tenure and promote me to associate professor that I should consider writing a book in the future. Second, at the 1997 American Society of Criminology Conference in San Diego, Francis T. Cullen, my mentor and friend, said, in discussing Jay s suggestion, that people would remember a scholar with a unique theory book, not a series of articles. He thought that he would mainly be remembered as an advocator of rehabilitation. I thus became aware of the issue of academic memory.

The initial adumbration of the book began in early 2001 after I returned from a one-semester sabbatical leave at Max Planck Institute of International Criminal Law and Criminology. Having decided on the topic of the book, I found that there were still details to surface only during writing. The book could become either a simple handbook or a complicated theoretical statement. I have decided that it should take the middle road. I have found that theorists have stood on the shoulder of the giants, but that the measurement of theory has not taken the same road. There is no systematic effort to examine the issue and the problems associated with it. This book hopefully fills this void in the literature and aims to help establish in some small way criminological theory as the basis of a scientific discipline *sui generis* without distorting the intent or content of each criminological theory.

I am indebted to many people for the successful completion of this book. On the top of the list is Francis T. Cullen, not only for his specific suggestions for this book, but also for all these years of unfailing friendship and intellectual encouragement. In fact, the book is dedicated to him and Paula Dubeck, and to the Department of Sociology and the Division of Criminal Justice at the University of Cincinnati. I thank my cohort graduate students (1986-1993) at the University of Cincinnati for their friendship and intellectual challenges, especially for Velmer Burton, Gregory Dunaway, David Evan and Sandra Browning. In retrospect, their excellent dissertations could be regarded as a prototype of the current book. Thanks go to my current and former students, both graduate and undergraduate, at Eastern Michigan University, who help me bring this theory book to their level of understanding. I also want to thank Jay Weinstein and Stuart Henry who generously shared their book proposals. Jay is my in-house confidant. He knew all about my publishing saga and was always ready with advice. Special thanks go to Jihong Zhao, John Winterdyk, Ira Wasserman, and Ling Ren, who read early versions of my manuscripts and graciously gave their constructive criticisms of early versions. At the time of difficulty, their encouragement was much appreciated. Kristy Schindler carefully edited Chapters 3, 4, 5, 12, and 13. Alethea Helbig provided valuable suggestions to improve the language of Chapters 1, 2, and 13. Last, but not least, I have adopted the current book title at the suggestion of Michael Braswell.

Finally, I am grateful to all my family: my daughter Nancy, my wife Meiling, my parents, and my parents-in-laws for their love and support. They probably feel I often spent more time with my computer and books than I do with them. I hope that when they see this book or read the comments on this book they will agree that the effort was worth it. Nancy actually helped to polish the language of Chapter 13. At the age of 15, she already shows her talent in writing. Unlike most wives named in prefaces, my wife is not an angel, but an ordinary complex human being, who constantly reminds me of the importance of humanistic approach in social sciences.

Liqun Cao
Monday, October 6, 2003

Chapter 1
Criminological Theory

Criminology is a fascinating and fast-growing academic discipline. It is fascinating because its subject matter constantly catches the imagination of the public and the media. There is a growing concern about etiology of crime and what should be done about it. The rapid rise and expansion of criminal justice/criminology as a separate academic discipline with its own subject matter happened only in the recent three decades[1]. Very few public universities nowadays do not offer a bachelor's degree of criminology or criminal justice, and criminology has also made its way to more prestigious universities. One important reason for such success is that it is only in recent decades that the political conditions have been propitious for an investigation into the ever enlarged problem of crime, and by implication, for a vested interest of society. As a result, time has become ripe for a separate academic discipline.

Of course, the success of criminology cannot rely solely on its interesting subject matter or on its political momentum. For continued growth, criminology has to face its own internal turmoil. There are three major obstacles inherent to the future development of criminology as an academic discipline. First, criminologists are divided among themselves as to the subject matter of their discipline and even to the definition of criminology. The tension between "criminal justice studies" and "criminology" certainly does not help work toward a common goal[2]. On top of this divide, the debate of whether criminology is a social science splits criminologists bitterly (see DiCristina 1995).

Second, traditional criminological theories have been criticized for being "discursive theory": conceptually rich but flabby arguments filled with provocative but fuzzy ideas (Gibbons 1994; Gibbs 1985; Leavitt 1999). It is said that this theorization resembles an art form in which scholars have turned out a host of theories that are interesting, insightful, and provocative, but that are also unclear and difficult to subject to any convincing kind of empirical confirmation or disconfirmation.

Third, measures of key theoretical concepts that predict delinquency and crime have not received much attention. The consequences of measurement error in explanatory variables can be very severe. Original key concepts may be misrepresented in the causal models and purely random measurement error in explanatory variables can bias estimates or regression coefficients. The results of such studies tend to mislead the readers. Traditionally, more attention has been paid to the measurement problems of crime and delinquency (see O'Brien 1985).

1

Relatedly, great advance has been made toward empirical testing of some specific hypotheses of theories, but progress in verification of criminological theory has been less impressive (Braithwaite 1989b; Gibbon 1994; Gibbs 1985; Leavitt 1999; Vold, Bernard, and Snipes 1998). One of the key functions of science — standardization of measurement — has not been seriously explored. Researchers are embargoing their own deduction process. Often, a variety of measures of the same concept exist. There are no comprehensive efforts toward standardization of key measuring instruments within any theories. It is well known that the standardization of measures is the most important part of the process of scientific theory building because it forces scholars to constantly refine their theoretical perspectives and methodological instruments, and because it compels them to constantly revalidate their theories and measures in the realm of reality (Kaplan 1968).

This book addresses some of these critical issues in the development of criminology. The first two chapters provide the foundation for the subsequent chapters and define the concepts used throughout the book. The current chapter begins with an argument that criminology is a behavioral science and ends with a brief history of criminology.

Criminology: A Definition

Criminology has emerged rapidly as an independent academic discipline in the last thirty years or so in the United States, partially because of the increased specialization of crime as a subject, partially because of the growing importance of the subject matter, and partially because of the political forces behind the criminal justice system. Observing that few countries sustain a robust criminology, Paul Rock (1997:xi) even claims that "criminology is almost wholly an American discipline conceived for an American audience and focused on American problems." He also admits, however, that American criminology "has moulded how people throughout the world have tried to make sense of crime and its problem."

There are many ways to define criminology, and there is a continued debate on whether criminology should confine itself to the domain of science. Instead of taking a polarized position on this important issue, I offer here a compromise to the heated debate. I propose two definitions of criminology: a broad one and a narrow one. The broad definition of criminology refers to any systematic study of crime and its related phenomena. Criminologists under this broad tradition draw inspiration from criminal jurisprudence, journalism, history, philosophy, any humanities, or any sciences, and from any serious study of crime. The narrow definition of criminology, in contrast, defines criminology as an interdisciplinary scientific study of crime[3]. It limits itself to the scope of science[4]. This book adopts this narrow definition of criminology, a definition also based on mainstream criminological thought.

It is recognized that conceptualizing the nature and the scope of the crime problem is the wellspring from which criminological inquiry flows (Brown et al. 1991). It shapes what is studied, and more importantly, what is not. The rise of crime in the 1960s through the 1980s stimulated increased public interest in the problem and generated an explosion in academic activities. With the rapid expansion of research, criminology has become increasingly fragmented in terms of substantive areas of specialization, epistemological methodology, and political orientations. Defining criminology as "the scientific study of crime" may fail to identify all criminological interests. Furthermore, criminology outside the United States, such as in most European countries, resides in law schools where it is considered as a sub-area of criminal law. In most other common law member societies, criminology is part of sociology, social sciences, or law schools.

Contemporary criminology in the United States has been greatly influenced by a scientific perspective. This perspective heavily relies upon accurate measurement of the matters of interest to criminologists. Consequently, the continued success of criminology rests upon the adequacy of efforts to measure the quantity, location, and other features of crime as well as the adequacy of criminological theories in explaining crime. This book differs from more extreme "empirical scientism," which rejects the contribution of other criminologies and regards their contributions as being "hot air" (Gibbs 1987). Recognizing that science is a unique way of knowing with many limitations and constraints (Ridley 2001), and that these other criminologies have their places within this academic discipline, I, nevertheless, argue that scientific methodology deserves a privileged place in criminology and criminal justice. As Matza (1964) argues, the history of modern criminology is intimately wrapped up with the increasing triumph of positivist criminology over the entire range of its intellectual competition.

To understand why scientific criminology deserves a privileged place, we must have a basic understanding of science and scientific principles. Science refers to a set of agreed-upon procedures for establishing and explaining facts, or the enterprise that "*gathers knowledge about the world and condenses the knowledge into testable laws and principles*" (Wilson 1998: 53, emphasis original). It is a particular way of knowing. The aim of science is to find satisfactory theory for social and natural phenomena, that applies to many different events (Hage and Meeker 1988). Scientific inquiry should lead everyone to the same results, but not necessarily to the same interpretation of these results. Scientists follow four major scientific principles when conducting their research activities: (1) empiricism, (2) objectivity, (3) skepticism, and (4) parsimony (Fizgerald and Cox 1975).

Empiricism requires that the scientist both develops and tests theories and hypotheses by relying as much as possible upon observation of the events being studies. While we cannot eradicate the selective aspects of the particular perspective we use, it is nevertheless crucial that scientists constantly compare their theories with observations of the events under study, and reject or modify theories that are contradicted by the observational evidence. Social scientists assume that the events we talk about are probabilistic rather than deterministic.

Objectivity refers to the scientist's attempt to ensure that measurement devices are precise and valid, and that the conclusions they have reached are based upon observation and accurate measurement rather than on personal predisposition. Objectivity in social sciences also refers to the belief that it is the duty of the social scientist to make no moral pronouncements. While subjective orientations cannot be completely eliminated, the scientist is especially concerned with attempting to become aware of them and to control them. Social scientists must be careful to state their biases, insofar as they are conscious of them, and to open up their measurement instruments to public scrutiny.

Skepticism implies that a scientist is willing to question everything, to accept little at face value, and to look behind the scenes in an attempt to determine the validity of an argument or conclusion. They maintain a healthy sense of curiosity and a desire to look behind closed doors to learn more about the subject. Skepticism also refers to the fact that scientists do not consider their conclusions to be permanent, universal, or absolute truths. Instead, they realize that their conclusions are tentative, may be shown to be inaccurate by future research, or may not hold in other places or at different times.

Parsimony requires that the scientist should attempt to reduce numerous possible explanations of a particular phenomenon to the smallest achievable number. In the case of the social scientist, ideally this would mean the development of one explanatory scheme for all human behavior. Competing explanations of the same phenomenon would either be incorporated into a more general statement or eliminated.

By constantly questioning existing theories and testing thoughts against reality, science helps liberate inquiry from bias, prejudice, and just plain common sense. To propose a relationship is a creative and imaginative act. To test a hypothesis against reality involves a different order of imagination—mainly the ability to find the bits and pieces of information elicited from reality that are essential to testing the credibility of a particular idea. Science is a procedure for making ideas as fruitful and productive as human ingenuity allows.

Criminology must establish itself in the tradition of science because science insists on objective evidence whereas common sense and many other ways of knowing are somewhat lackadaisical about verification of the explanations they advance. It is this insistence that sets the style of scientific communication, shapes its content, guides scientists' activities, and produces a kind of understanding of the world with momentous practical consequences not possible without science. In the mainstream of criminology, the verificational requirements of science are widely accepted, but a prevailing mystique of understanding has prevented them from being fully satisfied.

While mainstream criminologists regard criminology as a science and while we are quite content with our dominance within the discipline, we do not always use rigid scientific methods to guide our inquiry. This is particularly true regarding the measuring instruments of major criminological concepts. As a social science, criminology has not been through the process of standardizing its major concepts—one of the main functions of science (Kaplan 1968; Wilson 1998). This book attempts to fill the gap by summarizing the published descriptions of major criminological measures.

In following a scientific approach and seeking to isolate, define, and explain the critical features of crime and criminal behavior, this book highlights the significance of measurement instruments in the process of doing criminological research. A major purpose of criminology is to supply, through the sound application of research methods, accurate and objective data regarding crime and criminal behavior.

This book uses the narrow definition of criminology and emphasizes the scientific nature of criminology. Criminology is defined as an interdisciplinary scientific study of criminal behavior, the origins of law, and society's reaction to crime[5]. It draws upon other disciplines to provide a synthesized approach to understanding the problem of crime and its related issues, such as delinquency, deviance, victimology, and penology in contemporary society.

Criminology and Other Sciences

As late as the 1970s, most scientific study of crime was scattered among other academic disciplines, such as sociology, political science, psychology, economics, biochemistry, biological psychiatry, etc. Crime as a human behavior has elicited wide interest from a variety of social sciences. While these social sciences all have their own subject matter, crime is included in their broad scheme of interests as a sub-subject. In examining human relationships, these social sciences attempt to understand the social world objectively. Just as the world of nature contains ordered relationships that are not obvious but must be discovered through controlled observation, so the ordered relationships of the human or social world are not obvious and must be revealed by means of controlled and repeated observations.

The social sciences are divided into specialized fields based on their subject. The most relevant of the social sciences to criminology are economics, political science, psychology, and sociology. Political science focuses on politics and government. Political scientists study how people govern themselves: the various forms of government, their structure, and their relationships to other institutions of society. Political scientists are especially interested in how people attain ruling positions in their society, how they maintain those positions, and the consequences of their activities for those who are governed. In studying a constitutional government, such as that of the United States, political scientists also analyze voting behavior.

Economics also concentrates on a single social institution. Economists study the production and distribution of the material goods and services of a society. They want to know what goods are being produced at what rate and at what cost, and how those goods are distributed. They are also interested in the choices that determine production and consumption; for example, why a society produces a certain item instead of another.

Psychology is about processes that occur within the individual, within the "skin-bound organism." Psychologists are primarily concerned with mental processes: intelligence, emotions, perception, and memory. Some concentrate on attitudes and values; others focus on personality, mental aberration, and coping with the problems in life.

Sociology focuses on the impact of institutions and social group on individual behavior. It covers all major institutions in a society; politics and economics are only two of such institutions. Sociology examines structural factors and their impact on individual behavior.

Natural sciences are the intellectual and academic disciplines designed to comprehend, elucidate, and predict events in our natural environment. Many natural sciences, and in particular, biology, geology, physiology, and psychiatry are also relevant to the study of crime.

Criminology has many similarities to other sciences. Like political scientists, criminologists study the process of law making and the administration of justice. Like economists, criminologists are concerned with the consequence of the economy and its impact on criminal behavior. Like psychologists, criminologists are interested in how people adjust to the difficulties of life. Like sociologists, criminologists examine the consequences of social inequality on crime and social disorganization on crime. Like natural sciences, criminologists address the geographical distribution of crime, biological defects and their connection with crime, and possible human motivation related to psychics.

Given these overall similarities, what distinguishes criminology from all other sciences is its subject, not its methodology. The problems of methodology in criminology transcend all those found in any one discipline, dealing either with those common to groups of disciplines, or in more generalized form, with those common to all scientific inquiry. Criminology in the United States is "an eclectic science" (Pearson and Weiner 1985: 116), but has outgrown all the above-mentioned disciplines. Bianchi argued as early as 1956 that criminology is "an *independent* science, not subject to the control of sociology, psychiatry, or penal law or whatever science" (1956:2, emphasis in original). Nowadays, criminology has indeed become a distinct discipline, at least in the United States, that synthesizes the work of contributors from various component disciplines.

Although the subject of criminology appears narrow, its theoretical span is broad because of the variety of contributions and because of the involvement of so many disciplines. The narrow subject should not be confused with its complexity. The phenomenon of crime is multifaceted and potentially shaped by a range of factors that exists both internal and external to individuals, that crosses both the macro and the micro level, and that reflects various points in the life cycle (Cullen and Agnew 1999a). Criminologists are concerned not only about the causes of crime, but also about the justice of managing the problem of crime in our society. The highly complex nature of crime and its control warrants a specialized framework of concepts, which can only be mastered by a lengthy and focused career.

Criminological Theory

Like criminology, theory can have many meanings. Since I have adopted the narrow definition of criminology, my definition of criminological theory has to confine itself with the framework of scientific theory. Even so, there are no consensual meanings as to this narrower concept. Singleton and Straits (1999: 23) regard theory as "one of the most elusive and misunderstood terms in science."

In its simplest sense, "a theory is an explanation" (Bohm 2001)[6]. In less sophisticated terms, a theory is used interchangeably with a common sense, a guess, or even a faith. Most textbooks regard a theory as a framework that is used to study some aspect of the world. It is a way of looking at things. It is important to remember that it is also a way of not looking, since in order to attend closely to one perception, others have to be screened out (see Akers 2000; Pedhazur and Schmelkin 1991; Williams and McShane 1999 for more detailed discussion).

A scientific theory is one special kind of theory (Gibbons 1994; Vold et al. 1998). It is a set of ideas that provides tentative explanations for interrelated phenomena. These ideas are built upon certain assumptions, and they have to be quantifiable and testable. To put it more vividly, Popper (1968: 59) proposes that "theories are nets cast to catch what we call 'the world': to rationalize, to explain and to master it." DeGroot (1969: 40) states it more formally that "theory means ... a system of logically interrelated, specifically non-contradictory, statements, ideas, and concepts relating to an area of reality, formulated in such a way that testable hypotheses can be derived from them." Scientific theories, thus, imply causality and determinism. They suppose to make sense of facts, and facts provide the basis for testing and refining theories. As a result, facts and theory are mutually dependent.

There are several features that separate scientific theory from other theories. First, scientific theory focuses on proposing how social phenomena are related, and on why they are related in the way they are. It does not concern itself with how the things *should* be related. Second, any prediction a social theory makes is in terms of probability, and most proposed relationships are limited to the linear relationship. Empirical tests of a theory can only fail to support a hypothesis of the theory, or they can provide evidence in support of a hypothesis from the theory. They do not disprove or prove a theory directly. Third, the ultimate criterion for judging the validity of a scientific theory is its empirical accuracy (Gibbons 1994; Gibbs 1990; Akers 2000); that is, the claims made in a theory ought to be supported by empirical evidence. Truth is not a criterion for judging a scientific theory in that theoretical arguments are created for the purpose of gaining knowledge about reality.

A scientific theory is a deductively connected set of empirical generalizations (Brodbeck 1968; Merton 1968a). These generalizations, no matter how well established they may be, are always subject to possible refutation by future experience and are, therefore, hypothetical. A scientific theory is referred to as a hypothetico-deductive system, which involves formulating hypotheses, deducing propositions, and testing these propositions against the data; if the data don't confirm the proposition, then the hypothesis needs to be revised, further propositions tested, and so on (see the next chapter for a more detailed discussion).

It is important to recognize that personal life experiences shape the way in which people come to think about crime and its theories (Lilly, Cullen, and Ball 1995; Marx 1847; Williams and McShane 1999). Theory is human invention and both criminological theorists and the public are influenced by their life-experiences. As Hume (1748) warns, theories are inside our heads and that they are constructed to apply to observable events, but are not the events themselves. In addition, Kuhn (1970) argues that scientific enterprise is the collective framing dominated by tradition and "tacit knowledge." The formulation of problems and testing of theories are severely limited by conventions and beliefs. As society changes, views about crime will also change: during the colonial time, spiritual demons and the inherent sinfulness of humans were considered the major causes of crime; at the turn of the 20th century, the defective biological constitution of inferior people; in the 1960s, the denial of equal opportunity.

Criminological theory is at the core of criminology. Observation without a theory is chaotic and wasteful, while a theory without the support of observation is speculative. A scientific theory stimulates further discovery by providing new directions, and new observation invites an additional test of the original principles that led to its formation (Wilson 1998). A criminological theory is a set of explicit propositions that provides sensible and tentative relationships between criminal behavior and one or more well-defined conceptualizations of social phenomena, subject to empirical verification. It serves as a guide to interpret social reality and to chart the direction for future research. It is part of the broader social science perspective to explain human behavior and society (Akers 2000; Sheley 2000). As we have examined previously, mainstream criminological theories draw a wide span of inspiration and imagination from a variety of social and natural sciences. They are, however, united by their commonality of relying upon scientific methodology, the focus of the next chapter. One thing is clear: this book is intended as a detailed exposition regarding the issues of measurement instruments of major criminological theories, rather than as a critique of contemporary criminological theories *per se*.

A Brief History of Criminology

According to the principle of *Nullum crimen sine lege, nulla poena sine lege* (No crime or punishment without law), the history of a broad definition of criminology has to trace back to the history of law. The first known written law is supposed to have been the Babylonian Code of Hammurabi (about 1750 B.C.). In China, the first published law was the Law Book of Zheng State (about 536 B. C.) by its Prime Minister Zichan (Zhang et al. 1995). The development of criminology as a philosophy is as old as any other philosophical theory in almost all the major civilizations in the world.

The origins of criminology as a coherent body of thought are relatively recent. The systematic study of crime as a separate topic began with Cesare Beccaria (1738-1794) when he published his classic essay *On Crimes and Punishments* in 1763. His basic ideas grew out of the Enlightenment. One of the central tenets of his thinking was that the rights of man had to be protected against the corruption and excesses of existing institutions. Baccaria was convinced that the social contract, while restricting a citizen's behavior, did so in the best interests of society. Crime was usually defined from a strictly legal point of view. The construction of a rational and efficient penal calculus is necessary to stop the actions of the volitional legal subject. Beccaria left a rich legacy to our present-day justice system. The notion of free will was a guiding principal of the classical school. The belief that individuals were responsible for their own behavior, and therefore punishment was an appropriate response if a person transgressed the law, has helped to develop the due process model, the right to counsel, the determination of guilt, and the use of punishment for those found guilty (Vold et al. 1998).

Becarria's theory was limited, however, by the age in which the author lived. The theory was considered a rebellion against, and a rejection of, the theological worldview, considering it a fraud or at least an illusion. Becarria was largely a product of the Enlightenment or the "Age of Reason." He was regarded as a utilitarian social philosopher, whose primary concern was with legal and penal reform rather than with formulating an explanation of criminal behavior (Akers 2000). Becarria's theory is characterized as legal and administrative criminology (Cornish and Clarke 1986). As Foucault (1977:102) declared, "one will have to wait a long time before *homo criminalis* becomes a definite object in the field of knowledge." The spread and triumph of physical science would be felt by social scientists later, and the application of scientific method in the study of crime occurred a hundred years later.

Moral statisticians also contributed to our understanding of crime in the early 19th century. Adolphe Quetelet (1796-1874) and Andre Michel de Guerry (1802-1866) were two of the most famous. Andre Michel de Guerry de Champneuf was the French minister of justice in the late 1820s. He was instrumental in establishing the first official national statistics on crime, the *Compte generale de l'administration de la justice*. His successor, Andre-Michel Guerry, was in charge of gathering data for the *Compte generale* for the city of Paris. His book, *Essai sur la statistique morale de la France* (1833) has been called "the first to utilize relatively accurate criminal statistics to test ... hypotheses ... in the light of the facts...." (Unnithan et al. 1994: 11-12).

Quetelet was a Belgian mathematician who studied data gathered in France to investigate the influence of social facts on the propensity to commit crime. In addition to finding a strong influence of age and sex on crime, he uncovered evidence that season, climate, population composition, and poverty were related to criminality in his book *A Treatise on Man and the Development of His Faculties*. Andre-Michel Guerry and Quetelet were labeled as moral statisticians, not criminologists, because their statistical efforts are devoid of explicit theoretical ideas, but are full of moral lessons of the time (Einstadter and Henry 1995; Unnithan et al. 1994).

The scientific study of crime did not take place until the arrival of the positivist school (*suola positiva*) of criminology represented by the Italian physician Cesare Lombroso (1835-1909). Positivism is a philosophical approach whose basic premises are measurement, objectivity, and causality. Positivism is both skeptical and optimistic. It is skeptical in the sense that no theory, including criminological theory, can ever claim a *priori* support without empirical verification. It is optimistic in the sense that all behavior is the product of some antecedent causes which can be eventually found through empirical falsification or scientific evaluation. Although many of the ideas of Lombroso have fallen apart, he should still be credited with making major contributions to criminological thought. It was Lombroso who introduced the scientific method into the study of crime. It was Lombroso who caused a shift of focus from that of the crime, which the theorists of the Classical School had emphasized, to that of the criminal, the focus of the Positivist School. It was also Lombroso who caused a shift of focus from that of deterrence and prevention to that of rehabilitation (Fattah 1997; Vold et al. 1998; Wolfgang 1973).

Lombroso, thus, was crowned as the founder of scientific criminology[7]. Drawing on Darwin's evolutionary theory, Lombroso, in his book *L'uomo delinquente* (*The Criminal Man*, 1876), claimed that criminals were not as evolved as other individuals: they were savages in the midst of modern society, and it was their savage or primitive state that caused their criminal behavior. His work was criticized even during his time by his close ally, Garofalo, who in 1885 coined the term "criminology"– in Italian, *criminologia* (Adler et al. 1995). Lombroso's research, however, was important because it helped to establish what is known as the "positivist school" of criminology. This school is distinguished by its search for the causes of crime, be those causes biological, psychological, or sociological. It relies on the scientific method: the theories we develop must be tested against our observations of the world. Although Lombroso introduced the method of scientific methodology into the study of crime, it took a long time for scientific criminology to take its roots in the discipline. The use of empirical data to test a theory did not begin until the 1930s with Chicago delinquency studies. Since then, more and more sophisticated scientific methods have been introduced, and more and more rigid studies appear each year. Criminological theories have finally and gradually walked away from the tradition of social philosophy toward a more scientific status.

Notes

1.   Criminology as a subfield of law or sociology has a much longer history in the United States. American criminology began as a legal science under the leadership of John Wigmore, dean of the law school at Northwestern University (Knepper 2001). The legal profession, however, expressed little interest in the study of crime along the lines suggested by Wigmore. Criminology never became a specialty area for academic lawyers in the United States as it did in Europe. What became the American Society of Criminology began with August M. Vollmer, the chief of police in Berkeley, California. During the 1930s, he headed the institute for criminology and criminalistics at the University of California at Berkeley (Morris 1975). American Society of Criminology got its name in 1957 and since then has been dominated by sociologically-trained presidents (Jeffery 1990). The emergence of criminology as an independent academic unit within universities happened since the 1970s.

2.   Quarrelling about the disciplinary status of criminology and criminal justice is much less significant than is the job of spelling out the tasks that characterize criminology and criminal justice as variant emphasis of a common enterprise.

3.   Jeffery (1990) and Saccco and Kennedy (1996) regard criminology as an interdisciplinary perspective. In May 1970, under the editorship of C. Ray Jeffery, the American Society of Criminology's official journal got its current name: *Criminology: An Interdisciplinary Journal*. Although Binder (1988) agrees that criminology has assumed an interdisciplinary nature, he questions the prospects for interdisciplinarity in the visible future. In contrast, Akers (1992), Cote (2002), and Gibbons (1994) define criminology as "multidisciplinary" instead of "interdisciplinary." Akers and Cote regard criminology as an area of specialization within sociology, while Gibbons (1994:3) treats criminology as a "multidisciplinary field of study" posing "sociological, psychological, economic or other queries abut crime and criminal behavior." In Gibbons' mind, criminology is not a distinct discipline with distinctively criminological questions. In the same vein, Canadian criminologist James Hackler (1985: 445) considers criminology as a "subfield of sociology."

4.   As early as Sellin (1938), criminology was established within the domain of science in the United States. Jeffery (1990: 17) called for an interdisciplinary criminology residing in the tradition of science. He also found that such appeal went back as far as Enrico Ferri, who "advocated an interaction of criminal law and the behavior sciences as basic to penal philosophy."

5.   Similarly, Sutherland (1947) defined criminology as the study of the entire process of law-making, law-breaking, and law-enforcing.

6.   Vold et al. (1998) and Winfree and Abadinsky (1996) argue that a theory is a part of explanation. Tittle (1985:94) holds that "theories subsume many explanations of various specific phenomena in the domain of the theory...."

7.   Wolfgang (1973: 232) and Williams and McShane (1999:36) called Lombroso "the father of modern criminology," Sykes and Cullen (1992: 15) considered Lombroso as "the father of criminology," and Vold et al. (1998: 34) and Barkan (1997: 124) regarded Lombroso as "the founder of positivist criminology." Matza (1964:3) maintained that modern criminology "begins with the views of Lombroso." Foucault (1977) and Garland (1985) claimed that it was altogether misleading to designate the works of writers such as Becceria, Bentham, and Blackstone as criminology. Beirne (1993), however, disputed the

prevailing interpretation of Becceria's work. He argued that the difference between classical criminology and positivist criminology was not as distinct as it is assumed in the textbooks. Beccaria's chief object in *On Crimes and Punishments* was the application to crime and penal strategies of the "science of man." In other words, there was a deterministic tone implicitly at odds with conventional assumption about the exclusively humanist and volitional bases of "classical criminology." The label of "classical criminology," according to Beirne (1993), was the retrospective invention of distorted scholarly self-aggrandizement by Lombroso, Garofalo, and Ferri.

Chapter 2
Doing Criminological Research

In the previous chapter, we have achieved one important thing: we have spelled out the definition of criminology that will be used throughout this book. In the process, we have discussed why criminology is a behavioral science and the relationship between criminology and other sciences. We have also given the definition of criminological theory that will be used in this book, and we have investigated briefly the early development of criminology. The core argument of the book, however, has not been examined. It is in this chapter that the core argument will be raised and discussed in detail.

The last fifty years have witnessed striking advances in testing various hypotheses from criminological theories, but evaluations of the empirical status of a theory are always inconclusive. Throughout the years, new theories come and go, not because researchers have them falsified, but because the social context supporting the theory has changed (Lilly, Cullen, and Ball 1998). The solution to the increased number of midrange theories appears to be a variety of theoretical integration (Akers 1998; Cao and Deng 1998; Cao and Maume 1993; Cullen 1983; Cullen and Wright 1997; Elliott 1985; Hagan 1989; Tittle and Paternoster 2000; Vold et al. 1998), less discursive theorizing (Gibbons 1994; Gibbs 1985; Leavitt 1999), and returning to its root of political philosophy (Knepper 2001). For an alternative solution, this book argues that criminologists should strengthen one of the important features of scientific inquiry – movement toward standardization of key measures in each theory. In this way, the different studies testing the same theory can be compared over time, and the competition between theories within one model can falsify one of them.

Systematic evaluations of a theory's empirical validity have been conducted periodically. These evaluations in general focus on the data quality, results of research, techniques of analysis, and causal linkages, but seldom, if ever, do they examine a theory's measurement validity, resulting in a general inconsistency in the use of measures and reemergence of the new measures. One of the most important functions of science has been neglected in most of the previous efforts: movement toward standardization (Kaplan 1968). The process toward standardization is also described as one of the key features of science that separate it from other ways of knowing (Wilson 1998). Physics and chemistry could not achieve today's status without adopting universally accepted measures. The serious and difficult task of developing operational definitions and technical devices that constitute measuring instruments of major criminological theories remains, for the most part, yet to be accomplished in criminology. Although new attempts cannot be totally avoided if we want to model social reality, such efforts are not worked out anew with each research project; nor are they the arbitrary invention of each individual investigator. New research attempts must build on previous measures and with previous measures in mind, making sure that other researchers understand what he or she means. There are no logical or *prima facie* grounds upon which the development of comparable instruments for measuring social phenomena can be declared impossible. Generalization is only possible when the measures adopted are universally accepted within the criminological community. The ultimate test of the validity of any criminological theories will consist in the invention of widely accepted measurement devices and in the demonstration of their validity.

I will begin this chapter with a discussion of the scientific method, describing four major research methods in doing criminological research, and then focus on the traditional research model. A concerted effort to discuss measurement issues follows and this chapter concludes with a brief comment on the measurement issue in criminology.

Scientific Method

Scientific method is the research technique or tool used to gather data[1]. In contrast to faith, common sense, and intuition, it involves (1) objective observations, (2) precise measurements, and (3) full disclosure of research techniques and results. These permit others to repeat, confirm, or disconfirm studies and findings (Wilson 1998).

In doing criminological research, criminologists, like all social scientists, must, as far as possible, be aware of how their own attitudes, expectations, and values might affect their research. Scientific methods deliberately and systematically seek to minimize any personal bias on the part of researchers. Note that I use the verb "*minimize*." Wallace (1971:14), instead, used the verb "annihilate." I believe that total objectivity is hard to realize in practice. This position is consistent with both Weber's (1968) and Kuhn's (1970) views on the issue. Although Weber advocated "value-free" methodology in the sense that concepts should be clearly defined, agreed-upon rules of evidence should be followed, and logical interferences should be made, he never meant that a "value-free" social science is a reality. In fact, he proposed it as an "ideal model," not as a social reality. He always reminded us of the importance of the subjective interpretation of social action. People do not see the world "as is," but they learn to see it (Hanson 2002). Social

16

scientists thus are encouraged to minimize their bias and make their bias explicitly in their work. Similarly, Kuhn (1970) has argued that scientists, natural or social, do not possess neutral languages of observation. They cannot see the world from a paradigm-free standpoint.

It is recognized that it is far more difficult to measure human beings and their ever-changing thought processes (Gurwitsch 1974; Hanson 2002; Kaplan 1968; Singleton and Straits 1999). Unlike boiling water, which registers the same temperature from one measurement to the next, people's attitudes and behaviors do not remain constant. For example, just asking someone a question for the first time can subtly influence that person's answer to the same question at a later date. If a researcher asks your opinion of death penalty, you must stop and think. The next time your opinion is sought, it will have been affected by your having already thought about it. People change in many ways from one moment to the next, so that measurement in criminology can never be as exact or consistent as that found in the natural sciences.

The goal of objectivity is supported by measurement devices that leave as little as possible to guesswork. Such research instruments, as questionnaires, checklists, and interview forms allow different observers to obtain similar information. One can thus compare or combine research results to arrive at statements that cover more than one observation at one time. Deciding what to measure is the first problem faced by the researcher. Not everything can be measured directly, even such simple, abstract concepts as, for example, social class and crime. Something that can be counted must be selected to stand for the abstraction. The items that can be measured and counted are called empirical referents, meaning observable acts used as evidence of the abstract concepts. A systematic evaluation of indicators of abstract concepts has not been conducted periodically in the field of criminology, resulting in a lack of pressure toward more standardized measures.

Full disclosure refers to a scientific duty to make one's research materials fully available to colleagues. This is more likely to occur in an open society than in a closed society (Popper 1945). Every published report must provide information on who was studied, what was measured, and how, and the statistical procedures used to generate the findings. Researchers should be willing to provide additional information to those who might question the data or seek to replicate the study.

The four most widely used research methods for criminologists are surveys, field observations, secondary data analysis, and content analysis. Each of them has its strengths and weaknesses. A survey is a study, generally in the form of an interview or questionnaire (Dillman 1978), that provides criminologists with information concerning how people think and behave. Among our nation's best known surveys are the National Crime Victimization Survey and the National Youth Survey. As any one who ever studies criminology would know, these surveys have become an important part of our research life.

In preparing to conduct a survey, criminologists must exercise great care with developing questions, often referred to as instrumentation (Singleton and Straits 1999). An effective survey question must be simple and clear enough for people to understand. Questions that are less structured must be carefully phrased in order to solicit the type of information desired. Surveys can be indispensable sources of information, but only if the sampling is done properly and the questions are worded accurately. Data from a random survey offers the best case for generalization.

Field observations allow criminologists to examine certain behaviors and communities that could not be investigated through other research techniques. In some cases, the criminologist actually "joins" a group for a period of time to get an accurate sense of how it operates. Observers face a question that has both practical and ethical implications: to whom should they reveal the ultimate purpose of their observations? In our society, many people resent the feeling of being "studied." If the researcher disguises his or her identity, then the group has added a participant and observer who is being somewhat dishonest. In addition to the ethical dilemma, the disadvantages of this method include the very time-consuming nature of the technique and the limited generalizability of the results.

The term secondary data analysis refers to a variety of research techniques that make use of publicly accessible information and data. The Uniform Crime Reports, published annually by the Federal Bureau of Investigation, is one of the most important sets of government data that criminologists use routinely in their research. Generally, in conducting secondary data analysis, researchers utilize data in ways unintended by the initial collectors of information. For example, census data are compiled for specific uses by the federal government, but are available for criminologists too. The National Archive of Criminal Justice Data at the University of Michigan is a rich resource for researchers interested in secondary data analysis. There is one inherent problem, however, in relying on data collected by someone else: the researcher may not find exactly what is needed. Criminologists studying family violence, for example, can use statistics from police and social service agencies on reported cases of spousal abuse and child abuse. Yet such government bodies may have no precise data on all cases of abuse. Merging different sources of data is a common practice in doing criminological research.

Finally, many criminologists find it useful to study cultural, economic, and political documents, including newspapers, periodicals, radio, and television tapes, scripts, diaries, songs, folklore, and legal papers, to name a few examples. In examining these sources, researchers employ a technique known as content analysis, which is the systematic coding and objective recording of data, guided by some rationale.

Secondary data analysis and content analysis are both nonreactive, since people's behavior is not influenced. As an example, Emile Durkheim's statistical analysis of suicide neither increased nor decreased human self-destruction, whereas subjects of an experiment or observation research are often aware that they are being watched—an awareness that can influence their behavior (the Hawthorne effect). This is not a problem in either secondary data analysis or content analysis.

Other research methods are unobtrusive measures and experiments, both having questionable ethics, violating one or more of the following ethics in doing criminological research: 1. no harm to participants; 2. voluntary participation, 3. anonymity and confidentiality; 4. not deceiving subjects; 5. analysis and reporting; 6. legal liability. Because of these, these two methods are used less frequently in criminological research.

Traditional Research Model

Having put criminology into the framework of behavioral science, let us move on to discuss the traditional research model. Although there are many continuing controversies over the specifics, the traditional research model commonly followed by social researchers can be summarized as consisting of five parts (Lutz 1983). Theory is the beginning point of the traditional research model (see Figure 2.1). It can be defined as an integrated set of general statements that together offer an explanation for some portion of reality. The theory that is chosen guides the entire research process. It influences the selection of a researchable topic and the specific features of social life to be investigated.

Because the theory is composed of very general statements, it cannot be tested directly. The first step toward more testable ideas is to derive particular hypotheses from the theory. A hypothesis is a specific statement proposing what certain aspects of the entire research problem are like or how they are related to each other. Even though hypotheses use statements that are less general than those in a theory, they still employ concepts as their expressions. A concept is an abstraction representing empirical reality. *In general, it is not capable of being observed or measured directly*. We can think about social class, but we cannot see it directly.

The next step is to decide how the concepts in the hypotheses are to be measured or operationalized. This changes the hypotheses from statements concerning abstract concepts to statements concerning variables. A researcher may consider many different empirical representations or indicators. An indicator consists of a single observable measure. It is important to remember that *indicators provide imperfect representations of concepts* for two reasons: (1) they often contain errors of classification, and (2) they rarely capture all the meaning in a concept.

A variable is a measured characteristic that can take on different values for the research unit, typically referred to as attributes. Having been measured, a variable is therefore concrete, not abstract. A research unit is the individual, social group, community, or society that is the object of study. According to the variables' relationship stated in the hypothesis, variables can be either independent variables, dependent variables, or control variables.

Independent variables are the explanatory variables in a theoretical model. They influence another variable, but no outside or previous influence on itself is being investigated. A dependent variable is a variable that is thought to be influenced by another variable (the independent variable). When researchers examine a bivariate relationship within the conditions of a third variable, that third variable is said to have been controlled, and the variable is also called control variable.

The process of operationalization is referred to as the measurement step in the traditional research model. It includes decisions about such issues as what exact questions will be asked, how information will be collected, and if and how numbers will be assigned to the information collected. After the operationalization process, the theory has been transferred into a statistical model that can be tested through data analysis. A model is a set of hypotheses arranged to convey a causal process implied by the theory. As concepts are to theory, variables are the building blocks of a statistical model. A model is explicit and precise, and provides a clear exhibition of the structure of the arguments.

Although the theory and the model are sometimes used interchangeably, they really represent two separate domains. There is always a discrepancy between a concept and its variable in all social sciences. As a result, validity of a concept is always a concern for social scientists, including criminologists.

Data collection occurs next in the typical research model. It is the process of applying the measurement decisions to the research units in order to gather information. Data-gathering techniques provide safeguards against simply fulfilling the researchers' own expectations (Wallace 1971). Data construction, however, is irretrievably social (Pawson 1989). Once it is done, the researcher must next determine the patterns in the data and decide what they mean according to some set of procedures. This is the analysis step. Following the analysis the researcher compares the data to the initial hypotheses in order to reach conclusions about their accuracy. He/she decides whether the research hypotheses should be rejected or accepted. The findings are then examined in an effort to determine if in fact they support the original theoretical model.

The current book examines how the hypotheses are derived from the theory, and how the key concepts of the theory are operationalized. Particular attention is paid to the operationalization of concepts. I hope, through these efforts, to strengthen one of the most important functions of measurement: the process toward standardization.

Measurement

At this point, it is worthwhile to have some further discussion on some basic concepts of measurement. Measurement is the process of assigning numbers to units of analysis with the condition that these numbers obey the rule of arithmetic (Blalock 1982; Stevens 1968; Wallace 1971). The social phenomenon exists with or without our acknowledgement. Describing the phenomenon, however, depends on the language. Language shapes our concepts (Brodbeck 1968; Whorf 1956), and science without concepts is an impossibility—an ultimate limitation of current social sciences.

Accurate definition of concepts is the first step to measurement. The choice of operational definition is influenced by creativity, judgment, and practicality. When creating operational definitions, a researcher may consider many different empirical indicators. Whatever he/she chooses, every measurement is limited in the numerical description, and it omits certain properties and relations which are important in the conceptual frame (Kaplan 1968).

In assigning the numbers to represent a concept, it is important to know that there are four levels of measurement: nominal, ordinal, interval, and ratio (Stevens 1975). The lowest level nominal is simple classification of things, that are mutually exclusive and exhaustive, such as ethnicity, gender, region, etc. Nominal variables merely offer names or labels for characteristics. The numbers chosen for assignment to nominal categories are arbitrary.

Ordinal measurement can both classify as well as rank-order things. Many concepts are measured in this way (socioeconomic status, opinions of the police, fear of crime, etc.). Attitude and feelings can also be captured this way: high and low confidence; warm, warmer, and warmest, etc. In these examples, we gain a sense of ordering, but the distance between different categories is very subjective and thus is unknown. All we know is the rank-orders between these categories: 1 < 2, 2 < 3, 1< 3.

Interval measures have all the qualities of the nominal and ordinal levels, plus the requirement that equal distances or intervals between "numbers" represent equal distances in the variable being measured. Examples are Biblical time, Fahrenheit temperature, and IQ. Many scholars also regard measures of attitudes, such as Likert scale of "strongly agree" to "strongly disagree," as an interval variable (Borgatta and Bohrnstedt 1981; Labovitz 1970; Nunnally 1978; but also see Wilson 1971). Interval measures, however, do not have an absolute zero.

Finally, the most sophisticated measure is ratio that does have a true zero that represents the complete absence of the characteristic being measured. Examples are age, length of sentence, number of prior arrests, blood alcohol content, etc. Each of these levels of measurement from nominal to ratio builds successively upon the other. Each new level of measurement has all the properties of the earlier levels plus some additional properties of its own. In most social research, the distinction between interval and ratio levels of measurement is not very important compared with the differences among internal, ordinal, and nominal measures (Singleton and Straits 1999).

In addition, there is a distinction between discrete and continuous variables. Such discrete measures as the number of people in a family do not contain fractions, while continuous measures such as age do. Any measurement with a decimal point is continuous. A count is generally discrete. The difference between the two is that in discrete measurement only certain values are possible, while in continuous measurement an almost infinite number are possible.

Qualitative data are almost always categorical and nominal, and thus discrete. Quantitative data can be either continuous or discrete. Ordinal measurement is generally discrete, although it may be thought of as measuring some underlying continuum if it is orderable. As such, *ordinal measures are often treated as if they were continuous*. Interval and ratio data can be either discrete or continuous. In the selection of statistical techniques, the distinction between discrete and continuous variables has become the most meaningful criterion (Bohrnstedt and Knoke 1988).

In conducting studies, researchers need to be concerned with reliability and validity in the use of empirical referents. Reliability concerns whether the measuring instrument yields the same results on repeated trials or the extent to which a measurement consistently represents an intended characteristics. It is sometimes assessed by having different researchers use the same instrument in various settings. If the question, "How often do you use marijuana?" is asked in several separate studies and similar percentages of respondents answer "only on major holidays," "weekly," or "daily," the question would appear reliable. Researchers often speak of their procedures and data as being objective. One meaning of this term is identical to reliability. If a measuring instrument yields the same information from the same people no matter who the researcher is, that instrument is said to be objective. If it does not do that, the procedures and data that result are said to have bias. The reliability of a measure is simply its consistency, which can be assessed by either the split-half method or the test/retest designs (Allen and Yen 1979).

Does the question, however, really measure what it was designed to, in this case "drug problem"? This is the issue of validity, which is the extent to which a measurement truly represents an intended characteristic. In other words, validity refers to the accuracy of the extent of matching or congruence between an operational definition and the concept it is purported to measure. Many variables, such as anomie, cannot be captured as accurately as can distance or age, for example. Validity can be assessed by face validity, criterion validity, construct validity, internal and external validity (Allen and Yen 1979). The complexity of social reality and the elusive nature of language make it all the more worthwhile to invest more of our energy to the validity of measures after so many years of different attempts to test a variety of the criminological theories. Do the researchers derive their hypothesis correctly from the theory? To what extent are their measures of the key concepts valid? These are the two major questions that readers should keep in mind in reading the rest of the book.

Theory Testing and
Measuring Key Criminological Concepts

Methodology is the logic of scientific procedure or the philosophy of the research process. Inductive reasoning is based on observation and hypothesis testing. It goes from observation of facts to general conclusions and principles, whereas deductive reasoning goes from universal principles to individual cases. As the traditional research model indicates, a good scientific inquiry always contains both elements that make it possible for others to judge its worth.

Scientific knowledge is accumulated through testing theoretically deduced hypothesis in its many possible interpreted forms. One way to advance scientific theory is through bold hypotheses that can be submitted to attempts at falsification (Popper 1962). Studies lend confirmation to the theory by not disconfirming it. Over years, specific hypotheses from theory are tested either alone or in competition with hypotheses from another theory in different times and places. Eventually, accumulated unfavorable results would reach a point where the theory is no longer taken seriously. Scientific progress is thus made based on falsification[2]. Kuhn (1970) argues, in contrast, that the growth of science is the cumulative solutions of puzzles within a paradigm, not the substitution of one theory for another, and as such, lack of paradigm in social sciences makes it all more important for the competitive theory testing. Pawson (1989) proposes that empirical evidence must be constructed so that it is related to rival concepts or propositions. One of the problems of the present way of theory testing, however, is the insufficient attention paid to the comparable and/or agreed-upon measures in theory. This has prevented us from reaching a more definite conclusion on the validity of any theory.

As discussed, measurement is the backbone of methodology. Many of key criminological definitions are not well-defined by the original theorists. Consequently, researchers tend to provide their own interpretations of the original concepts and conduct their studies according to their own conceptualizations. For example, the Chicago School ventured a sociological concept called social disorganization, which was defined enumeratively in terms of such indicators as population density, social mobility, poverty, anonymity, and heterogeneity, suggesting that these factors reduce the effectiveness of social control. After several decades of empirical research, Cohen (1959), however, notes, "Few terms in sociology are so variously and obscurely defined as social disorganization." Although the theory suggests that social disorganization leads to deviant behavior of all kinds, it is, as Cohen points out, "difficult to determine what, if anything, is the line of demarcation between social disorganization and deviant behavior" (Cohen 1959: 474). After a lengthy and systematic analysis, Sainsbury (1956) concluded that of his three indices of social disorganization--divorce, illegitimacy, and juvenile delinquency--the last one (juvenile delinquency) is actually measuring poverty rather than social disorganization! These examples illustrate that it is one thing to develop a logical definition of a phenomenon, but quite another to operationalize the definition, and still quite another to understand exactly what really is measured in the research.

Progress in criminological theories has been hampered by murky conceptualization and ambiguous measures of key theoretical concepts. Given that most criminologists believe that we are doing "scientific" research and our work distinctly emphasizes precision in measurement, negligence in this area is surprising and unforgivable. This negligence may result from what Gibbons (1994:7) calls "the bifurcation of theory and methodology at universities." Theories are frequently identified as abstract and speculative thinking, divorced from empirical evidence. In contrast, methodology is often disparaged as atheoretical "mindless number crunching." This division into two separate spheres grossly misrepresents the nature of scientific inquiry. This divide in criminological/criminal justice curriculum, in turn, leads to what Merton calls "bifurcation of theory and empirical research" (1968a: 476). When theories are evaluated, only interesting results of empirical research are discussed, and the issues of measurement are too boring to mention. Criminological knowledge, however, can not be cumulated because different studies used different measures to test the same theory. The original theory has never been modified in light of the empirical evidence. This book attempts to make concerted efforts at examining unique measures of the most popular criminological theories in the next ten chapters. It aims to contribute to criminological theory-building as the basis of a scientific discipline *sui generis* without distorting the intent or content of each theory. I hope to sensitize the difficulties embedded in the hypothetico-deductive procedure in theory testing, and I want to highlight the issue of measurement.

From the next chapter on, I will present individual criminological theories first, and then list unique measures that capture the key concepts of a theory. The criminological theories are taken from what I consider to be the mainstream of criminology. This book is not, of course, a comprehensive survey of all criminological theories, nor of all empirical measures of a theory. The dangers of oversimplification are not entirely avoided in the course of condensing the relevant examples. The focus is on the various derivative measures of a theoretical concept rather on the theory itself. Attempts at determining the conclusive empirical status of a theory, of which there are meager beginnings, are not considered, since the measures of these theories have not yet been unanimously agreed upon by the criminological community.

Notes

1.   Readers should be aware of postmodernism's critiques of positivism or modernism. Postmodernism represents an attempt to reconceptualize the way people experience relationships and social structure. It is fundamentally opposed to many of the key modernist assumptions, and especially so in criminology, which is seen as one of several instrumentalist knowledge (Foucault 1977). Beyond that, it is difficult to define postmodernism. According to Einstadter and Henry (1995: 278), postmodernism "challenges the whole idea of how reality is conceived. It questions the superiority of 'science' as a mode of analysis and explanation (just as it questioned high art). It questions all attempts to reduce life to essences or causes. It questions any attempt by communities or individuals as 'experts' to prioritze their knowledge over the knowledge of others, and it asserts that no one can claim their knowledge is privileged."

2.   Although falsification in a pure Popperian sense is both unrealistic and unpractical, Popper has made an important point in distinguishing science from pseudosciences, and it is premature to abandon falsification as a method in social research.

Figure 2.1 Traditional Research Model *

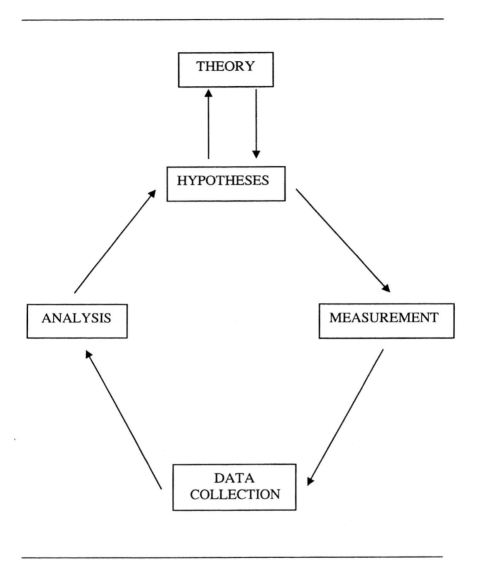

* This figure is adopted from *Understanding Social Statistics* by G. M. Lutz (1983:3).

Chapter 3
Rational Choice Perspective and Routine Activity Approach

This chapter is the beginning of a series of chapters that will focus on one of two specific criminological theories and list unique measures that capture the key concepts of a theory. We will discuss mainly the rational choice perspective[1] and routine activity approach, but their compatibles, such as deterrence theory, opportunity theory, lifestyle theory, and situational theory will also be mentioned briefly. The chapter will be divided into four parts: the root of the theoretical tradition, rational choice perspective, routine activity perspective, and the measures of the key concepts followed by a summary with discussion.

The Root of the Theoretical Tradition

Rational choice perspective and its variations can trace their roots in the classical school of criminology, which is also said to be the philosophical foundation of criminology. The classical school of criminology emerged in the late 18th century and early 19th centuries when Europe was experiencing great transformation from a predominantly agricultural society to an industrial society. The traditional authority of monarchies was increasingly tenuous as philosophers and scholars involved in the Enlightenment intellectual movement promoted the ideas of free will, democracy, optimism, reason, toleration, humanitarianism, the belief that all human problems could be solved and a belief in progress. Demonological explanations of behavior, including criminal and deviant behavior, gradually lost their popularity. Social contract theory (1762) advocated by Jean-Jacques Rousseau (1712-1778) was the basis of classical theory. Also Montesquieu's (1689-1755) *The Spirit of the Laws* (1748) influenced the classical thinking. Classical Theory popularized the philosophy which held that human beings have free will and that behavior is guided by hedonism.

The criminal justice systems in the mid-18th century European societies were planned to ruin citizens (Radizinowicz 1966). Once arrested, the accused had few legal protections. He/she was cut off from legal assistance, subjected to torture, and kept in secret from family and friends. Witnesses against the accused testified in secret.

Under this social background, social philosophers began to call for rethinking the prevailing concepts of law and justice. Cesare Beccaria (1738-1794), born from an aristocratic family, published *On Crimes and Punishments* in July 1764 at the age of 26. The essay was a revolt against despotism, absolutism, and the Italian administration of justice practices.

29

Fearful of condemnation by those who wielded control over Italy's antiquated system of law and criminal justice, Beccaria first published his work anonymously. Although his life was not in danger, he had invoked accusations of "sedition, impiety, and heresy," and by 1765 his essay was condemned to the Pope' list of banned reading for its "extreme rationalism." The book was a success, however, and almost immediately became a landmark. He was publicly praised by Catherine the Great of Russia and Maria Theresa of Austria-Hungary, and he was quoted with admiration by such luminaries as the philosopher Voltaire, the legal theorist Blackstone, and those architects of the new American republic, Thomas Jefferson and John Adams.

Beccaria's argument can be summarized in relatively simple terms. First, in order to escape war and chaos (Hobbes: war of all against all), individuals gave up some of their liberty and established a contractual society. This established the sovereignty of a nation and the ability of the nation to create criminal law and to punish offenders. Second, because criminal laws placed restrictions on individual freedoms, they should be restricted in scope. They should not be employed to enforce moral virtue. To prohibit human behavior unnecessarily was to increase rather than decrease crime. Third, the presumption of innocence should be the guiding principle in the administration of justice, and at all stages of the justice process the rights of all parties involved should be protected. Fourth, the complete criminal law code should be written and all offenses and punishments should be defined in advance. Fifth, punishment should be based on retributive reasoning because the guilty had attacked another individual's rights. Sixth, the severity of the punishment should be limited and it should not go beyond what is necessary for crime prevention and deterrence. Seventh, criminal punishment should correspond with the seriousness of the crime; the punishment should fit the crime, not the criminal. Eighth, punishment must be a certainty, inflicted quickly, and should not be administered to set an example; neither should it be concerned with reforming the offender. Ninth, the offender should be viewed as an independent and reasonable person who weighed the consequences of the crime. Tenth, the aim of a very good system of legislation was the prevention of crime. It is better to prevent crimes than to punish them. Beccaria argues that every punishment which was not soundly based upon absolute necessity was tyrannical and that the more cruel and severe the punishment, the more the minds of men grew "hardened and calloused."

Another scholar of the same time period Jeremy Bentham (1748-1832), a jurist and philosopher, also advocated utilitarian philosophy: Actions are evaluated by their tendency to produce advantages, pleasure, and happiness, and to avoid or prevent mischief, pain, evil, or unhappiness. According to Bentham, punishment has four main objectives: 1. to prevent all criminal offenses; 2. to convince the offender to commit a less serious one; 3. to insure that a criminal uses no more force than necessary; 4. to prevent crime as cheaply as possible. Bentham claimed that since the aim of law is to eliminate mischief, law itself must limit its sanctions to the most parsimonious necessary to achieve the desired goal: "all punishment is mischief: all punishment itself is evil. Upon the principle of utility, if it ought at all to be admitted, it ought only to be admitted in as far as it promises to exclude some greater evil." As a corollary, the law should not be involved in the control of any activities which do not harm others, do not contradict their self interest or threaten the Social Contract (see Einstadter and Henry 1995).

The writings[2] of Beccaria and Bentham form the core of what today is referred to as the classical school of criminology: 1. free will to choose between right or wrong; 2. a person's choice of criminal solutions may be controlled by fear of society's reaction to such acts; 3. punishment should be proportional to crime. The classical school of criminology was nurtured by reformers responding to the abuse of power and blatant inequities in the administration of justice. It is essentially an economic theory of crime that focuses on the criminal acts as defined by law. Those who commit crimes are rational, hedonistic, free actors, and not different from noncriminals. The belief that the punishment should fit the crime and that people should be punished for what they did and not to satisfy the whim of a capricious judge or ruler was widely accepted. The classical school of criminology is characterized as legal and administrative criminology (Cornish and Clarke 1986) and denounced as "armchair criminology" (Curran and Renzetti 1994: 22).

The influence of the classical school of criminology is well reflected in *Declaration of the Rights of Man* (1789): "The law has the right to prohibit only actions harmful to society. The law shall inflict only such punishments as are strictly and clearly necessary.... no person shall be punished except by virtue of a law enacted and promulgated previous to the crime and applicable according to its terms." A prohibition against "cruel and unusual punishments" was incorporated into the Eighth Amendment to the U.S. Constitution. The classical school of criminology has "stood the test of time" and many people appear to support deterrence policies.

Several recent criminological developments which can be said to be the spinoffs of the classical school of criminology are deterrence theory (Gibbs 1975; Wright 1993; Zimring and Hawkins 1973), environmental criminology (Brantingham and Brantingham 1981), geography of crime (Harries 1990), hot spot analysis (Sherman et al. 1989), life-style theories of victimization (Hinderland et al. 1978), rational choice perspective (Clarke and Cornish 1983; Cornish and Clarke 1986), routine activity perspective (Cohen and Felson 1979), and social context theory (Miethe and Meier 1994). Despite their varying emphasis on explanation and control of crime, these perspectives all share a similar image of criminals in which temptation and opportunity are central to the explanation of crime. They all assume, implicitly or explicitly, that offenders are purposive or goal-oriented. Only two of these theoretical perspectives will be extensively discussed in this chapter: rational choice perspective and routine activity approach. I will discuss rational choice perspective in the following section and then routine activity approach in the section after it.

Rational Choice Perspective

Classical theory dominated the reform of the criminal justice in Europe and America for about one hundred years when the positivist school of criminology began to challenge it. For many years, the classical school of criminology has not been popular with academics. Despite the long history and continuing importance, empirical research designed to test the core elements of classical school of criminology was rare until the late 1960s. The core assumptions of classical theory – that the criminal is rational and that crime could be prevented through increased certainty, severity and celerity of punishment — had never been vigorously tested. Most discussions of the theory revolved around the humanitarian, philosophical, and moral implications of punishment rather than the empirical validity of the theory.

In the 1970s, however, many new versions of the classical school of criminology emerged in legal reform and in criminology. The rehabilitation of known criminals came under attack (the most well known being Martinson's "What Works?" 1974). Punishment must not be used for reformation of criminals, for this would encroach on the rights of the individual and transgress the social contract. To control the crime, Van den Haag (1991) argues for decreasing its advantage and increasing cost.

Rational choice perspective has its origin in work on "situational crime prevention" (Clarke 1980). Currently it is an effort to synthesize strands of work in four different academic disciplines: sociology, environmental criminology, economics, and cognitive psychology (Clarke and Felson 1993). It is based on the "expected utility" principle in economic theory. The expected utility principle simply states that people will make rational decisions based on the extent to which they expect the choice to maximize their profits or benefits and minimize their costs or losses. This is the same general assumption about human nature made in classical criminology.

Rational choice theory is largely an individual-level theory and its theorists argue that any attempt to explain criminal choices requires a crime-specific focus because the situational context of decision making and the information being handled will vary greatly among offenses. The rational choice perspective is proposed as a general, all-inclusive

32

explanation of both the decisions to commit a specific crime and the desistance from a criminal career. The decisions are based on the offenders' expected effort and reward compared to the likelihood and severity of punishment and other costs of the crime (Cornish and Clarke 1986). Offenders seek to benefit by their criminal behavior. This involves decision making and choices, constrained by time, cognitive ability, and information, resulting in a limited rather than normative rationality. When analyzing criminal choices there is a need to be crime-specific and to treat decisions relating to the various stages of involvement in crimes separately from decisions relating to the criminal event, such as target selection. There is a fundamental distinction between criminal involvement (criminality) and criminal events (or crime) in the views of rational choice perspective.

Crime is an event; criminality is a personal trait. Criminals do not commit crime all the time; noncriminals may on occasion violate the law. Criminal involvement refers to the processes through which individuals choose to become initially involved in particular forms of crime, to continue, and to desist. The decision processes at these three stages are influenced by different sets of factors and needs to be separately modeled. Some high-risk people lacking opportunity may never commit crime; given enough provocation and/or opportunity, a low-risk, law-abiding person may commit crime. The offender is seen as choosing to commit an offence under particular conditions and circumstances. The decision making is not always fully rational, or even properly considered; instead the perspective emphasizes notions of the limited rationality. The offenders thus are variable in their motives, which may range from desires for money and sex, to excitement and thrill seeking. Offenders' ability to analyze situations and to structure their choice, to switch between substitutable offenses may also vary, as may their specific skills to carry out a crime.

Routine Activity Approach

Elements of rational choice are also found in lifestyle theory[3] (Hindelang et al. 1978) and routine activity perspective (Cohen and Felson 1979). Both rational choice and routine activity perspectives put more weight on the situational determinants of a criminal event, and both recognize the crucial distinction between criminality and crime, including the need for crime-specific explanation. Routine activity approach, however, is proposed as a causal criminological theory in the sense that it links changes in routine activities to changes in crime rates[4]. Furthermore, routine activity approach functions largely at the macro, population level (Clarke and Felson 1993).

Routine activity approach derives its name from the fact that Cohen and Felson (1979) begin with the assumption that the convergence in time and space of three minimal elements of a criminal event are related to the normal, legal, and "routine" activities of potential victims and lack of guardians. The three elements for direct-contact predatory criminal event refer to a suitable target, the absence of capable guardian, and a motivated offender. A lack of any one of these elements will be sufficient to prevent a crime. A change in any one of these elements would change the crime rates, but that the presence of all three would produce a multiplier effect on crime rates.

Built their theory on the human ecological theory, Cohen and Felson (1979) argue that illegal acts are events, which occur at specific location in space and time. The spatial and temporal structure of routine legal activities plays an important role in determining the location, type, and quantity of illegal acts occurring in a given community or society. The motivated offender is anybody who for any reason might commit a crime. This factor is given in any community. Routine activity approach focuses on examining the manner in which the spatial-temporal organization of social activities helps people to translate their criminal inclinations into action.

A suitable target of crime is any person or object likely to be taken or attacked by the offender. Capable guardians are not limited to a police officer or security guard in most cases. The most likely persons to prevent a crime are neighbors, friends, relatives, bystanders, or the owner of the property targeted. There is a conscious effort to distance routine activity perspective from the rest of criminology which is far too wedded to the personal motivation of the offender, moral implications of the victim, and the criminal justice system as central to crime explanation. Defining this key element as "an absence rather than a presence is surely the ultimate in depersonalizing and depsychologizing the study of crime" (Clarke and Felson 1993:3).

Cohen and Felson (1979) present data on post-war trends (into the 1970s) in family activities, consumer products, and businesses that seem to be compatible with the trend in type and rate of crimes in the United States. They found that crime rates increase as the number of adult caretakers decreases because of female participation in the work force, as easily transportable wealth increased, creating a greater number of available targets, and as excess of motivated offenders-baby boomers increase. Since then, Anderson and Bennet's cross national study, Cao and Maume's research (1993) on robbery, Maume's study (1989) on rape, Messner and Blau's study on metropolitan crimes (1987), Stahura and Sloan's study of suburban crimes (1988) all extend their original thesis and find supportive evidence of the approach.

Sherman et al. (1989) report findings consistent with routine activities theory in their study of the "hot spots" of predatory crime. They note that prior research on routine activities used data on the characteristics of individuals or households as measures of lifestyles that affect the convergence of victim, offender, and guardians. Their research focused on the "criminology of place" by using Minneapolis police "call data" (i.e., crimes reported to the police by telephone). They believe that there is something about these hot spots that relates to the convergence of victims and offenders in the absence of guardians. Jensen and Brownfield (1986) point to another variable which is seldom controlled for in studies of routine activities: the deviant or non-deviant nature of the activities in which victims are engaged. They found that activities most strongly related to adolescents becoming victims of crime are not the normal conforming routine activities (dating, going out at night, shopping, or going to parties), but rather the deviant activity of committing offenses. In other words, those who commit crimes are more likely to be victims of crime. Engaging in offense behavior itself, of course, does not fit Cohen and Felson's definition of "routine" activity. Moreover, as Jensen and Brownfield (1986) point out, since criminal behavior is correlated with victimization, variables taken from theories that explain criminal behavior should also be correlated with victimization.

Measurement of the Key Concepts

Rational choice perspective is not a measurement-oriented perspective[5]. Data containing the variables of the decision to commit a specific crime and the development of, or desistance from a criminal career are very hard to collect. The interactive nature of offense and offender characteristics also defies efforts of measurement. Even though it is called rational choice perspective, it only assumes a limited rationality.

A considerable amount of illustrative evidence, however, tends to support rational choice perspective (Clarke and Cornish 1983; Clarke and Felson 1993; Cornish and Clarke 1986). These studies range from white-collar crime to burglary. Most of them only indirectly test a partial argument of rational choice perspective and it seems that the perspective is better applicable to explain white-collar crime than street-level crime, where many acts are under the influence of drugs and alcoholic, or many offenders are in a desperate situation. The supportive evidence from white-collar crime, however, seems less relevant because the perspective is supposed to prevent crime through environment re-designing. That is, its policy implication is to prevent the street level crime, not white-collar crime.

Beyond the narrow focus on rational choice, the related concept of perceptual measure of deterrence is also elusive. Some perceptual measures of deterrence which captures individuals' perceptions of legal penalties were proposed. One widely adopted item is "How likely is it that someone like you would be arrested if you committed X?" (Jensen et al. 1978; Klepper and Nagin 1989; Miller and Iovanni 1994; Nagin and Paternoster 1994; Paternoster et al. 1983; Tittle 1980). Since only limited rationality is assumed, the subjective studies on perception in deterrence research are less relevant in the overall testing the rational choice perspective.

The objective deterrence aspect of rational choice perspective usually evaluates the effects of legal sanction on crime with variables such as arrest, sentencing, imprisonment, and capital punishment. The arrest rate (the ratio of arrests to crimes known to the police), or the proportion of arrested offenders who are prosecuted and convicted in courts are considered objective measures of the certainty or risk of penalty. The maximum sentence provided by law for an offense, or the average length of sentence for a particular crime, or the proportion of convicted offenders sentenced to prison rather than to probation are some of the usually adopted measures for severity of punishment. It is hypothesized that an inverse or negative relationship between these official measures of legal penalties and the official crime rate measured by crimes known to the police. That is, when the certainty and severity of criminal sanctions are high, official crime rates would be low (Gibbs 1975; Ross 1982; Tittle 1980).

One of the major statistical problems in testing the relationship between various certainty and severity of punishment is the possible definitional dependency, or ratio correlation bias, between the measures of the independent and dependent variables (Logan 1977). The independent variables consist of the ratio of sanctions to crime (i.e., arrests/crimes). The dependent variable is the per capital crime rate (i.e., crimes/populations). The common term crime has been either identical or very highly correlated between the two ratios in the data, and they are likely to be measured with errors. Thus, there is always a question of whether the observed inverse correlation might be a spurious mathematical artifact of the common term. Another problem associated with using arrest or imprisonment as the deterrence effect is that it may reflect the effects of incapacitation rather than the fear of legal sanctions.

For the routine activity approach, the key concept of routine activities is defined as "recurrent and prevalent activities which provide for basic population and individual needs ...... formalized work, as well as the provision of standard food, shelter, sexual outlet, leisure, social interaction, learning, and childbearing" (Cohen and Felson 1979: 593). Most empirical studies also incorporate lifestyle theory's variables such as exposure and proximity to crime and target attractiveness. Cohen and Felson (1979) assume that motivation to commit crime and supply of offenders is constant in a population. What needs to be measured among the three elements are suitable targets and lack of guardians.

Table 3.1 presents measures of key routine activity concepts in some of the most important studies at the macro-level. Only the measures of routine activity in predicting crime rates are listed. There are many empirical studies with the dependent variable as victimization. Routine activity approach is regarded by many as largely a victimization theory, not a crime theory (Akers 2000). Routine activity theorists, however, like to consider it both a crime theory and a victimization theory. Although crime and victimization share some commonality, these are two different variables. Furthermore, although I report measures of routine activity at the population level, there are studies applying the approach at the individual level (Bernburg and Thorlindsson 2001; Osgood et al. 1996; Schwartz et al. 2001; Wooldredge et al. 1992).

As is clear in Table 3.1, the measures of routine activities are quite varied from one study to another. In Cohen and Felson's longitudinal study (1979), household activity ratio is captured by a single unmeasured indicator composed of the number of married and husband-present female labor force participants plus the number of non-husband-wife household divided by total number of household. This variable provides "an estimate of the proportion of American household in year t expected to be most highly exposed to risk of personal and property victimization due to the dispersion of their activities away from family and household and/or their likelihood of owning extra sets of durables subject to high risk of attack" (1979: 601). It is found to have a positive relationship with official index crime rates. The other two elements of routine activity perspective – lack of guardians and motivated offenders – are only assumed in this study because the household activity taps only the exposure to crime.

Similarly, using cross-sectional data from the 124 largest Standard Metropolitan Statistical Areas around 1980, Messner and Blau (1987) test the routine activity approach with two different measures: a household activities index and a non-household activities index (see Table 3.1). Again, both measures capture the exposure to crime while leaving absence of guardians and motivated offenders unmeasured. The analyses indicate that these two measures affect each of the eight index crimes as predicted.

In studying metropolitan rape, Maume (1989) creates two measures of criminal opportunity: a criminal opportunity index and racial inequality index (see Table 3.1). First, a general criminal opportunity index includes the potential targets in the SMSA (the percentage of women who are separated/divorced), the motivated offenders (the number of employed men aged 16-64 per 100 women of the same age), overcrowding (the proportion of housing units with more than one person per room), and lack of guardians (the percentage of housing units that were renter-occupied). Second, the index of racial differences in lifestyles consists of the same four variables except calculating the variables separately by race and taking a ratio. Maume argues that income differences could affect rape activity because income constrains lifestyle. For the first time, all three elements of routine activity theory are allegedly included in one single index, however inexplicit and indirect. The results indicate that the opportunity indexes were the strongest predictors of geographic variation in rape. Building on Maume, Cao and Maume (1993) create a lifestyle/routine activity index to study metropolitan robbery (Table 3.1). Their index measure, however, taps only suitable targets and absence of guardians. The lifestyle index is found to be the strongest predictor of urban robbery.

Applying routine activity perspective in explaining suburban crime rates, Stahura and Sloan (1988) propose a full model with all three elements of routine activity approach measured explicitly (see Table 3.1). Note, however, that they regard the motivated offenders as an unmeasured variable based on four indicators – percentages of the poor, of the black, of the young and of the unemployed. Stahura and Sloan's (1988) construct of motivated offenders is debatable. It is one thing that the young, the unemployed and the black are overrepresented in criminal offenses, and it quite another to claim that this overrepresentation indicates criminal motivation. In most other studies, including Cohen and Felson's original study, the percentage of the young is a control variable, not a motivation variable. Similarly, race is generally used as a control variable, not a motivation variable (Cao and Maume 1993; Maume 1989; Messner and Blau 1987). Stahura and Sloan's measure of formal guardianship is unique because it includes both direct guardianship of police per 100,000) and police expenditures, and indirect guardianship of percent female not in labor force. However, the percentage of females not in the labor force only partially captures the informal guardianship. Other aspects of informal guardianship, such as neighbors, friends, relatives, or bystanders, are not measured.

In contrast, applying routine activity approach to the international minor theft arrest data, Anderson and Bennett (1996) use proxies to represent the three elements of the theory. They regard the motivated offenders as status inequality measured by education (index of concentration in which educational disparity serves as the base), accessible targets as gross domestic products per capita, and guardianship as unemployment rate. In addition, they have extended the theory to include proximity measured as the percentage urban. These measures of routine activities are, of course, highly tentative. Their dependent variables are women's minor theft arrest rates and men's minor theft arrest rates. Their results suggest that routine activities theory appear to explain minor theft arrest rates most accurately for men in developed nations.

Summary and Discussion

The rational choice perspective was originally developed to provide policymakers with a useful framework to guide thinking about crime prevention and control (Clarke and Felson 1993). It is rooted in the classical school of criminology, which is characterized as legal and administrative criminology. It represents a systematic common sense theory and is not meant to be a causal criminological theory. It has developed models of *partial rationality* that incorporate limitations and constraints on choices through lack of information, moral values, and other influences on criminal behavior.

To address the speculative nature of rational choice perspective, it seems logic to expand it to include variables beyond its narrow focus on the decision-making process of a specific crime and beyond rationally expected utility. However, when rational choice perspective is modified in this way, the level of rationality it assumes is indistinguishable from that expected in other criminological theories. As Akers (2000) contends, the expanded rational choice model is no longer appropriate to call itself rational choice perspective.

Routine activity approach is proposed as a causal criminological theory. Many researchers have reported findings that are consistent with routine activity approach. As our review shows, however, the measures of the key concepts of routine activity approach are quite different from one study to another. Conceptualization of the key concepts has not reached any consensus among scholars. Few research has attempted to test the full model of the approach. Some proposed measures of variations in the motivation for crime or variations in the presence of motivated offenders are highly debatable. Many times, researchers claimed to have measured this element only provide a highly debatable and indirect measure of this key concept. For example, in the study of Stahura and Sloan (1988), offender motivation is assumed from variations in the demographic correlates of crime. The other two major elements of routine activity approach – suitable targets of crime and absence of capable guardians – are usually not directly measured either. More work needs to be done to devise direct empirical measures of the key concepts. Finally, it is worth noting that this perspective is less applicable to violent crimes in the home (Mawby and Walklate 1994) and is particularly limited when dealing with crimes without direct contact. Many white-collar crimes are without direct contact and the organization of contemporary world has made crime without direct contacts much more available to motivated offenders. Despite these limitations, routine activity approach remains a dynamic criminological theory in 21st century.

Notes

1.   Clarke and Felson (1993:7) maintain that the term *perspective* is used to indicate that it provides "not a substantive theory of crime, but rather an organizing perspective or 'blueprint' from which theories for specific crimes could be developed or within which existing ones could be usefully located."

2.   Fattah (1997) argues that Cesare Beccaria (1738-1794) in Italia, Jeremy Bentham (1748-1832) in England and Paul Johann Anselm von Feuerbach (1775-1833) in Germany are three representative writers of classical school of criminology. However, the writings of Feuerbach in English are difficult to find.

3.   Hindelang, Gottfredson and Garofalo (1978) argue that lifestyle differences associated with routine activities explain group differences in falling victim to a crime. They labeled their theory as lifestyle theory. Most textbooks nowadays combine this theory with routine activity theory. This book follows the practice and does not differentiate the two theories.

4.   Akers (2000: 35) contends that routine activity approach is only indirectly a theory of the commission of criminal behavior even though it draws upon etiological theories. It is primarily a theory of criminal victimization.

5.   Clarke and Felson (1993: 9) admit that rational choice perspective is not causal theory.

Table 3.1 Measures of Routine Activity Approach

I.   Anderson and Bennett (1996)
        1.   attractive and accessible targets = GDP per capita
        2.   proximity = percent urban
        3.   motivation = status (educational) inequality
        4.   guardianship = unemployment rate

II.   Cao and Maume (1993)
        1.   lifestyle/routine activity index = percentage of
                households without a car + percentage of households
                with more than one person per room + percentage of
                housing units that were rent-occupied + percentage of
                people who rely on the public transportation +
                percentage of people who were divorced or separated

III.   Cohen and Felson (1979)
        1.   household activity ratio = (No. of married and husband-
                present female labor force participants + No. of non-
                husband-wife household)/ total No. of households

IV.   Maume (1989)
        1.   general criminal opportunity indexes = percentage of
                women (aged 16 or older) who were separated or
                divorced + No. of employed men aged 16-64 per 100
                women of the same age + proportion of housing units
                with more than one person per room + percentage of
                housing units that were renter-occupied
        2.   racial differences in lifestyles = ratio of the black v.
                white of the above four variables

V.   Messner and Blau (1987)
        1.   TV viewing index = television viewing time each day of
                the week
        2.   non-household activities = supply of sports and
                entertainment establishments (cinemas and drive-ins,
                entertainment producers, and profit making professional
                and semi professional sports establishments)

IV.   Stahura and Sloan (1988)
        1.   motivated offenders = percentage poor + percentage
                black + percentage young + percentage unemployed

2. criminal opportunities = percentage of multiple housing + No. of commercial industrial
3. guardianship = police per 100,000 + police expenditures + percentage of females not in labor force

---

Chapter 4
Biological, Personality, and
Neutralization Theories

It is generally agreed that the beginning of criminology dates back to the middle of the 18th century when Becarria published his book *On Crimes and Punishments* in 1763. The beginning of scientific criminology, however, arrives when Cesare Lomboros published his book *Criminal Man* in 1876. The monograph, with its intention to unlock the causes of crime through rigorous empirical research, fundamentally has changed the nature of criminology. In this chapter, I am going to discuss biological theory and psychological theory together because of many similarities of these two theoretical traditions. Both challenge the basic assumption of the classic school of criminology that crime is the product of rational choice. In different ways, both believe that criminal conduct is caused by forces beyond the control of the criminal. Finally, both are convinced that the solution to crime is treatment or rehabilitation.

I will first discuss the contribution of the positivist school of criminology and introduce the psychoanalysis theory and personality study of crime. Then I will focus on neutralization theory. Finally I will present the measures of the key theoretical concepts that are supposed to be associated with crime.

The Biological Search for Crime Causation

With the publication of Charles Darwin's *Origin of Species* in 1859 and *Descent of Man* in 1871, the scientific quest to unlock the secrets of human origin and behavior received considerable momentum. In Italy, a physician by the name of Cesare Lombroso (1835-1909) was studying the executed criminals in an effort to scientifically determine whether law violators were physically different from people of conventional values and behavior. He wore many hats of academic and professional positions: he was a medical doctor, psychiatry and anthropology professor, phrenologist, scientist, and clinician. Influenced by Charles Darwin's evolution and the eugenics movement (from eu = good and genes = inherited traits), he applied scientific method to the measurement of criminal *craniums*. Through years of observation and research, he proposed a general theory of criminal behavior which claimed that criminality was a result of degeneracy or atavism. By atavism, Lomboros meant that criminals were left-over specimens of primitive human ancestry and that criminals' skulls could be identified by certain physical signs that betrayed their savage nature.

Lombroso's army experience gave him ample opportunity to study the physical characteristics of soldiers convicted and executed for criminal offenses. Through careful measurements of various bodily organs of nearly ten thousand prisoners and soldiers, Lombroso drew the conclusion that criminals were, by birth, a distinct type. In additional to heredity, environmental conditions promoted crime – alcoholism, lack of education, temperature swings (hot temperatures were related to violent crime), and imitation of well-publicized crimes. Lobrorso's theory was later labeled as the positivist school of criminology. It was a product of the "realism" movement which placed a high value on action, power, and success. It discounted sentiment, idealism, and the belief in the supernatural. Although Lombroso was not the first who connected biological explanation with criminal behavior, nor was he the first to use statistical measures in his research, he was the most famous and the most influential one, mainly due to his timing. Lombroso, Ferri (who made the positivist school popular), and Garofalo were considered the "unholy" three because of their belief in evolution as opposed to Biblical interpretation of the origin of men and women.

Despite his fame, Lombroso's findings were falsified by later research. Lomboro had failed to examine noncriminals for the purpose of comparison, and there was no evidence of primitive people's supposed characteristics. In 1913, Charles Goring delivered what is generally regarded as the finishing stroke with the publication of *The English Convict*. Goring carefully compared some 3000 English convicts and a large number of noncriminal Englishmen and concluded that

> We have exhaustively compared, with regard of many physical characters, different kinds of criminals with each other, and criminals, as a class, with the law abiding public. From these comparisons, *no evidence has emerged confirming the existence of a physical criminal type, such as Lombroso and his disciples have described*. (Goring,1972: 173, emphasis in original)

Although his biological explanation of crime is considered simple and naive today, Lombroso has made significant contributions that continue to have an impact on criminology. Lombroso is considered a pathfinder in his time. It was Lombroso who called our attention to the scientific methodology in the study of crime. Therefore, he is credited with pushing the study of crime away from abstract metaphysical, legal, and juristic explanations as the basis of criminology "to a scientific study of the criminal and the conditions under which he commits crime" (Wolfgang 1973: 286). Lombroso demonstrated the importance of examining clinical and historical records, and he emphasized that no detail should be overlooked when searching for explanations of criminal behavior.

The study of physical traits as indicators of criminality did not die with Goring's study. In fact, Goring himself reported a statistical difference between criminals and noncriminals in terms of weight and stature. He further judged, without any measuring devices such as IQ, that convicts were less intelligent. Body types and crime in the 1930s, psychogenic causes of crime, IQ testing, testosterone and criminal aggressiveness, chromosome studies in the 1970s, and personality disorders can all be regarded as evidence of Lombroso's theoretical orientation. Other contemporary efforts attempt to link violence with certain neurotransmitter imbalance such as low serotonin, hypoglycemia (which occurs when glucose in the blood falls below levels necessary for normal and efficient brain functioning), hormonal influences, allergies, and environmental contaminants (increasing amounts of lead, copper, cadmium, mercury, and inorganic gases such as chlorine and nitrogen dioxide have been found in the ecosystem).

Biological explanations of criminal behavior are based on the assumption that structure determines function. People behave differently because they are structurally different – the results of genes, hormones, or body types. The biological theories of crime have not been popular for a while, but we continue to demand that crime be reduced to a simple cause and solution. The biological theories of crime causation give us hope that we can isolate a simple concrete cause of crime and that we can find fast, effective solutions with technological advances in biology and medicine.

The Psychoanalytic and Personality Study of Crime

By the early 1900s, research on crime causation had shifted its emphasis from the body to the psyche. Crime was a bursting forth of instinctive impulses, and the criminal was acting out what most civilized men and women had learned to restrain. Like biological theories, the criminal was still regarded as abnormal, but the abnormality was centered in the mind. Organic disorders resulting from injury or disease have obvious physical basis while functional disorders have no apparent physical basis.

Any discussion of personality theory has to begin with an introduction to psychoanalysic theory developed by Freud. All modern personality theories in psychology have come into existence either because they have chosen to reject psychoanalysis concepts or because they have felt motivated to extend, refine, or elaborate upon the basic principles of psychoanalysic perspective (Shoham and Seis 1993:14).

Sigmund Freud (1856-1939) was a trained physician, psychiatrist, psychologist, and philosopher. He developed psycho-analytic theory to understanding human behavior, drawing heavily on psycho-biological concepts. His research shed light on human unconsciousness, the part of us consisting of irrational thoughts and feelings of which we are not aware, but

45

which can cause us to commit deviant acts. He proposed that our personality or mind had three parts: id, superego and ego. The id, our biological and psychological instinctive drives or our pleasure principle, according to which humans directly seek pleasure, discharge tension and avoid the state of "unpleasure" or pain. Freud viewed the id as amoral raw need, reflecting the immature instinctive passions of the primitive animal within. It is also considered the source of drive, energy, creativity, and even positive and negative aggression. The superego is the force of self-criticisms and conscience, and reflects requirements that stem from a person's experiences in a cultural milieu. It is our moral conscience, a "psychic police officer" that police the person, the conveyor of ideal images, and ultimately an ego-ideal or role model of how to behave in ways that are right and correct. The superego is seen as controlling the id, largely through unconscious processes, popularly known as conscience. The ego forms first as an "outgrowth of the id," an adaptive compromise between the id and the external world of reality. It is a facilitator of the id, and the executive of personality, and represents what is possible in reality, given the logic of the person's capability and the opportunities and constraints presented by situations. It is the balance among the impulsiveness of the id and the restrictions and demands of the superego, and the requirements of society.

Freud proposed five stages of human development and how the basic conflicts between id and superego were played out in different ways at different points of the life cycle. Although he did not discuss criminal behavior to any great extent, his theory does provide enough material for people to apply it to explain criminal behavior. According to these extensions, criminal behavior is symptomatic of three deep-seated psychological problems (Bohm 2001).

First, crime is considered symptomatic of an individual's inability to sublimate sexual and aggressive drive. The greater part of human progress and most cultural achievements have been the product of our success in diverting the animal drives of human being from direct and selfish forms of expression into constructive and socialized avenues of manifestation. Psychologists call this process sublimation (redirection). If successful, sexual and aggressive drives will find legal outlets (reading, hobbies, marriage etc.). If unsuccessful, they will be either acted out or repressed (rendered unconscious). If the drives are repressed, they may be acted out anytime in later life, again possibly as criminal behavior. Repressed sexual and aggressive drives, if not acted out, can lead to mental conflict that manifests itself in anxiety (distress or worry).

Second, crime is a failure to resolve the Oedipus complex (or Electra complex of girls for their fathers), which Freud saw as a normal, inevitable aspect of parent-child relationship. If the process proceeds naturally, the boy will develop normally, that is, to develop a strong superego capable of controlling the id. If early childhood socialization does not proceed normally (a cruel father or absence of a father), however, the superego will be defective or damaged, and the individual will not develop conventional moral standards. If he experiences injustice, the superego may lose its inhibitory power. If the superego fails to develop at all, the result is a psychopathic personality.

Third, crime is an unconscious desire for punishment. On the one hand, criminals unconsciously seek to be caught and punished to expatiate this repressed guilt. Criminals commit crimes to provide punishment from authority in an attempt to justify pre-existing guilt; the act reflects a need to hurt the self. One major culprit in such a scenario is an overdeveloped superego, which produces constant and excessive feelings of guilt. This constant guilt serves to motivate a desire to be punished, albeit temporary. On the other hand, the society's thirst for accounts of crime indicates that our society is suffused with repressed criminal impulses seeking an outlet. Punishing a lawbreaker fulfills our unconscious desires for aggression. In this way, the lawbreaker is said to shoulder the guilt we refuse to accept ourselves (Sykes and Cullen 1992).

Within criminology, the work of Freud has generated a lot of studies in personality, particularly antisocial personality disorder, sociopath, and psychopath. Personality is usually used to describe the collective and/or most prominent psycho-behavioral traits exhibited by an individual. Personality traits are defined as permanent patterns developed by individuals that guide how they perceive, relate, and think about themselves and their environment. The term "psychopath" was first used in the late 19th century, when "psychopatic inferiority" referred to patients with severe behavioral disorders (Yochelson and Samenow 1976:89).

Although these three terms are often used interchangeably and refer to the similar personality disorder, antisocial personality disorder, sociopath and psychopath have subtle differences. Psychopaths are the products of psychological or biological factors, such as an unresolved Oedipal or Electra complex; sociopaths are the products of social factors, such as broken homes; and antisocial personality disorder is a mental illness. All of them overlap with criminality, but are not identical with it.

Freud saw society as an overwhelming apparatus of social control which required the sacrifice of individual autonomy (Shoham and Seis 1993: 18). Society was seen as a necessary but definite evil, serving to elevate progenesis over self-enhancement. For Freud, civilization requires and is only possible with the sacrifice of self-interested behavior. Unconscious desires, after all, are genetically determined, civilization is forced upon us, and children cannot be held responsible for the traumas that they experience. Rational consciousness plays a much smaller role in producing our behavior than the instinctual forces which lie below the threshold of consciousness. Much of psychoanalytic theory undermines the belief that humans are motivated by rational utilitarian concerns.

In addition, Freud has identified a variety of defense mechanisms for an individual to maintain a normal outlook and happy life. Among them are perceptual vigilance (seeing only what one wants to see), perceptual defense (blocking out what one does not want to see), repression (forcing ideas out of consciousness), rationalization (intentionally misperceiving or redefining a situation), introjection (internalizing external objects and making them a part of one's personality), and projection (interpreting situations based on internal states or emotions). Some of these defense mechanisms have been refined and extended by Sykes and Mazta (1957) to develop one of unique criminological theories – neutralization theory.

Neutralization Theory

The techniques of neutralization theory by Sykes and Matza (1957) can be regarded as an extension of Freud's psycho-analytical theory's defense mechanisms. It is a unique social psychological theory of crime and most criminological textbooks treat it as either a part or variation of social control theory or social learning theory (see Akers 2000 for a detailed discussion). While referring to techniques of neutralization as a "theory" of delinquency, Sykes and Matz (1957) leave it open that neutralization could be considered as one component of some more general "theory." Because of its focus on the meaning of crime to the criminal, it is also regarded as a symbolic interactionist theory by Vold et al. (1998). Because of its use of Freud's defense mechanisms, Bohm (2001), however, discusses the neutralization theory together with psychological theories of crime. This text follows Bohm's reasoning and treats the theory as one of psychological theories.

In advancing the techniques of neutralization theory, Sykes and Matza (1957) observe that (1) delinquents sometimes voice a sense of guilt over their illegal acts; (2) juvenile offenders frequently respect and admire honest, law-abiding persons; and (3) delinquents draw a line between those whom they can victimize and those whom they cannot. Consequently, Sykes and Matza conclude that delinquents are not immune to the demands of conformity.

> *It is our argument that much delinquency is based on what is essentially an unrecognized extension of defenses to crime, in the form of justification for deviance that are seen as valid by the delinquent but not by the legal system or society at large.* (Sykes and Matza 1957: 666, emphasis in original)

Neutralization theory therefore argues that an individual will obey or disobey societal rules depending upon his/her ability to rationalize as appropriate a particular infraction. Sykes notes that "an individual justifies action by unconsciously distorting reality, and the ego-image is protected from hurt or destruction under the attacks of self-blame" (1956: 258). Since most juvenile delinquents do not have an overt commitment to delinquent values and do not conceive of themselves as criminals, they have to neutralize their guilt when they commit delinquent acts.

Five techniques of neutralization are widely used by juvenile delinquents to provide a mechanism by which they can break the ties to conventional society that would otherwise inhibit them from violating the rules. These techniques are 1) denial of responsibility (I couldn't help it); 2) denying the injury (I didn't hurt anybody); 3) denial of the victim (They had it coming to them); 4) condemnation of the authorities (Everybody's kicking on me); 5) appealing to higher principles or authorities (I didn't do it for myself; conflict between friendship and law – help a buddy, never squeal on a friend). Sykes and Matza argue that neutralizing verbalizations are essentially unrecognized extensions of legally acceptable excuses for crime. These techniques prepare the juveniles for delinquency and represent glancing blows at the dominant normative system rather than the creation of an opposing set of norms. They are extensions of patterns of thought prevalent in society rather than something newly created. These techniques not only increase the likelihood of delinquent behavior, but also expect to have the same effect on adult criminality (Sykes and Cullen 1992).

In stating their theory, Sykes and Matza made it clear that they considered techniques of neutralization to be types of "definitions favorable" to crime and delinquency, as referred to in Sutherland's differential association theory. However, they challenged the idea that delinquency stems from a set of norms antithetical to those of the dominant culture. That is, delinquency stems from membership in an oppositional subculture, the hallmark of which is "a system of values that represents an inversion of the values held by respectable, law-abiding society" (Sykes and Matza 1957: 664). Techniques of neutralization are needed to shield the individual from the force of his own internalized values, and delinquents often appear to suffer from feelings of guilt and shame.

Contradictory evidence exists regarding the premise of neutralization theory. That is, there is a controversy on whether delinquents and non-delinquents are different in their value orientation. Sykes and Matza's data were criticized because institutionalized delinquents might have tried to make themselves look good. Hindelang (1970 1974), for example, found that delinquents and non-delinquents do have different moral values. As so, delinquents do not really feel guilty and thus have nothing to neutralize. Buffalo and Rogers (1971) and Regoli and Poole

(1978) reported, on the other hand, that delinquents do claim conformity to conventional behavior. Yochelson and Samenow (1976) found that even the most hardened, consistent offenders were unwilling to admit that they were criminals, although they could easily recognize criminality in others. Other researchers (Agnew 1994; Minor 1984; Thurman 1984) test the validity of the techniques of neutralization and find some evidence in support of the theory.

Measurement of the Key Concepts

For most students of criminology coming from one of social sciences, the measurement and laboratory experiments of biological theories are beyond them. The author of this book also shares this trained incapacity to discuss in any detail about tests of biological theories of crime. Consequently, no key concepts of biological measures of crime causation will be presented in this section. Interested readers can check out articles by Ellis and Walsh (1997) and Fishbein (1990), the book by Rowe (2002), and the edited book by (Wasserman and Wachbroit 2001). Freud's theory of psychoanalysis and its derivatives of personality theories, on the other hand, are criticized for being too philosophical and clinical. In other words, they are "not empirically testable" (Martin et al. 1990:84).

The theories of personality are aimed at diagnostics and treatment. As such, standardization of measurement is well developed by psychologists and psychiatrists. Despite their utility and validity in diagnostics and treatment, these are not good measures for criminologists to examine the causes of crimes. They generally ignore social factors in crime causation. The use of these measuring instruments requires careful training and resources to get hold of them. In addition, the measurement involves many dimensions of personality and taking the diagnostic survey itself is more than several hours' work. As a result, few criminologists use them (but also see Caspi et al. 1994).

The most widely adopted survey of personality, the Minnesota Multiphasic Personality Inventory (MMPI), for example, has a list of 550 true/false statements developed to aid in psychological diagnosis (Hathaway and Meehl 1951). Scale 4 of the MMPI, also known as the "psychopathic deviate" scale, is considered to be consistently correlated with delinquent and criminal behavior. It was originally standardized on a group of incarcerated offenders. Other commonly used personality instruments are the Eysenck Personality Questionnaire, the California Psychological Inventory, and multidimensional Personality Questionnaire. The scales from these surveys are excellent clinical tools for detecting criminal deviants in an ostensibly normal population, but a theory that is based on observed correlations between these scales and delinquency may be tautological.

Similar criticisms can levy against psychiatric measurement of antisocial personality disorder. We use this disorder as an example to illustrate our point. The fourth edition of the official *Diagnostic and Statistical Manual of Mental Disorders* (DSM-4) of the American Psychiatric Association states that "the essential feature of Antisocial Personality Disorder is a pervasive pattern of disregard for, and violation of, the rights of others" (2000: 701). For the diagnosis to be given, the individual must be at least 18 years old when he/she demonstrates at least three of the seven criteria listed in the DSM-IV (see Table 4.1). This disorder appears to be associated with low socioeconomic status and urban settings. It has a chronic course but may become less evident as the individual grows older, especially near the age of 40. It must be distinguished from a host of other disorders and especially criminal behavior, which is "undertaken for gain that is not accompanied by the personality features characteristic of this disorder" (2000: 705). It tends to be inherited and more likely to happen for the first-degree biological relative of those with the disorder than among the general population.

The measurement of neutralization suffers from its unstandardization. In general, neutralization may be defined nominally as a method whereby a person renders behavioral norms inoperative, thereby freeing themselves to engage in behavior which would otherwise be considered deviant. It is important to note that neutralization itself is not necessarily "right or wrong" in a strict moral sense. Some of the previous studies (Austin 1977; Ball 1966) were criticized for adopting measuring instruments that confuse the concept of neutralization with commitment to unconventional norms.

There are many studies that claimed to have measured the concept of neutralization or the techniques of neutralization. Table 4.2 just lists three of the best examples of operationalization of techniques of neutralization. Rogers and Buffalo (1974) made up items to cover all five techniques of neutralization, but in their subsequent transformation into the Guttman scale, they added two items of "assessment of responsibility for delinquent behavior." In their final Guttman scale, two items of techniques of neutralization (what I did was not so bad, no one was really hurt [denial of injury] and the trouble was an accident, which I could not help [denial of responsibility]) were dropped out. Their final version of the Guttman scale contains four techniques of neutralization plus two items assessing responsibility for delinquent behavior (I have no one to blame but myself for being sent to the Boy Industrial School and I deserved to be sent to the Boy Industrial School).

Thurman's operationalization of techniques of neutralization (1984) contains every component of the five techniques in Sykes and

Matza's original article. Heeding to Minor's (1981) call for the extension of techniques of neutralization, Thurman, however, adds two more techniques of neutralization – defense of necessity and metaphor of the ledger – to his final scale (see Table 4.2). His index of neutralization has seven additive items. The Cronbach's alpha of the index is .78. His data indicate that neutralization significantly explains expected future deviance among those adults who are morally committed. Later, Thurman (1991) uses the same scale in studying taxpayer noncompliance and again finds evidence in support of neutralization in predicting both underreporting income and overdeducting tax.

Finally, Agnew claims that the validity of Matza's model depends on showing that neutralizations precede delinquent acts, causing the criminal behavior to follow. Sectional data could not do that. Agnew (1994) uses National Youth Study's longitudinal surveys to test the techniques of neutralization theory. He carefully separates the acceptance of neutralization techniques from the general approval of deviance. Respondents are asked whether they approve of violence whatever the reasons are. His analysis indicates that neutralization has the greatest effect on violence among those with delinquent peers and those who disapprove of violence. These conditioning effects shed light on the mixed results of previous research, and they help explain why neutralization only has a weak-to-moderate main effect on deviance in many studies. In both waves of the National Youth Survey, and in both studies of his tests of the theory (1994; 1986), however, there is only one dimension of techniques of neutralization: denial of the victim (see Table 4.2).

Summary and Discussion

Biological and psychological theories emphasize that each offender is unique, physically and mentally; consequently, there must be different explanations for each person's behavior. As a group, biocriminologists and psychocriminologists are not overly concerned with legal definitions of crime. Their studies focus on basic human behavior and drives – aggression, violence and lack of concern for others. These theories "complement sociological theories in several fundamental ways" (Cullen and Agnew 1999b: 5). They provide us with good reference to understand the heuristic nature of human behavior, including the causes of crime, but their measures are more laboratory or clinic-oriented diagnostics and are not ready to be adopted by most criminologists who are not trained for the usage.

In general, personality diagnosis has come under attack as an incomplete and as a circular argument because characteristics are listed for the diagnosis after people have committed antisocial acts. In addition, many of the studies focus almost exclusively on the individual personality, ignoring social conditions and life situations. Being more concerned with therapy than with legal definitions, many psychiatric and psychological theories tend to be speculative rather than scientific. They overemphasize the case study approach and are prone to observer bias. They often fail to use control groups and experimental groups are usually institutionalized populations.

Extending the psycho-analytical theory's defense mechanisms, Sykes and Matza propose their techniques of neutralization theory. Neutralization theory has made a "small but apparently lasting contribution to our theoretical accounting of criminal behavior" (Hamlin 1988). One debate on the validity of the theory is organized around its premier: whether delinquent and non-delinquent share similar value and morality. Another debate focuses on whether neutralization is necessary for delinquency (Hirschi 1969). In general, it is agreed that the five techniques of neutralization are valuable tools for analyzing delinquent behavior. The measures are less complex and thus offer the hope of standardization. The insight of Sykes and Matza is worthy of continued consideration in the study of crime.

Table 4.1   Diagnostic Criteria for Antisocial Personality Disorder

---

A.   There is a pervasive pattern of disregard for and violation of the rights of others occurring since age 15 years, as indicated by three (or more) of the following:

    1.   failure to conform to social norms with respect to lawful behaviors as indicated by repeatedly performing acts that are grounds for arrest

    2.   deceitfulness, as indicated by repeated lying, use of aliases, or conning others for personal profit or pleasure

    3.   impulsivity or failure to plan ahead

    4.   irritability and aggressiveness as indicated by repeated physical fights or assaults

    5.   reckless disregard for safety of self or others

    6.   consistent irresponsibility, as indicated by repeated failure to sustain consistent work behavior or honor financial obligations

    7.   lack of remorse, as indicated by being indifferent to or rationalizing having hurt, mistreated, or stolen from another

B.   The individual is at least age 18 years.

C.   There is evidence of Conduct Disorder with onset before age 15.

D.   The occurrence of antisocial behavior is not exclusively during the course of Schizophrenia or a Manic Episode.

---

* It is adopted from the fourth edition of the official *Diagnostic and Statistical Manual of Mental Disorders* (DSM-4) of the American Psychiatric Association (2000: 706).

Table 4.2   Measures of Techniques of Neutralization Theory

I.   Agnew (1994)

        1978 National Youth Survey (the scale's alpha = .66):
        1.   It's alright to beat up people if they started the fight.
        2.   If people do something to make you really mad, they deserve to be beaten up.
        3.   It is sometimes necessary to get into a fight to uphold your honor or "put someone in his/her place."

        1979 National Youth Survey (the scale's alpha = .77):
        1.   It's alright to beat up people if they started the fight.
        2.   If people do something to make you really mad, they deserve to be beaten up.
        3.   It's alright to physically beat up people who call you names.
        4.   If you don't physically fight back, people will walk all over you.
        (strongly agree, agree , neither agree nor disagree, disagree, and strongly disagree)

II.   Rogers and Buffalo (1974):
        1.   I got into trouble because I got in with the wrong boys (denial of responsibility).
        2.   The trouble was an accident, which I could not help (denial of responsibility).
        3.   What I did was not so bad, no one was really hurt (denial of injury).
        4.   If anyone was hurt by what I did, they either deserved it or could afford it (denial of the victim).
        5.   Unfair teachers are to blame for my being sent to the Boy's Industrial School (condemnation of the condemners).
        6.   The judge and the court were against me from the start (condemnation of the condemners).
        7.   I got into trouble because I couldn't run out on my friends (the appeal to higher loyalties).
        (strongly agree, agree , undecide, disagree, and strongly disagree)

III. Thurman's Neutralization Scale (1984) (alpha = .78.):
1. It is okay to break the law if you aren't sure what the law is (denial of responsibility).
2. It is okay to break the law if no one gets hurt (denial of injury).
3. It is not as wrong to violate the law when the victim involved is a dishonest person (denial of the victim).
4. It is not as wrong to break laws which seem unfair and unjust to you (condemnation of the condemners).
5. It is al right to break the law if it is done to aid a friend in need (appeal to higher loyalties).
6. It is all right to break the law under circumstances where it seems like you have little other choice (defense of necessity).
7. It is more acceptable for an honest and law-abiding citizen to break the law than it would be for a frequently dishonest person to do so (metaphor of the ledger).

(strongly agree, agree, disagree, strongly disagree)

Chapter 5
Social Disorganization Theory

In the previous chapter, various biological and psychological theories of crime and delinquency have been examined. These theories focus their attention on individual characteristics and differences. They, in general, argue that it is various detectable individual traits, physical or psychological, that separate criminals from non-criminals. From this chapter on, I shall focus on various sociological and social psychological theories of crime and delinquency.

Sociologists, in general, do not regard crime as an aberrant, pathological set of responses of individuals, or as an epiphenomenon that will necessarily vanish in a more just society (Blumberg 1981:1). Criminal behavior is often seen as adaptive responses to environmental pressures. The sociological explanations of crime, thus, highlight the role that social structures, social institutions, and social processes play in shaping human behavior. The foundations of sociological criminology can be traced to the works of Karl Marx (1818-1883) and Emile Durkheim (1858-1917). The causes of crime lie in the socio-economic structure and environmental factors triggering for those predisposed to crime. Marx's contribution to our understanding of crime will be presented in Chapter 11. This chapter and the following few chapters will discuss Durkheim's opulent contributions.

One of Durkheim's most significant contributions is his claim that crime is a "normal" and necessary social behavior since it has existed in every age, in both poverty and prosperity, crime seems part of human nature. The existence of some crimes implies that a way is open for social change, and that the social structure is not rigid or inflexible. Consequently, creativity and independent thinking can develop. Crime can also have benefits because it calls attention to social problems so programs would be designed to relieve the human suffering. Crime functions to promote social solidarity by uniting people against crime. Punishment of criminals is the payoff to citizens who obey the law. Crime thus seems to be "the price society pays for the possibility of progress" (Vold et al. 1998:129).

Durkheim's theory emerged during a period of profound social change in France – the transition from a largely agricultural society to a mostly industrial society. Durkheim regards human nature as selfish. Individuals have unlimited desires that, if left unchecked, would results in chaos. Collective conscience or a set of strong norms is necessary for a stable society. Social institutions are developed in order to serve to regulate behavior and integrate people into the group (see Chapter 9 for a further expansion of Durkheim's analysis on social control). Rapid change in technology and organization affect social structures because they alter human environments and expectations, which in turn, decrease the effectiveness of informal mechanisms of social control and integration. A weakened collective conscience or ineffective social control makes life unpredictable and results in anomie (see Chapter 6 for a more detailed discussion of this topic). The unpredictability causes disorganization which can lead to crime (Durkheim 1893; 1895; 1897).

Social Disorganization Theory

Social disorganization theory is one of the first sociological theories developed in the U.S. In addition to its emphasis on the geographical distribution of crime, the theorists propose a theoretical causal model to explain the crime rate. Building on Durkheim's argument that rapid social change is associated with increases in crime due to the breakdown of social controls, they argue that social order, stability, and integration are conducive to conformity, while disorder and malintegration are conducive to crime and deviance. They suggest that the less there exists solidarity, cohesion, or integration within a group, community, or society, the higher there will be the rate of crime and deviance. Shaw and McKay (1942) assume that a competitive, open housing market naturally makes certain areas of the city more attractive for settlement and, in turn, more residentially stable than others. This process leads to variation in the ability of neighborhoods to regulate themselves, which results in the variation in the delinquency rates. Shaw and McKay argue specifically that three structural factors lead to the disruption of urban community social organization, which also accounts for variations in delinquency[1]. These three factors are low economic status, ethnic heterogeneity, and residential mobility. Social disorganization theory attempts to explain high rates of crime and delinquency in urban communities of disadvantaged lower-class and racial/ethnic groups resulted from rapid industrialization, urbanization, and immigration. It also provides grounds for the later study of delinquency, criminal gangs and subcultures.

In the United States, rapid social change and urban development were the central feature of the landscape in the 1920s (Lilly et al. 1995). The American economy was thrown into full gear by the World War I. Long strides were made toward the increased mechanization or technologicalization of both industrial and agricultural production. Demands for large-scale and efficient production were bolstered by major technological advances in the fields of communication and transportation. These developments propelled business organization toward greater centralization, combination and control of industrial effort.

Change, as the Chicago theorists would note, led to further change. The increased mechanization of agriculture produced technological unemployment. This resulted in a drift of farm workers to cities. There they joined large populations of foreign-born workers, an increasing number of women workers who had entered the industrial labor force during the war, and black workers who had migrated from the south to the urban industrial centers of the north and west.

These rapid changes paved the way for the rise of the Chicago school of sociology. The Chicago school emerges in the writings and research of sociologists at the University of Chicago during the 1920s. By emphasizing social causation, as opposed to rational choice or illness, the Chicago school departed from the individualistic focus of classical and pathological theorizing. Moreover, in demanding that sociological theory be tied to a rigorous scientific investigation of social life, the Chicago school separated itself from a previous generation of speculative, sentimental, and reform-oriented social pathologists. It developed a model of naturalistic social causation. Crime was viewed as a natural by-product of rapid social change. High rates of nonconformity occurred when too much change in too short a time disrupted the normative order of society.

The Chicago school devoted a great deal of its attention to ecological studies of the city. Park, Burgess and McKenzie (1928) were concerned about how neighborhood structure developed, how isolated pockets of poverty developed, and what social policies could be used to alleviate urban problems. They proposed that as cities expanded in size, they grew radially in a series of concentrated zones or rings. The zone in transition contained rows of deteriorating tenements, often built in the shadow of aging factories. As the least desirable living area, the zone had to weather the influx of waves of immigrants and other migrants who were too poor to reside elsewhere. Social lives in the transitional zones, thus, weakened the family and communal ties that bound people together and resulted in social disorganization. This disorganization in turn was the source of social pathology, including crime and delinquency.

The observations were explained by reference to the theory of urban ecology that viewed the city as analogous to the natural ecological communities of plants and animals. Allying the concepts of dominance, invasion, and succession, the theory maintained that there are dominant uses of land within the zones. When those uses characteristic of an inner zone encroach on the adjacent outer zone, invasion occurs and that territory becomes less desirable. The Chicago School was used as the basis for a broadly ranging study of juvenile delinquency by Clifford R. Shaw and Henry D. McKay.

From the ecological perspective, human behavior is determined by social conditions that affect the social and physical environment of which humans are a part. Human beings are viewed as conformists, acting in accordance with group values and norms. Behavior is seen by Chicago school sociologists as relative, a view which implies that there are limitations on free will and on humans' freedom of action. This limited free will later was adopted by most criminologists.

Society is seen as a conglomerate of human communities, each forms through functional systems of relationships that emerge in localized territories. The pluralistic vision of culture conflict in relation to crime is implied in the notion of the "struggle for space" and emerges in the writing of Sellin (1938). Early ecological approach represents an acceptance of the established mainstream values, a pressure toward relinquishing "old ways," and a rationalization and justification for those who dominate others, culturally and organizationally.

The persistent patterns of geographical characteristics of population aggregates are associated with differential rates of crime. Social disorganization refers to (1) the breakdown in conventional institutional control, both formal and informal; and (2) the inability of a community structure to realize the common values of its residents. Crime is found disproportionately in the "soul-searing conditions" of the city slums, where there is social, cultural, and economic deprivation. The Chicago sociologists emphasize that residents in this area are not biologically or psychologically abnormal. Rather, their crime and deviance are simply "the normal reaction of normal people to abnormal social conditions" (Plant 1937: 248). Criminal and delinquent traditions develop under these conditions and are culturally transmitted from one generation to the next. Industrialization, urbanization, and other social changes in modern society are seen as causing social disorganization by undermining traditional social order and values. These macro-social processes account for the aggregate-level relationship, independent of individual predisposition.

The uneven distribution of crime along the lines of the climate, populations, poverty and geography was first noted by French lawyer and statistician Guerry (1833) and Belgian mathematician and astronomer Quetelet (1835). These scholars, however, failed to develop a social theory in explaining these differences. In the U.S., the development of human ecology in Chicago influenced Shaw and McKay. Through painstaking research, Shaw and McKay used juvenile court statistics to map the spatial distribution of delinquency throughout Chicago to test the hypothesis derived from human ecological theory. Their data analysis confirmed the hypothesis that delinquency is highest in the zone in transition and was inversely related to the zone's affluence and corresponding distance from the central business. Consequently, Shaw and McKay (1942) concluded that crime is a product of transitional neighborhoods that manifest social disorganization and criminogenic environment.

For Shaw and McKay, population turnover and racial/ethnic heterogeneity in the slums are assumed to increase the likelihood of disorganization. Regular institutions pertaining to internal control are difficult to function when residents are not interested in communities and are ready to leave at the first opportunity. The development of primary relationships that result in informal structures of social control are less likely when local networks are difficult to establish or in a continual state of flux. Racial and ethnic heterogeneity impedes effective communication and obstructs the efforts to solve common problems of the communities. As a result, weak structures of both formal and informal controls decrease the costs associated with deviation within the group, making high rates of crime and delinquency more likely (Bursik 1988).

Measurement of the Key Concepts

The key concepts in social disorganization theory are not as complex as the concept of social disorganization itself. Cohen (1959: 474) notes, "Few terms in sociology are so variously and obscurely defined as social disorganization." Although the theory suggests that social disorganization leads to deviant behavior of all kinds, it is, as Cohen points out, "difficult to determine what, if anything, is the line of demarcation between social disorganization and deviant behavior." Schmid (1928) for example, used rescue missions, pawnshops, employment agencies, houses of prostitution, and homicides as indices of social disorganization. Similarly, Lander (1954) defined delinquency as social disorganization. As a result, there is a confusion as whether delinquency is a dependent variable or an independent variable.

Traditionally, the tests of social disorganization theory focus on three structural factors: low economic status, ethnic heterogeneity, and residential mobility. Over the years, these measures have improved in accuracy. Heitgerd and Bursik's test (1987) of social disorganization theory illustrates this point (see Table 5.1). Using data from a longitudinal design, social disorganization is captured by four variables. These four variables are further divided into two groups: internal dynamics and extern dynamics of the community. The internal dynamics include house, race, and residential stability within a community. The variable house is an unmeasured variable with three indicators: the percentage of dwelling units that are owner-occupied, the percentage of unemployment, and the percentage of households averaging more than one person per room[2]. This unmeasured variable captures the concept of economical well-being and over-crowding. The racial/ethnic composition is an index of the residual change scores for the percentage of nonwhite and the percentage of foreign-born. Residential stability is measured by the percentage of residents over the age of five who had lived in the same dwelling unit for at least five years. The external dynamics is created by averaging the nonwhite scores for all areas immediately adjacent to each of the local communities. The advantage of this study is to get a sense of longitudinal changes in a community and its impact on the delinquency rates. The results partially support social disorganization theory. Previously, Bursik and Webb did a similar study in 1982.

Sampson and Groves (1989), on the other hand, open up a new ground for testing social disorganization theory. They attempt to capture the illusive concept of social disorganization in its original sense. They ague that rapid rates of population turnover and the increases in structural density lead to a greater proportion of strangers in a neighborhood, who are less likely to intercede on behalf of local residents in crime-related situations. To better capture the sense of social disorganization, they organize their variables into two groups: exogenous and intervening variables. The exogenous variables are very similar to variables of Shaw and McKay (1942) and the following studies since then. They tap into the concepts of socioeconomic status, ethnic heterogeneity, residential stability, family disruption, and urbanism. Note that they use socioeconomic status to replace the traditional measure of poverty in social disorganization theory. It is also worthy noting the operationalization of ethnic heterogeneity. To capture the full range of heterogeneity, an index employed in Blau's research (1977) of the intergroup relations is adopted:

The index racial/ethnic heterogeneity = $(1 - \text{sum } p_i^2)$,

where p_i is the fraction of the population in a given group. This index takes into account both the relative size and the number of groups in the population, with a score of one reflecting maximum heterogeneity and zero maximum homogeneity. Ever since this study, most new studies of social disorganization theory adopt this measure of ethnic/racial heterogeneity (Osgood and Chambers 2000; Markowitz et al. 2001; Warner and Pierce 1993).

The most innovative variables in Sampson and Groves' study are intervening variables which include local friendship networks, unsupervised peer groups and organizational participation. According to Sampson and Groves, these factors are considered direct indicators of social organization; thus their relative absence suggests social disorganization. Using data from the British Crime Survey, their study indicates that crime rates are lower in areas characterized by higher friendship ties in a locality, higher levels of participation in organization, and greater control of teenage groups. They, however, also admit that their measures of disorganization are only an approximation of the concepts suggested by Shaw and McKay. Their data were reanalyzed by Veysey and Messner (1999) with covariance structure modeling (LISREL). The results of the reanalyses largely support Sampson and Groves' findings, but Veysey and Messner (1999) dispute Sampson and Groves' interpretation.

Markowitz et al. (2001), also using the British Crime Survey data, emphasizes the concepts of neighborhood cohesion, disorder, and fear of crime in social disorganization theory (see Table 5.1). Their operationalization of cohesion overlaps with that of Sampson and Groves (1989). Their measures of disorder and fear are their interpretation of social disorganization theory. The major contribution of their study is the estimate of nonrecursive models of relationship between disorder, burglary, cohesion and fear of crime. The results suggest a feedback loop in which decrease in neighborhood cohesion increases crime and disorder, including fear, in turn, further decreasing cohesion.

Gottfredson, McNeil, and Gottfredson (1991) conduct a multi-level study to partially test social disorganization theory. In their study design, social disorganization theory is regarded as a community level exogenous variable. The concept of social disorganization is tapped by five indicators of the community. These five indicators are (1) the ratio of female-headed households with children under 16 years old to husband-wife-headed households with children under 16; (2) the proportion of families on welfare; (3) the proportion of families with incomes 1.24 times the poverty level or below; (4) the proportion of persons aged 14 and over who are married with spouse absent, separated, or divorced; and (5) the proportion of males aged 16 or over in the labor force who are unemployed. Their study indicates that social disorganization is significantly related to interpersonal aggression, but not to theft, vandalism or drug involvement.

Many new tests of social disorganization theory continue to model according to Shaw and McKay's original study. They do not have any new measures to offer (Osgood and Chambers 2000; Warner and Pierce 1993). Instead, they have extended the application of the theory to different environments. Warner and Pierce (1993), for example, apply traditional independent variables of social disorganization theory – poverty, racial/ethnic heterogeneity, residential mobility, family disruption, and structural density (see Table 5.1), and their interactions – to explain calls to the police in Boston. Interestingly, although social disorganization theory is developed to explain delinquency and crime in urban areas, Osgood and Chamber (2000) extend it to explain suburban crime rates. One recent innovative interpretation comes from Warner's test of the cultural component of social disorganization (2003). Built upon the extension of social disorganization theory by Kornhauser (1978), Warner constructs two indexes of cultural variables to test the theory: social ties and cultural strength. Although she finds evidence in support of her test of social disorganization theory, the dependent variable of the study is informal social control. This re-orientation of social disorganization theory is worth further exploring.

Summary and Discussion

Sociologists in general emphasize crime and deviates as social phenomena. Human kind is not, by nature, inherently deviant. Deviant impulses are socially induced. Social disorganization theory, as principally developed and elaborated by Shaw and McKay, has merit in that it has pointed to social causes of delinquency that seem to be located in specific geographic areas. It is a thoroughly social viewpoint on the study of delinquency and social control. It transcends many of the individualistic limitations and biases of previous perspectives. The theory asks us to imagine that delinquent and criminals are people just like ourselves (Pfohl 1985). The theoretical models are grounded on the statistical analysis of large aggregate data bases, such as U.S. Census Bureau, National Crime Survey, and Uniform Crime Report data. Because of Shaw and McKay, studies of juvenile delinquency have become an inseparable part of the study of crime. Since the late 1980s, survey data have also been used to test the theory (Gottfredson et al. 1991; Markowitz et al. 2001; Sampson and Groves 1989; Simcha-Fagan and Schwartz 1986). After almost a century's empirical scrutiny, the theory continues to show its viability.

Social disorganization, however, has its limitations because it fails to ask why middle-class crime occurs, why some youths are insulated from a delinquent career, how accurate official statistics are, and why crime occurs in rural areas. It is difficult to judge the extent to which social disorganization theory has been verified as an explanation of crime (Akers 1998). Bursik (1988), for example, points out that changes in economic, racial/ethnic, and other socioeconomic conditions within urban areas may alter the geographic distributions of delinquency rates. Such changes may not always result from "natural' competition for limited spaces, but might also reflect the intentional efforts of those who have some control over land-use patterns. Shaw and McKay's model leaves the impression that the composition and internal organization of local communities are relatively independent of the broader political dynamics of a city or a society. Moreover, are physical, economic, and population characteristics objective indications of disorganization, or does the term disorganization simply reflect *a value judgment* about lower-classes lifestyle and living conditions[3]?

For the measures of social disorganization theory, the lack of theoretical clarity has led to different interpretations of the theory, which results in some very different measures (see Table 5.1). One of the measures – racial/ethnic heterogeneity proposed by Blau (1977) seems to have received a wide acceptance within this theoretical tradition: ($1 - $ sum p_i^2). Despite its limitations, social disorganization theory has enjoyed a revived appreciation in the 1980s and 1990s (Bursik 1986; 1988; Bursik and Webb 1982; Markowitz et al. 2001; Osgood and Chambers 2000; Rose and Clear 1998; Sampson and Groves 1989; Warner and Pierce 1993). The expansion of its measures to include survey data adds a new dimension to test the theory. The theory is rich in sociological imagination and it continues to be one of the most important criminological theories of the 21st century. The current discussion only focuses on the structural side of social disorganization theory. The cultural side of social disorganization theory, which gives rise to differential association theory and subculture of violence theory, will be discussed in Chapters 7 and 8 respectively.

Notes

1.   Shaw and McKay (1942) also began a new line of research by substituting crime with delinquency in their pioneering study.

2.   Remember these three variables also appear in the tests of routine activity theory where the percentage of dwelling units that are owner-occupied and percentage of households with more than one person per room are components of the lifestyle index (Cao and Maume 1993). The percentage of the unemployed is interpreted as one motivational factor by Stahura and Sloan (1988).

3.   Sutherland (1947) used the term "differential social organization" by emphasizing that these urban neighborhoods may not be so much *disorganized* as simply *organized around* different values and concerns. Previously, Whyte (1943) argued that what appeared from the perspective of the larger society to be disorganization, or lack of organization, might from another perspective be quite organized.

Table 5.1 Measures of Social Disorganization Theory

I.   Gottfredson, McNeil, and Gottfredson (1991)

1.   disorganization = ratio of female-headed households with children under 16 to husband-wife-headed households with children under 16 + proportion of families on welfare + proportion of families with incomes 1.24 times the poverty level or below + proportion of persons aged 14 and over who are married with spouse absent, separated, or divorced + proportion of males aged 16 or over in labor force who are unemployed

II.   Heitgerd and Bursik (1987)

A.   Dependent Variable:

1.   delres = the differences between delinquency rates in 1970s and the rates that can be predicted on the basis of the 1960 data

B.   Internal Dynamics:

1.   house = residual change scores for percentage of dwelling units that are owner occupied, unemployment rate, and percentage of households averaging more than one person per room

2.   race = residual change scores for percentage nonwhite and percentage foreign-born

3.   residential stability = percentage of residents over the age of five who had lived in the same dwelling unit for at least five years

C.   External Dynamics:

1.   ext-nwres = averaging the race scores for all areas immediately adjacent to each of local communities

III.   Markowitz, Bellair, Liska and Liu (2001)

A.   Neighborhood Cohesion (aggregate-level reliability = .70)

1.   the percent who went to a club or committee meeting in the last week

2.   the percent who said that "neighbors mostly help each other"

3.   the percent who reported being "very satisfied" with living in the area

B.   Disorder (aggregate-level reliability = .83)
The percentage of those who considered each of the following as "a very big problem" in their area was computed and added across the five items:
1.   Noisy neighbors or loud parties;
2.   teenagers hanging around on the streets;
3.   drunks or tramps on the streets;
4.   rubbish and litter lying about;
5.   vandalism or graffiti.
C.   Fear of Crime:
1.   The percent who felt "very unsafe" walking alone after dark;
2.   the percent who were "very worried" about being burglarized;
3.   the percent who were "very worried" about being robbed.

IV.   Sampson and Groves (1989)
A.   Exogenous:
1.   socioeconomic status (percent college educated, percent in professional and managerial positions, and percent with high income)
2.   ethnic heterogeneity $(1 - \text{sum } p_i^2)$
3.   residential stability (percentage of residents brought up in the area within a 15-minute walk from home)
4.   family disruption (proportion of divorced and separated adults among those who had ever married, and percentage of households with single parents with children)
5.   urbanization (dummy with 1=central city and 0=all others)
B.   Intervening:
1.   local friendship networks (how many of their friends reside in the 15-minute walk local community)
2.   unsupervised peer groups (how common it was for groups of teenagers to hang out in public in the neighborhood and make nuisances of themselves)
3.   organizational participation (percentage of residents who participated in committee, club, and other organizational activities in the week before)

V.   Warner and Pierce (1993)
1.   poverty = percentage of the population living below the poverty level

2. racial heterogeneity $= (1 - \text{sum } p_i^2)$
3. mobility = percentage of residents who have not lived in the same house for the past five years
4. family disruption = percentage of households headed by a female
5. structural density = percentage of structures with five or more units

---

Chapter 6
Anomie Tradition

Another important contribution of Emil Durkheim (1858-1917) to criminology is his thesis of anomie, which has been greatly enriched by American criminologists led by Robert K. Merton (1910-2003). Anomie tradition has developed into several variations. This chapter, however, discusses only three most distinct branches of the theory and their measures.

Anomie tradition is one of the most influential criminological theories in the United States. Originally, Durkheim (1897) used the term anomie to refer to a state of normlessness or lack of social regulation in modern society as one condition that promotes deviance and suicide. A society beset by anomie was said to lack the regulatory constraints necessary for the adequate social control of its members. Merton (1938) borrowed the concept and used it to explain why crime rates vary in different societies and why crime rates vary within a society between different groups. He argues that an integrated society maintains a balance between social structure and culture. Anomie is the form that societal malintegration takes when there is a dissociation between valued cultural ends and legitimate societal means to those ends. It is the discrepancy between socially engendered goals and the availability of legitimate means to achieve such goals.

Both Durkheim and Merton agree that the source of deviance is anomie, the sense of normlessness and frustration that is a product of the way that society is organized. Organization or disorganization of society causes anomie, which leaves people confused about what norms should regulate their behavior. Merton's anomie theory, however, shifts the emphasis of anomie from a failure to develop adequate moral regulation to differential access to opportunity social structure[1]. Unlike Durkheim, Merton argues that human desires are not natural, rather they are created by cultural influences (Cullen 1983; Passas 1995). His anomie theory explains both the crime as a general adaptation to human societies and the crime rate specific to the U.S. society.

Anomie Theory

Merton's essay "Social Structure and Anomie" (1938) is possibly the most frequently quoted paper in sociology (Cole 1975) and criminology. It exerts tremendous impact on the studies of crime in the United States. Merton argues that people are basically good. Only under pressure (strain) do they deviate. Merton believes that two elements of all modern cultures interact to produce potential strain – culturally defined goals and socially approved means for obtaining these goals. When societies place equal emphasis on goals and means, individuals achieve satisfaction from both goal achievement and following institutional means for achieving goals. When societies have an imbalanced emphasis between goals and means, anomie results. Anomie is rampant when societies emphasize certain common success-goals, such as monetary success, for the population at large, but do not provide equal access for everyone to achieve that goal. Anomie increases the probability of committing crimes, in particular instrumental crime (Bernard, 1987). Some societies, such as the United States, stress the goals of acquiring material success. Socially permissible means to acquiring wealth include hard work, education, and thrift. The United States, however, is a class society and the socially permissible means are stratified across class and status lines. Those with few economic resources soon find that they are denied the access to legally acquire money and other success symbols. When socially mandated goals are uniform throughout society and access to legitimate means is bound by class, the anomie/strain is produced among those who are locked out of the legitimate opportunity structure. Consequently, people may develop criminal or delinquent solutions to the problem of attaining societal goals.

Merton proposed five modes of adaptation to a state of anomie within a society: conformity, innovation, ritualism, retreatism and rebellion. Except conformity, the other four adaptations to anomie are considered deviant, in one way or another. While the conformity is the mostly widely employed adaptation in any stable society, the rebellion is the least possible form. Innovation refers to an acceptance of cultural goals but a rejection of legitimate means. In a society emphasizing equality for all like the United States, this means that all individuals are encouraged to aspire to economic success, but the reality is that not every body has equal access to the opportunity structure of the United States. As a result, many economically disadvantaged people who accept the cultural goals have to reject the legitimate means to success. The technically most effective procedure, whether culturally legitimate or not, becomes typically preferred means to institutionally prescribed conduct. This may result in a wide variety of innovative criminal violation of laws in the road to the riches. Anomie is more applicable to the prediction of instrumental crimes than expressive crimes (Bernard 1987; Messner and Rosenfeld 1994).

Retreatism represents the rejection of both goals and means. This may lead individuals to lose themselves in the drug or alcohol world, or to sexually promiscuous behavior and survival activities such as pimping. Individuals are deemed "double failures" since they have failed both criminal and conventional activities. Ritualism refers to the rejection of cultural goals, but obeys the legitimate means of a society. Merton tries to make us see that "some social structures exert a definite pressure on certain persons in the society to engage in nonconforming conduct rather than conformist conduct" (1938: 672). The following sections examine the other two major intellectual lines of causal theories derived from Merton's anomie theory.

Strain Theory

Another line of interpreting anomie theory is made by re-labelling the theory as strain theory. Bernard (1995) and Burton and Cullen (1992) maintain that this interpretation of Merton's theory in criminology was largely provided by Hirschi (1969) and fleshed out by Kornhauser (1978). This version has largely confined the theory to the domain of juvenile delinquency and within a single society. It is further reduced to its cores— the gap between aspirations and expectations and the perceptions of blocked opportunity for juveniles. Strain theory was the dominant delinquency theory from the early 1950s up until about the 1970s (Cole 1975). The gradual transformation of anomie theory into strain theory began with Albert Cohen's book *Delinquent Boys* (1955).

In an effort to apply Merton's anomie theory in the study of delinquency gang, Cohen specifically suggested that delinquent and law-abiding behavior both depend largely on one's sociocultural environment and social interaction. Delinquent subcultures develop primarily among juveniles from poorer working class family background who are relatively unskilled at competing in a middle-class world. This results in their status frustration. Delinquent behavior of lower-class youths is actually a protest against the norms and values of the middle-class American culture. Many working-class kids join together in teenage gangs and engage in behavior that is "nonutilitarian, malicious, and negativistic" (Cohen 1955).

Cohen's version of anomie theory is in basic agreement with Merton's theory, because it perceives blocked goals as producing deviance-inducing strain. In Cohen's view, however, rather than the inability to gain material success, it is the inability to gain status and acceptance in conventional society that produces the strain among juveniles. Cohen makes it clear that delinquency is not a product of inherent class inferiority. Rather, it is a result of the social and economic limitations suffered by members of the less-fortunate groups in society. Cohen, thus, has substituted the goal of status among peers for Merton's goal of achieving wealth.

Building on Merton and Cohen, Richard Cloward and Lloyd Ohlin's theory of differential opportunity (1960) extends anomie theory in explaining juvenile delinquency[2]. The authors agree with Merton that people who perceive themselves as failures within conventional society will seek innovative ways to gain success; some will question the legitimacy of conventional codes of conduct as an appropriate guide for their own behavior and instead begin to use illegal means. They are interested in knowing why delinquent subculture arises in certain neighborhood in the social structure. They suggest that not all adolescents adapt to anomie/strain in the same way because, not only are conventional opportunities stratified unequally in the social structure, but so too are illegal opportunities. They identify three delinquent subcultures or gang types: 1. criminal gangs, which seek monetary gain through crime; (2) conflict gangs, which specialize in violence; and (3) retreatist gangs, which are drug-related. The response taken depends on the means available in the neighborhood.

General Strain Theory

Discontented with classic strain theory's obtensible empirical weakness, Robert Agnew (1992) has proposed an extension of classic strain theory — general strain theory. He agrees with the basic statement of classic strain theories of Merton (1938), Cohen (1955) and Cloward and Ohlin (1960) that the sources of deviance and crime are strain. He argues, however, that classic strain theories focus on only one type of negative relationship: relationship in which others prevent the individual from achieving positively valued goals. His general strain theory provides a more comprehensive account for the cognitive, behavioral, and emotional adaptations to strain. These forms of strain may be more important than the traditional aspirational related strain. Specifically, general strain theory identifies three major types of deviance-producing strain or negative relationships with others: the failure to achieve an individual's goals, the removal of positive or desired stimuli from the individual, and the confrontation of the individual with negative stimuli. According to Agnew, each type of strain increases the likelihood of experiencing such negative emotions as disappointment, depression, fear, and most importantly, anger. Delinquency operates as one way of coping with "negative social relations" and their resultant psychological state, even though it may be socially unacceptable.

Agnew (1992) attempts to offer a more general explanation of criminal activity among all elements of society rather than restrict his views to lower-class crime. He argues that since strain is not confined only to the disjunctures between means and ends, a number of other measures beyond the discrepancy between aspirations and expectations can now be used. In specifying the types of strain (especially the second and third) and outlining factors that influence each adaptation, Agnew moves strain theory closer to social bonding and social learning theories, thereby incorporating a number of explanatory variables from those theories. In order to improve strain theory's power of explaining delinquency, Agnew has set his general strain theory solidly on the ground of social-psychological level of explanation, and as an unintended consequence, has taken away the classic strain theory's distinguished structural nature, substituting it with individual-psychology.

Measurement of the Key Concepts

Anomie Theory. Although Merton's anomie theory was meant to be both for cross-national and for cross-sectional research at both the macro and the micro levels, most efforts have been made to test the theory with cross-sectional data within a single society at the micro-level. Tests of the theory with cross-national data at the macro level, in contrast, have become a road less travelled (Messner 1988; Burton and Cullen 1992; Bernard 1987) and few tests at this level are quite tentative and explorative in nature (see Messner and Rosenfeld 1997[3]). As such, the following discussion will focus on the tests of the theory at the micro-level.

The concept of anomie is very elusive and controversial. Like many other early criminological theories, anomie theory is not put forth in precise and readily testable propositions. Merton himself did not provide an operational definition of anomie in his 1938 essay or in any of his later theoretical clarification. He has provided many clues on the meaning of anomie in his later works (1964). He proposed that a state of normlessness is the widespread de-legitimation of social norms: "withdrawal of allegiance from one or another part of prevailing social standards is what we mean, in the end, by anomie" (1964: 218). Later, in the same article, Merton (1964: 227) again defines anomie as "a lack of consensus on norms judged to be legitimate." Thus the concept of anomie can refer to values and judgements of people with respect to the violation of norms.

It is ironic that Merton's anomie theory is often "tested without reference to his concept of anomie" (Cullen and Wright 1997:199). There are, however, a few exceptions to this rule[4]. Srole (1956) is credited with proposing the term "anomia" to represent the anomic state of the individual. He developed the term in his article "Social integration and certain corollaries: An exploratory study." He considered anomia as social malintegration in individuals, and more specific, as interpersonal alienation. As a result, he designed a five-item scale to measure anomic state of mind as a part of broader concept of alienation (see Table 6.1). His measure has not been used in the criminological literature.

A more widely used measure of anomie in the criminological literature appears in The National Youth Surveys (see Table 6.1). It was based on Elliott's (1985) deduction from Seeman's (1959) interpretation of anomie, which refers to normlessness as a part of alienation. This measure is also shaped by Cohen's argument (1955) that anomie refers to the inability of juveniles to gain status and acceptance in conventional society. It is more specifically designed to measure juveniles' anomie, not adults' anomie. Relying on this measure and using data from National Youth Surveys, Menard's studies (1995; 1997) indicate the anomie theory is able to explain the variation in delinquency.

Despite many advantages of this measure of anomie and its subsequent adoption in research, it has three problems. First, it does not actually reflect Merton's original meaning that anomie refers to de-legitimation of particular social norms. Instead, every item clearly contains an element of justification for breaking the norm. Second, the measure fails to capture the pivotal role of money in Merton's theory. It only reflects the deviations from norms that are driven by a juvenile's simple desire to achieve a goal, unnecessarily monetary or utilitarian in nature. Third, the index is more specifically designed or tailored to a juvenile population rather than to an adult population.

In absence of a satisfactory measure for anomie, Cao (1999) proposes another measure of anomie to test the hypothesis that "contemporary American culture appears to approximate the polar type in which great emphasis upon certain success-goals occurs without equivalent emphasis upon institutional means" (Merton, 1968, p. 190). Anomie is operationalized as an index of acceptance of legitimacy of six instrumental criminal/deviant scenarios (see Table 6.1). This measure improves on previous operationalization of anomie in three ways. First, it reflects Merton's original meaning of anomie that a lack of consensus on norms judged to be legitimate is anomie. Second, it captures Merton's original argument that anomie refers to the extent that the technically most effective procedure becomes typically preferred conduct. In other words, anomie is the extent of the de-legitimation regarding "particular" or "specific" norms resulting from rules and legal codes of a society. Third, the index covers a wider range of instrumental crimes – white-collar and street crimes – for adults. The extent that the general population tolerates these money-related criminal or deviant behaviors is a clear indication of extent of acceptance of innovation as a mode of adaptation. There is a connection between America's strong emphasis of monetary success and crime in Merton's original theory and its later interpretations (Agnew 1984; Bernard 1987; Burton and Cullen 1992; Messner and Rosenfeld 1997). Apparently, the measure indicates this aspect of anomie: the extent of individuals' readiness to disregard the rules or to use the technically most efficient and available means "in netting the socially approved value." The Cronbach's alpha of this index is .72.

Strain Theory. Most other research on anomie theory shifts its attention from anomie to strain. Researchers occasionally have departed from the standard test of strain theory (see Agnew et al. 1996; Cao and Deng 1998), but most existing studies share the following features: they do not try to explain social class difference in the crime rates and they use self-report surveys to measure whether juveniles' perceptions that their life prospects are restricted increase involvement in delinquency. Strain is largely operationalized either by (1) the perception of blocked opportunity or by (2) the perceived gap between desired success goals and lack of opportunity (Burton and Cullen 1992; Burton et al. 1994).

Short, Rivera and Tennyson (1965) developed one of the early measures of strain: the perception of blocked opportunities in education and occupation (Table 6.2). Their blocked educational opportunities varies from 0 to 12 with higher scores presenting less blocked educational opportunity and their blocked opportunities varies from 0 to 10 with higher scores presenting less blocked occupational opportunities. Both scales are hypothesized to be negatively related to delinquency. Several later studies produced some variations of the strain measure based on this research (Cernkovich 1978; Cernkovich and Giordano 1979; Segrave and Halsted 1983). In general, these studies have supported a correlation between delinquency and strain.

Another measure of strain proposed by Farnworth and Leiber (1989) represented a better operationalization of strain in terms of the perceived gap between desired success goals and lack of opportunity (see Table 6.2). Most previous studies measure the gap between youth's educational and/or occupational aspiration. Farnworth and Leiber (1989), however, argued that the appropriate operationalization of strain theory is to measure the disjunction between economic aspirations and educational expectations, and that this approach is closer to Merton's thesis that economic success is the dominant cultural goal and that education is the principal legitimate means for attaining such success. Thus, educational expectations and aspirations are quantified: no college=0, some college=1, college graduation=2, and then an index of educational strain is created by subtracting educational expectation from educational aspiration. The differences range from 0 to 2. It is found that within categories of educational aspiration, the higher the level of educational strain, the higher the delinquency rate.

Finally, two studies testes strain theory with data of adults. This is a departure from most studies of strain theory (Agnew et al. 1996; Cao and Deng 1998). In Agnew et al.'s study (1996), the survey instruments were designed by Cullen, Burton, Evans and Dunaway and the data were collected in a large mid-west city. Strain is defined as dissatisfaction with one's monetary situation. It is a function of (1) the importance placed on monetary success; (2) the amount of money desired; (3) the importance placed on alternative goals; (4) one's position in the stratification system; (5) expectations of future monetary success; and (6) degree of relative deprivations, based on comparisons with the financial situation of others. Strain is captured by three composite index measures of dissatisfaction with monetary status, expectations for a lot of money, and relative deprivation (Table 6.2).

Cao and Deng (1998) conduct another innovative test of the strain theory in an integrated model of shoplifting by employing three measures of strain: immediate goals, blocked opportunity, and perceived solution (see Table 6.2). They notice that previous measures of strain focus on the long-term goals, such education and occupation, but most people are brought up with a culture of immediate gratification. Therefore, measures of the immediate needs may be a better indicator of strain than long-term goals of education and occupation, and the immediate blocked opportunity of general goals, financial situation and comparison may be a better indicator of strain than long-term goals of education and occupation. Moreover, Cao and Deng propose a measure based on Cloward and Ohlin's call for the delinquent coping that bridges strained individuals and availability of the opportunity (Cullen 1983; 1988). This results in a measure of perceived solution. Their measures, of course, are uniquely designed to predict the behavior of shoplifting, and their application to explain other types of delinquency needs modification. Their analysis indicates that the perceived solution is the strongest predictor of shoplifting. This is so even after controlling the measures of differential association theory and a measure of seduction theory in an integrated model.

General Strain Theory. Based on Agnew's general strain theory, Agnew and White (1992) used the data from the first wave of the Rutgers Health and Human Development Project to test the theory. Eight dimensions of strain are identified (Table 6.3). Most of them are multiple items measures[5], but the last two measures are one-item measures. In addition, a general strain scale is created from five aspects of strain: negative life events, life hassles, negative relationship with adults, parental fighting and neighborhood problems. The tests are considered a conservative one because only negative relations with others are classified as strain measures while positive measures are classified as social control variables. Even so, the results support the hypotheses of general strain theory. Agnew and White, however, admit that their test of general strain theory is incomplete because they fail to measure the type of strain to achieve positively valued goals.

Mazerolle and Maahs (2000) used the data from the National Youth Surveys and developed four measures of strain (see Table 6.3). Their measures of general strain theory are different from Agnew and White's. They capture four dimensions of the negative strains: negative relations with adults, school/peer hassles, neighborhood problems[6], and negative life events. Negative relations with adults contain 20 items on child's perception of teaches' and parents' evaluation of them. The reliability of the measure is .86. School/peer hassles have seven items with the Likert scale responses and reliability of the index is .72. Neighborhood problems consist of seven items with response ranging from not a problem or somewhat of a problem to big problem and the reliability of the scale is .74. Negative life events contain thirteen items from divorce to father moved in/out last year with a reliability of .50. Finally, consistent with the tradition started by Agnew and White (1992), a composite strain index is formed by these four measures.

Summary and Discussion

Anomie tradition has drawn attention to the interplay between social structure, cultural context, and individual action. Different versions of anomie theorists disagree over some fundamental dimensions of their versions of the theory, however, and emphasize different aspects of its components. Merton's original anomie theory assumes individual appetites are "culturally rather than structurally induced" and societal anomie comes from differential opportunities in the social structures that have not met the culturally raised appetites. No acceptable direct measure of anomie has ever been created at the macro-level. For the individual level data, three measures of anomie are proposed. Srole's measure is largely a measure of alienation and is never used in the criminological literature. The measure out of National Youth Survey used by Menard is limited for juvenile delinquency and for nonutilitarian behavior of adolescents. The proposed measure by Cao (1999) for the general population looks promising and may generate more efforts in this area.

Strain theory focuses on a key issue in anomie theory: the goal-oriented and achievement-directed behavior and the result of the social structure and culture that shape this interaction. The society is described as suffering strain because of a dysfunctional mismatch between the goals or aspiration it sets for its members and the structure of opportunities it provides for them to achieve these goals. In other words, strain results in an unleashing of individual aspiration without a corresponding provision of normative or moral guidelines to moderate the level of raised aspirations. Interpreted in this way, strain theory builds its measure around the gap between aspiration and expectations and around perceptions of blocked opportunity. Apparently, the existing measures of various kinds are not good enough in capturing the variation of delinquency. Burton and Cullen (19920 provide an excellent critique of the measures of strain theory and pinpoint the ways the theory can be interpreted differently. Recent efforts have shifted to tap strain of one's satisfaction of financial situation (Agnew et al. 1996; Cao and Deng 1998).

Agnew's version of general strain theory is less compatible with anomie theory or classic strain theory in its notion of goal-seeking actors within a social and cultural structure. Agnew argues that juveniles not only seek goals but exercise pain-avoidance behavior. His contribution is to identify three such sources of strain among adolescents. Delinquency, thus, operates as one way of coping with negative social relations and their resultant psychological states. It is important to remember that Agnew presents his theory as a foundation for further theoretical development rather than a fully developed alternative to earlier anomie/strain theories. More recently, he adds a macro-component to his general strain theory (1999). Overall, the anomie tradition has lost its dominance over the research on the causes of crime (Cullen and Agnew 1999c), but with its sociological richness, it remains one of the influential theories of crime. New efforts in extending the theory at the macro-level are also worthy watching (Messner and Rosenfeld 1994).

Notes

1.　　　Hilbert (1989) argues that Durkheim regards crime as normal and healthy, for it is a primary means the *sui generis* society has for protecting itself against the withering away of the collective conscience. In contrast, Merton tends more or less toward silence on crime's status as healthy and necessary. There is no room in Merton's work for suggesting that if it were not for crime society would face an even more profound crisis. Indeed the "crisis" seems to be crime itself or the related catalogue of social problems.

2.　　　Cullen (1988) rejects the prevailing categorization that treats Cloward and Ohlin's theory as a simple variation of Merton's paradigm. He argues that Cloward and Ohlin's work has not been fully understood and illegitimate opportunity theory is drawn far more from the Chicago school than from Merton's structuralism. Interested readers are encouraged to "revisit" the original work of *Delinquency and Opportunity* (Cloward and Ohlin 1960).

3.　　　Messner and Rosenfeld (1997) tested their institutional anomie theory with cross-national data, but they did not try to measure anomie. Instead, they developed a measure of decommodification based on levels and patterns of welfare expenditures. In a previous test of institutional anomie theory, Chamlin and Cochran (1995) did not introduce any unique measure.

4.　　　In extending Srole's study and further exploring the relationship between anomy and various dimensions of personality, McClosky and Schaar (1965) proposed an anomy scale ten years later. Their psychological anomy referred to "the feeling that the world and oneself are adrift, wandering, lacking in clear rules and stable mooring" (1965:19). Sampson and Bartusch (1998) advanced a measure of legal cynicism in the classic Durkheimian sense – a state of normlessness in which the rules of the dominate society are no longer binding in a community. It is my belief, however, that these measures are too broad, and neither of them have captured Merton's original argument that anomie would develop to the extent that the technically most effective procedure, whether culturally legitimate or not, becomes typically preferred to institutionally prescribed conduct (Merton 1938).

5.　　　Agnew and White (1992) did not report the alpha reliability of all strain's multiple measures.

6.　　　Note that this measure of strain is very similar to a measure of social disorganization theory proposed by Markowitz, Bellair, Liska and Liu (2001) (see Table 5.1, Chapter 6). Previously, similar measures are labelled as "incivility" by Lewis and Salem (1986) and "neighborhood disorder" by Skogan (1987) and "community disorder" by Cao et al. (1996).

Table 6.1   Measures of Anomie Theory

I.   Cao (1999)
Anomie is an index of the following six items with the same lead
question: "Please tell me for each of the following statements
whether you think it can always be justified, never be justified,
or something in between:

1.   claiming government benefits which you are not entitled to;
2.   avoiding a fare on public transport;
3.   cheating on tax if you have the chance;
4.   buying something you knew was stolen;
5.   someone accepting bribe in the course of their duties;
6.   failing to report damage you've done accidentally to a parked vehicle."

(from 1=never through 10=always, the Cronbach's alpha = .72)

II.   Menard (1995):

1.   Sometimes it is necessary to lie to your parents in order to keep their trust.
2.   It may be necessary to break some of your parents' rules in order to keep some of your friends.
3.   In order to gain the respect of your friends, it is sometimes necessary to beat up on other people
4.   You have to be willing to break some rules if your want to be popular with your friends.
5.   To stay out of trouble, it is sometimes necessary to lie to teachers.
6.   At school, it is sometimes necessary to play dirty in order to win.

(from "strongly agree" to "strongly disagree" with Cronbach's alpha = .75-.81)

III.   Srole (1956):

1.   There is little use writing to public officials because often they aren't really interested in the problems of the average man.
2.   Nowadays a person has to live pretty much for today and let tomorrow take care of itself.
3.   In spite of what some people say, the lot of the average man is getting worse, not better.
4.   It's hardly fair to bring children into the world with the way things look for the future.

5.   These days a person doesn't really know whom he can count on.

(from agree to disagree)

_____

Table 6.2   Measures of Strain Theory

I.   Agnew, Cullen, Burton, Evans, and Dunaway (1996)
    A.   Dissatisfaction with Monetary Status (alpha = .74):
    1.   Every time I try to get ahead, something or someone stops me
    2.   Right now I'm satisfied with how much money I have to live on
    3.   I've often been frustrated in my efforts to get ahead in life.
    4.   In the long run, I expect to be satisfied with how much money I'll have to live on.
    5.   I will have enough money to live comfortably on when I retire.
    B.   Expectations for a lot of Money (alpha = .74):
    1.   I expect to be better off financially this time next year.
    2.   In the long run, I expect to be better off financially than I am now
    3.   My chances for making a lot of money in life are not very good
    C.   Relative Deprivation (alpha = .73):
    1.   I get angry when I see people having a lot more money than I do spend their money on foolish things.
    2.   It bothers me that most people have more money to live on than I do.
    3.   It is frustrating to see people driving nicer cars and living in better homes than I do.

II.   Cao and Deng (1998)
    A.   Immediate Goals (alpha = .71):
    1.   I have to have the latest clothes
    2.   I have to have the latest electronics goods?
    B.   Blocked Opportunity (alpha = .75):
    1.   I am satisfied with my opportunities to reach my goals.
    2.   I am satisfied with my present financial situation.
    3.   I am satisfied when comparing myself with other American families.
           (strongly agree, somewhat agree, slightly agree, slightly disagree, somewhat disagree strongly disagree)
    C.   Perceived Solution:
    1.   Shoplifting could offer an easy and quick solution to my needs.
           (0=no and 1=yes).

III. Farnworth and Leiber (1989):
    A. Goals and Means
    1. Economic aspirations: "I want to make lots of money." (0-4).
    2. School aspirations: "How much schooling would you like to get eventually?" (0-3)*
    3. School expectations: "How much schooling would you expected to get eventually?" (0-3)*
    4. College aspirations: Aspirations for college completion (0-1).
    5. College expectations: Expectations for college completion (0-1).
    B. Strain1 (Dysjunction between economic goals and educational means):
    1. High commitment to financial goals, no expectation for college degree (0-1).
    2. Economic aspirations minus school expectations (0-4).
    C. Strain2 (Educational aspirations/expectations dysjunction):
    1. School aspiration greater than school educational expectation (0-1).
    2. Educational aspirations minus educational expectations (0-2).

(* 0=some high school; 1=hihg school graduation, on-the-job apprenticeship, trade or vocational school; 2=some college or junior college, college, and 3=college graduation.)

IV. Short, Rivera, and Tennyson (1963)
"If you think that the statement is true about the area, say 'True'; if you don't think it's true, say 'False.'"
    A. Legitimate Educational Opportunities (0-12):
    1. In our area it's hard for a young guy to stay in school.
    2. Most kids in our area like school.
    3. Most of the guys in our area will graduate from high school.
    4. In our area, there are a lot of guys who want to go to college.
    5. College is too expensive for most of the guys in the area.
    6. As far as grades are concerned, most of the guys in our area could get through college without too much trouble.
    B. Legitimate Occupational Opportunities (0-10):
    1. It's hard for a young guy in our area to get a good paying honest job.

2. Most of the guys in the area will probably get good paying honest jobs when they grow up.
3. For guys in this area honest jobs don't pay very well.
4. Guys in this area have to have connections to get good paying jobs.
5. In this area it's hard to make much money without doing something illegal.

Table 6.3   Measures of General Strain Theory

I.   Agnew and White (1992)
          A.   Individual Index Measures of Strain:
          1.   Negative Life Events (15 items)
          2.   Life Hassles (9 items)
          3.   Negative Relationship with Adults (2 items)
          4.   Parental Fighting (2 items)
          5.   Neighborhood Problems (5 items)
          6.   Unpopular with Opposite Sex (2 items)
          7.   Occupational Strain (1 item)
          8.   Clothing Strain (1 item)
          B.   General Strain Scale (a summary of standardized scores
                    of the following):
          1. Negative life events; 2. Life hassles; 3. Negative relationship
          with adults; 4. Parental fighting; 5. Neighborhood problems.

II.   Mazerolle and Maahs (2000)
          A.   Neighborhood Problems (scale mean = 8.8, s = 2.3,
                    range = 7-21, alpha = .74):
          How much of a problem are each of the following in your
          neighborhood?
          1.   Vandalism, buildings and personal belongings broken
and torn up
          2.   Winos and junkies
          3.   Traffic
          4.   Abandoned houses
          5.   Burglaries and thefts
          6.   Run-down and poorly kept buildings
          7.   Assaults and muggings
          (not a problem, somewhat of a problem, big problem)
          B.   Negative Life Events (scale mean = 14.0, s = 1.3, range
                    = 13-21, alpha = .50):
          Which of the following events have occurred in your home or to
          members of your family during the past year?
                    Divorce, Separation, Remarriage, Serious illness/death,
                    Serious accident, Suspension/expulsion/school dropout
                    of children, Children in trouble with the law, Father
                    unemployed, Mother unemployed, Children changed
                    schools, Family move, Mother moved in/out, Father
                    moved in/out.
          (yes or no)

C.	Negative Relations with Adults (scale mean = 38.7, s = 7.8, range = 20-74, alpha = .86):
1.	Teachers don't call on me
2.	I am an outsider with my family.
3.	I feel lonely with my family.
4.	Teachers don't ask me to work on projects.
5.	My family is not interested in my problems.
6.	My parents think I need help.
7.	My parents think I am a bad kid.
8.	My parents think I break rules.
9.	My parents think I am messed up.
10.	My parents think I get into trouble.
11.	My parents think I do things against the law.
12.	My teachers think I need help.
13.	My teachers think I break rules.
14.	My teachers think I am messed up.
15.	My teachers think I get into trouble.
16.	My teachers think I do things against the law.
(strongly agree, agree, neither agree nor disagree, disagree, strongly disagree)
D.	School/Peer Hassles (scale mean = 16.1, s = 3.9, range = 7-34, alpha = .72):
1.	I'm not asked to take part in school activities as much as I'd like.
2.	I don't feel that I fit in very well with my friends.
3.	I often feel like nobody at school cares about me.
4.	My friends don't take much interest in my problems.
5.	I don't feel as if I really belong at school.
6.	Even though there are lots of kids around, I feel lonely at school.
7.	Sometimes, I feel lonely when I'm with my friends.
(strongly agree, agree, neither agree nor disagree, disagree, strongly disagree)
E.	General Strain Index:
1.	standardizing and summing the four scale measures of strain: scale mean = 0.0, s = 2.5, range = -.3.3 to 11.6, alpha = .76).

Chapter 7
Theories of Differential Association
And Social Learning

One year after Merton put forward his anomie theory, Edwin H. Sutherland (1883-1950) proposed his theory of social differential association in 1939. The theory, however, had immediate impact on the study of crime because it was printed in a very successful criminological textbook – *Principles of Criminology*. In those days, criminological theory was, in general, presented as a sociological theory of crime. Presented in a criminological textbook, social differential association theory was regarded as "a watershed in criminology" (Matsueda 1988: 277). In the following years, it stimulated many theoretical refinements and efforts in making new criminological theories. This chapter only examines Sutherland's social differential association theory and Akers' social learning theory.

Differential Association Theory

Sutherland (1939;1947) put forth the theory of differential association as a scientific theory of crime with logical abstraction, differentiation of levels of explanation, and analytic induction. His insights stemmed from his earlier research on white-collar crime and professional theft. Sutherland was influenced by two theorists – Gabriel Tarde (1843-1904), an early French criminologist, and Thorsten Sellin (1896-1994). Tarde (1890) presented a theory of crime as normal learned behavior. Tarde rejected his contemporary Lombroso's theory that crime was caused by biological abnormality. Instead, he argued that criminals were primarily normal people who were brought up in an atmosphere in which they learned crime as a way of life. He phrased his theory in terms of "laws of imitation," which were similar to Aristotle's laws of learning except that the "laws of imitation" focused on associations among individuals rather than associations among sensations within one individual (Martin et al. 1990; Vold et al. 1998). Sellin (1938), on the other hand, examined the crime from a historical standpoint and argued that crime originated in the passage of criminal laws, which, in turn, was a cultural expression of normative conflict.

Greatly concerned with a scientific generalization, Sutherland attempted to propose a systematic and formal presentation of the theory in which a set of interrelated propositions were put together to explain all of the observed correlates of crime. He observed that many modern societies exhibit normative conflict reflected in cultural patterns favoring criminal behavior existing alongside patterns unfavorable to crime. He theorized that people are variously exposed to these opposing cultural messages, mainly through interpersonal interaction. The major components of his theory are outlined in the form of propositional statements, composed of nine principal points (1947):

1. Criminal behavior is learned (v. born).
2. Criminal behavior is learned in interaction with other persons in a process of communication.
3. The principal part of the learning of criminal behavior occurs within intimate personal groups.
4. Learning criminal behavior includes (a) learning the techniques of committing crime, and (b) learning the specific direction of motives, drives, rationalizations, and attitudes.
5. The specific direction of motives and drives is learned from perceptions of various aspects of the legal codes as being favorable or unfavorable.
6. A person becomes delinquent when he or she perceives more favorable than unfavorable consequences to violating the law.
7. Differential associations may vary in frequency, duration, priority, and intensity.
8. The process of learning criminal behavior by association with criminal and anti-criminal patterns involves all of the mechanism that are involved in any other learning.
9. While criminal behavior is an expression of general needs and values, it is not explained by those general needs and values, since noncriminal behavior is an expression of the same needs and values.

As a result of more intimate, longer, more frequent, and more intense association with cultural "definitions" favorable to criminal behavior relative to those unfavorable (an "excess"), individuals are said to learn criminal behavior, including techniques, attitudes, drives, and rationalizations. The differential association means that individuals commit an act of crime in response to an excess of attitudes favoring law violation at that time and that principally they have attained this excess in association with others. People learn to commit crime from exposure to antisocial definitions.

In formulating his theory, Sutherland carried on a dialogue with the prevailing criminological theory of the time – social disorganization theory – with an intention to supplementing it. He argued that areas with high crime rates are not necessarily disorganized. Instead, these areas may be organized differently, which is conducive to criminality. He thus proposed to use differential social organization to replace social disorganization in these settings. At the community or societal level, norms, values, and behavior patterns are differentially organized to make it more or less likely that an individual will come into contact with, and be influenced by, criminal values.

Since its first appearance, many efforts have been proposed to modify or reformulate Sutherland's theory (Burgess and Akers 1966; DeFleur and Quinney 1966; Glaser 1956; Jeffery 1965). While all of these suggested revisions have added some insight into Sutherland's formulations of differential association, they have not fundamentally altered the basic assumptions of the theory. "Essentially, the reformulations of the differential association according to the concepts of set theory or learning theory have formally stated what was already implicit, if not explicit, in Sutherland" (Showmaker 1996: 140).

Social Learning Theory

One of the most influential reformulation of Sutherland's differential association theory comes from Burgess and Akers (1966). In heeding the earlier advice of C. Ray Jeffery (1965) to couch the concepts and principles of differential association in terms of operant behavior theory, Burgess and Akers (1966) produced a full reformulation in their "differential association-reinforcement" theory. Since then, Akers and his colleagues (1973; 1979; 1985; 1989) continue to refine the theory by providing empirical evidence in support of the theory. Akers later re-labeled the theory as "social learning theory."

Social learning theory is a general perspective emphasizing "reciprocal interaction between cognitive, behavioral and environmental determinants" (Bandura 1977). Variants of social learning can be found in virtually any social behavioristic approach in social sciences, and in particular, in psychology and sociology. In the field of criminology, social learning theory refers to mainly Akers' behavioristic reformulation of Sutherland's differential association theory of crime. The theory retains the principles of differential association, combining them with, and restating them in terms of, the learning principles of operant psychologists.

Beyond a brief comment that more is involved than direct imitation, Sutherland did not explain what the mechanisms of learning are. Social learning theory, in contrast, is an effort to integrate Sutherland's theory with differential reinforcement and other principles of behavioral acquisition, continuation, and cessation so that it explains criminal and delinquent behavior more thoroughly.

In the 1980s, the most important developments in social learning theory emphasized the psychological process of operant conditioning (See Akers 1985). Akers borrows a series of concepts from behavioral learning theory. "Operant" behavior (the voluntary actions of the individual) is conditioned or shaped by rewards and punishments. Other concepts include "respondent" conditioning (the conditioning of involuntary reflex behavior), discriminative stimuli (the environmental and internal stimuli that provides cues or signals for behavior), and schedules of reinforcement (the rate and ratio in which rewards and punishments follow behavioral responses, and other principles of behavior modification). According to Akers' social learning theory, crime is initially learned through direct imitation or modeling; the subsequent likelihood of sustaining criminal behavior is determined by differential reinforcement, the relative rewards and punishments following the act.

Reinforcement can be direct or vicarious, whereby simply observing another's criminal behavior being reinforced will reinforce the observer's own criminal behavior. Definitions of crime are learned through this process and affect behavior directly, as well as indirectly, by serving as cues (discriminative stimuli) for law violation. Reinforcement can also be positive and negative. Positive reinforcement is the presentation of a stimulus that increases or maintains a response. The stimulus, or reward, can be either material, such as money, or psychological, such as pleasure. Negative reinforcement is the removal or reduction of a stimulus whose removal or reduction increases or maintains a response. The stimulus in negative reinforcement is referred to as an aversive stimulus. Aversive stimuli, for most people, include pain and fear. Criminal behavior is reduced through extinction or punishment. Extinction is a procedure in which behavior that previously was positively reinforced is no longer reinforced. In other words, the rewards have been removed. As a result, Akers and his colleagues have successfully developed operational indicators of imitation, differential reinforcement, and definitions of deviance.

There are four concepts that are central to Akers' revised version of the theory: differential association, differential reinforcement, imitation, and definition. In addition, Akers (1998) proposes that one's age, sex, race, class, and other characteristics indicate a person's position in the social structure. These characteristics relate to the groups of which persons are likely to be members, with whom they interact, and how others around them are apt to respond to their behavior. These variables affect which behavioral models and normative patterns to which persons are exposed and the arrangements of reinforcement contingencies for conforming or law-violating behavior. In the general model of social learning, social structure is hypothesized to have an effect on the individual's behavior through its effect on the social learning process.

Akers' own definition of social learning theory is quite broad. He claimed that five major variables have been consistently validated in the delinquency prediction literature. These five variables are prior problem, deviant peer associations, parental and family factors, deviant attitudes, and school factors. Akers believes that all of these variables can reasonably be defined as an operational indicator of social learning concepts (Akers 1998:155-6).

Measurement of the Key Concepts

Differential Association Theory. Sutherland's differential association theory was originally proposed as a macro-level criminological theory. In its broadest level, even its co-founder Donald Cressey (1960) agreed that differential association theory is untestable. Most tests of social differential association theory are at the micro-level with delinquent data. Uncertainty as to the exact meaning of the theory has prevailed because Sutherland left most of his concepts imprecisely defined and he did not explicitly spell out how the conceptual variables affect each other (Matsueda 1988; 1982; Tittle et al. 1986).

Matsueda (1982) provides one of the best tests of the differential association theory with the juvenile data from Richmond. He carefully measures the three key concepts of Sutherland's theory – definition favorable to criminality, attachment to peers, and deviant friends (see Table 7.1). The index of definition favorable to criminality is composed of seven Likert items. The attachment to peers is composed of two items and deviant friend is a single item scale. Matsueda is not happy with the index measure of definition favorable to criminality because the relatively low reliability coefficients indicate that the indicators may have "undesirable measurement properties." It seems that two items in the index do not fit the overall theoretical orientation of the index. These two items are "I have a lot of respect for the Richmond police" and "Policemen try to give all kids an even break." The research, however, demonstrates that differential association theory was supported over control theory, providing empirical evidence that differential association theory can endure empirical scrutiny. Relying on the same measures, Matsueda and Heimer (1987) later found that the effects of broken homes and attachment to parents are mediated by the learning of definitions of delinquency, another piece of empirical evidence in support of differential association theory.

The most comprehensive test of Sutherland's differential association theory is conducted by Tittle, Burke and Jackson's research on predicted future criminal behavior for adults over 15 years old (1986). Almost all of the key theoretical concepts in Sutherland's theory are captured in this study. The intensity of association with criminals and attitudes favorable to criminal behavior are both measured with Guttman scale (see Table 7.1). The association with criminal definitions is created to capture the criminogenic influences. "Excess association" has been taken to "mean a higher position on the resulting continuum of association with crime-favorable definition," on the assumption that all individual are equally exposed to non-criminal definition (Tittle at al. 1986:410). The attitudes favorable to criminal behavior tap ideas about rightness and wrongness, the appropriateness of legal regulations, and self-justifying rationales. The most unique variable of this test is a measure of criminal motive. Sutherland proposed that specific direction of motives and drives are part of learning process. Another variable – perceptions of crime – captures the favorable normative expectations of one's friend circle. Finally, a variable arrest fear was deduced from their interpretation of differential association theory.

The dependent variable of this study is quite unique. It is the probability of future criminal behavior, measured for six specific offenses – tax cheating, illegal gambling, assault, $50 theft, $5 theft, and marijuana smoking. The study controls for age, education, family income, parental involvement, city size, church attendance, community interest, chances of discovery, gender, race, employment, and religion. The results on the whole support Sutherland's claim that differential association plays a substantial role in all of the models.

Replying on the same data set and variables, Jackson et al. (1986) found that excess association with definitions favorable to crime and/or deviance tends to increase crime, but this effect is mainly indirect, through increasing motivation to engage in deviant acts. The same differential association process holds for a range of crimes and also for the two noncriminal deviate acts, suggesting that Sutherland's theory is more widely applicable than he himself claimed.

Following the newly emerging trend of predicting specific delinquency with specific independent variables, Johnson et al. (1987) proposed two unique measures in their model: proportion of drug-using friends and friend-derived ratio of pro to con drug definitions (see Table 7.1). To construct the measure of proportion of drug-using friends, the number of best friends that were reported to have used the particular drugs (drink alcohol, smoke cigarettes, sue marijuana, or use amphetamines or depressants) was divided by the number of people the respondent listed as best friends. For friend-derived drug definitions, respondents were asked to report the attitudes that they had received from their friends toward use of that particular drug. Responses to prodrug items were summed and divided by the sum of antidrug times. The resultant quotients represent ratios of prodrug to antidrug definitions toward the four drug categories. It is found that both variables have a direct effect on drug use.

In an effort to modify differential association theory, Warr and Stafford (1991) argue that Sutherland's theory is an attitude formation theory that focuses on the influence of peers' views but neglects their behavior. They maintain that the distinguishing feature of Sutherland's theory is "its insistence that attitude transference is the mechanism by which delinquency is socially transmitted" (1991: 853). They test their ideas with data from the National Youth Survey. Three independent variables are identified: respondent's attitudes, friends' attitudes, and friends' behavior (see Table 7.1). Both attitudes and behavior are specific (classroom cheating, petty thief and marijuana use). Warr and Stafford measure the deviant attitudes with an index that asks: "How wrong is it for someone your age to ...?" Similar measure has also been adopted by Heimer and Matuseda (1994), Heimer (1997), and Thornberry et al. (1994). Warr and Stafford found that in predicting delinquency, the effect of peers' attitudes is small in comparison to that of peers' behavior and the effect of peers' behavior remains strong even when peers' attitudes and adolescent's own attitude are controlled.

McCarthy (1996) offers another alternative interpretation of differential association theory and tests his idea with data collected from adolescents lived on the streets and shelters in Toronto. He argues that Sutherland's theory had been tested without enough attention being paid to one of its key element: tutelage in criminal methods. According to Sutherland, both skills and symbolic elements are central to the differential association process and together they intervene between deviant associations and crime. He uses six crime-specific questions to measure tutelage, three for drug selling and three for theft (see Table 7.1). Five categories of answers are possible: (1) not approached; (2) received offers from friends whom the respondent believed were not actively involved in trafficking; (3) approached by friends or adults assumed to be actively involved in selling; (4) received solicitations from both non-selling and selling friends; (5) propositioned by other friends and adults involved in drug trafficking. McCarthy also measures deviant attitudes with a three-item index. The results provide considerable support for introducing tutelage to improve models of differential association theory.

In testing whether differential association theory can explain violent behavior, Heimer (1997) introduced the mediation hypothesis in her model. This hypothesis proposed that social structure and group interactions influence delinquency mainly by shaping the learning of definitions of delinquency, which are attitudes, values and belief about the law. Relying on the data from National Youth Survey, she creates an index of definition favorable to violence and measures friends' aggression (see Table 7.1), which contains items logically similar to Agnew's measure of neutralization (see Table 4.2). Her results show that violent delinquency is a product of learning definitions favorable to violence, which itself is determined directly and indirect by association with aggressive peers, socioeconomic status, among other things.

In an attempt to create an integrating theory of crime, Cao and Deng (1998) developed two measures of differential association theory: definition favorable to criminality and deviant association in their study of shoplifting. Their definition favorable to criminal is composed by four modified items from National Youth Survey (see Table 7.1). Two of them tap the specific and two of them tap the general justification and acceptability of violation of law among general population. The reliability of the index is .81. The measure of deviant association is composed of three items. The index's reliability is .68 and it captures not only whether the respondent has shoplifting friends but also the extent that shoplifting is socially approved among those friends and that the friend's involvement in shoplifting. Their analysis indicated that deviant association is a more robust predictor of shoplifting.

Social Learning Theory. Empirical tests of Akers' social learning theory are less of a problem. Akers et al. provided the most comprehensive test of social learning theory in 1979. Most recent studies are based on that study. Akers' survey with all measures of social learning theory is 35 pages long. Most concepts are measured by multiple dimensions. Altogether, sixteen aspects of social learning theory are measured (Table 7.2). About ten of these measures are considered new to social learning theory. Others can be easily derived from Sutherland's differential association theory or neutralization theory. These variables are arranged into four categories: imitation, differential association, differential reinforcement, and definitions favorable and unfavorable. Obviously, a detailed description of all these items is beyond the current book. Interested readers should contact Akers for the survey.

A simplified test of social learning theory can be found in Winfree et al. (1994). In examining the gang, Winfree et al. explore the conceptual and empirical ties between membership in gangs, misconduct, and social learning theory. Three aspects of differential associations are measured: peer gang members, peers' disapproval, and significant adult disapproval (see Table 7.2). Three aspects of differential reinforcers are captured: peers' reactions, parents' reactions, and net effects. The net effects are the summery of all good things about gang members (from 1 to 5) and all bad things about gang members (from -1 to -5). A negative summed response was taken to reflect a negative net effect of the gang-specific social/nonsocial reinforcers and punishers; a positive summated score indicated a positive net effect. In addition, differential definitions are measured with a four-item index. It is concluded that variables drawn from social learning theory, including differential reinforcers, differential association, and personal pro-gang definitions, performed as expected.

Summary and Discussion

After more than half a century's empirical scrutiny, Sutherland's theory of differential association remains one of prime criminological theories. Most tests of the theory are partial and comprehensive tests are few. The measures of differential association theory, however, are not always consistent and there is a need to move toward standardization. Following the established tradition of differential association theory, social learning theory adds the concepts from the learning principles of operant psychology and develops measures of predictor variables specific to each specific type of crime. This practice may account for the fact that tests of the theory are generally favorable in support of social learning theory over other theories where the explanant variables are general in nature and are better to explain delinquency instead of any specific types of crime. Akers' modification and transformation have significantly enriched Sutherland's theory. The measures of his theory at the micro-level, however, suffer from their over-comprehensiveness. The development of a more parsimonious model with fewer more powerful, but readily administered measures is needed if social learning theory intends to have a wider acceptance among criminologists. Akers' new push of his theory at the macro-level (1998) is also worthy watching.

Akers' efforts, however, have not fundamentally changed the basic assumptions of differential association theory. Both differential association theory and social learning assume that the criminal is a rational goal-seeking actor. They also assumes that humans start out as social blanks until socialized into conforming social roles by primary groups such as families and friends. What people become is a product of social learning, of tendencies poured into his human vessel that lead it to engage in one type of action or another (Einstadter and Henry 1995). As a result, both theories are limited in scope. Neither of them accounts for the initial motivation to learn criminal behavior. Both are better at explaining the transmission of criminal behavior than its origins. They both assume a passive and unintentional actor who lacks individuality. Because of this limited conception of human nature, learning theories generally also ignore the differential receptivity of individuals to criminal message (Beirne and Messerschmidt 1991).

Despite their theoretical limitations, both social differential association theory and social learning theory have received empirical support. Whether they are tested alone, or with other criminological theories, the main arguments are largely supported. As a result, these theories are regarded as "the leading theories of crime" (Cullen and Agnew 1999d: 79) and will continue to play a vital part in directing the attention of criminology to the process of learning criminal behavior.

Table 7.1   Measures of Differential Association Theory

I.   Cao and Deng (1998)
      A.   Definition Favorable to Criminality (alpha = .81)
      1.   It is OK to shoplift when people are unemployed.
      2.   It is OK to shoplift if people are poor.
      3.   To get ahead, you may have to do something which is not legal.
      4.   It is all right to do things that are not legal if you can get away with it.
(strongly agree to strongly disagree)
      B.   Deviant Association (alpha = .68)
      1.   Do you have any friends who have shoplifted?
(1=no, 2=a few, 3=some, 4=many)
      2.   How much would your best friends approve of your shoplifting activity?
(1=strongly disapproval, 2=somewhat disapproval, 3=slightly disapproval, 4=slightly approval, 5=somewhat approval, 6=strongly approval)
      3.   How likely it is that one's best friends would be caught by the police?
(1=very likely, 2=somewhat likely, 3=slightly likely, 4=slightly unlikely, 5=somewhat unlikely, 6=very unlikely)

II.   Heimer (1997) (National Youth Survey)
      A.   Disapproval of Aggression
      1.   How wrong is it for an adult like you to hit or threaten to hit someone without any reason?
(1=very wrong, 2=wrong, 3=a little bit wrong, 4=not at all wrong)
      B.   Definitions Favorable to Violence:
      1.   In order to gain respect from your friends, it is sometimes necessary to beat up on other kids.
      2.   It is all right to beat up another person if he/she called you a dirty name
      3.   It is all right to beat up another person if he/she started the fight
      4.   Hitting another person is an acceptable way to get him/her to do what you want.
(1=strongly disagree, 2=disagree, 3=neither agree or disagree, 4=agree, 5=strongly agree)

C.   Friends' Aggression
1.   During the previous year, how many of your friends have hit or threatened to hit someone?
(1=none, 2=very few of them, 3=some of them, 4=most of them, 5=all of them)

III.   Johnson, Marcos and Bahr (1987) (National Youth Survey)
A.   Proportion of Drug-using Friends
1.   How many of your best friends a) drink alcohol, b) smoke cigarettes, c) use marijuana, or d) use amphetamine or depressants?
2.   Best friends users/total best friends
B.   Friend-derived Ratio of Pro to Con Drug Definitions
1.   Attitudes from their friends toward use of each particular drug: 1) cigarettes, 2) alcohol, 3) marijuana, and 4) amphetamines and depressants.
2.   Sum of "it's okay to use the drug and occasional use is harmless fun"/Sum of "use of the drug is harmful to health and it is wrong to use it and too many people use the drug.

IV.   Matsueda (1982)
A.   Definition Favorable to Criminality
1.   Most things that people call "delinquency" don't really hurt anyone
2.   It is all right to get around the law if you can get away with it
3.   I have a lot of respect for the Richmond police
4.   Policemen try to give all kids an even break
5.   To get ahead, you have to do some things which are not right
6.   I cannot seem to stay out of trouble no matter how hard I try
7.   Suckers deserve to be taken advantage of.
(strongly agree, agree, undecided, disagree, strongly disagree)
B.   Peers Relationships
1.   Would you like to be the kind of person your best friends are?
(0=no, 1=in a few ways, 2=in most ways)
2.   Do you respect your best friend's opinions about the important things? (0=no, 1= a little, 2= pretty much, 3= completely)

C.	Deviant Friends
	Have any of your close friends ever been picked up by the police?
(0=no, 1=1, 2=2, 3=3, 4=4 or more)?

V.	McCarthy (1996)
	A.	Deviant Attitudes (alpha= .594)
	1.	It is alright to break the law
(0=never, 1=in a few cases, 2=sometimes, 3=often, 4=most cases)
	2.	It is not always wrong to damage, destroy or take other's property
	3.	People should have the legal right to take the drugs they want.
(0=strongly disagree, 1=disagree, 2=undecided, 3=agree, 4=strongly agree)
	B.	Tutelage in Theft (alpha=.681) or Drug Selling (alpha=.753)
	1.	Has anyone offered to help you steal/sell drugs?
(0=no offers, 1=offers from friends not known to be involved, 2=offers from involved friends or adults, 3=offers from uninvolved and involved friends, 4=offers from involved friends and adults)
	2.	Did anyone help you steal/sell drugs?
(As above except with "help" replacing "offers" and none-offenders coded as zero)
	3.	How did you find out that you could make money stealing/selling drugs?
(As above except "talked with" replaces "Offers from" and those who reported knowing from other experiences coded as zero)

VI.	Tittle, Burke, and Jackson (1986)
	A.	Association with Criminal Definitions (Guttman scale: Coefficient of reproducibility of .90 and coefficient of scalability of .62):
	1.	How many people do you know personally who ever got in trouble because they did (each of) the things (tax cheating, illegal gambling, and assault) we have been talking about?
	2.	Of all the people you know personally, how many of them do these things ($50 theft, $5 theft, and illegal gambling) at least once a year? 5=all of the people; 4=most, 3=about half, 2=less than half, 1=neardly anyone

100

3.   How many people who get the chance do each of the things (illegal gambling, tax, cheating, $5 theft, marijuana smoking) we have been talking about at least once a year? 5= almost everybody, 4=more than half, 3=about half, 2=less than half, 1= hardly anyone.

B.   Tolerance (attitudes and rationalizations favorable to criminal behavior. Guttman scale: Coefficient of reproducibility of .90 and coefficient of scalability of .67):

1.   Now I want you to tell me how morally wrong each of the following things (illegal gambling, marijuana smoking, tax cheating) is. 5=not wrong at all, 4=not very wrong, 3=somewhat wrong, 2=wrong, 1=very wrong

2.   How serious is each of the things we've been discussing?.... Please show me the step that tells how serious you believe it is for someone like yourself to (criminal act--illegal gambling, marijuana smoking, tax cheating, $50 theft, $5 theft, assault). 5=not serious at all, 4=not very serious, 3=somewhat serious, 2=serious, 1=very serious.

3.   It ought to be against the law to (commit crime--illegal gambling, marijuana smoking, tax cheating). 1=agree strongly, 2=agree a little, 3=neither agree nor disagree, 4=disagree a little, 5=disagree strongly

4.   People in the community have the right to expect you not to gamble for money.

C.   Perceived Acceptance -- favorable normative expectations:

1.   If tomorrow you were to (illegal gambling, marijuana smoking, tax cheating, $50 theft, $5 theft and assault), how much respect would you lose among people you know personally if they found out about it?
(none, almost none, a little bit, quite a bit, a great deal)

D.   Motive:

1.   There are a lot of things that pope would like to do, even though they may not do them, for one reason or another... I'd like you to tell me whether you would like to do these things: illegal gambling, marijuana smoking, tax cheating, $50 theft, $5 theft, assault.
(almost always, a lot of the time, once in a while, or never)

E.   Predicted Future Criminal Behavior:

1.   Imagine that you were in a situation tomorrow where you had an extremely strong desire or need to commit (illegal gambling, marijuana smoking, tax cheating).

Show me the step that tells what the chances are that you would actually do each of the crime?
(5-point from "almost no chance" to "excellent chance")

VII.   Warr and Stafford (1991) (National Youth Survey)
         A.   Respondents' own Attitudes:
                How wrong is it for someone your age to …
         1.   … cheating?
         2.   … larceny?
         3.   … marijuana?
         (1=not wrong at all, 2=a little bit wrong, 3=wrong, 4=very wrong)
         B.   Friends' Attitudes as Perceived by the Respondent:
         1.   Will your friends approve or disapprove (cheating, larceny, marijuana)?
         (1=strongly approve, 2-approve, 3=neither approve or disapprove, 4=disapprove, 5=strongly disapprove)
         C.   Friends' Delinquent Behavior
         1.   During the past year, how may of them (cheated, larceny, and use marijuana)?
         (1=none, 2=very few of them, 3=some of them, 4=most of them, 5=all of them)

Table 7.2   Measures of Social Learning Theory

I.   Akers, Krohn, Lanza-Kaduce, and Radosevich (1979)
    A.   Imitation
    1.   Index of imitation: Total of all the "admired" models (on TV or in the movies, parents, peers, other adults) whom the respondent reports having observed using alcohol and marijuana, ranging from 0 to 10.
    B.   Definitions Favorable or Unfavorable to Use
    1.   Techniques of neutralization scale: An index of six Likert scale items (1=strongly agree and 4=strongly disagree) measuring three techniques: "denial of injury," "denial of responsibility," or "condemning the condemnors."
    2.   Law-abiding or law-violating definitions
        A scale of items measuring obedient or violating attitudes toward the law in general and alcohol and rug laws in particular.
    3.   Positive or negative definitions of use
        Respondents own approval or disapproval of use
    C.   Differential Association
    1.   Significant adults' norm qualities
        Respondents' perception of the approving-disapproving attitudes toward use held by adults whose opinions they value.
    2.   Significant peers' norm qualities
        Respondents' perception of the approving-disapproving attitudes toward use held by other teenagers whose opinions they value.
    3.   Differential peer association scale
        A scale of three measuring how many of respondents' best friends, friends with whom they associate most often, and friends whom they have known for the longest time use the substance.
    D.   Differential Reinforcement: Social
    1.   Praise for not using: Respondents' report as to whether or not friends, parents or both encouraged them not to use.
    2.   Friends' rewarding or punishing eeactions: Respondents' reports of anticipated or actual positive or negative sanctions of friends to respondents' use of the substance, ranging from encouraging their use to turning them in to the authorities.

3.   Parents' rewarding or punishing reactions: Respondents' reports of anticipated or actual positive or negative sanctions of parents to respondents' use of the substance, ranging from encouraging their use to turning them in to the authorities.

4.   Informal parental deterrence: Respondents' perceived probability that their parents would catch them if they used the substance.

5.   Formal deterrence: Respondents' perceived probability that the police would catch them if they used the substance.

6.   Interference with other important activities: Respondents' perception of the extent to which using the substance would interfere with their participation in activities (i.e., school work, athletics, etc.) important to them.

E.   Differential Reinforcement: Combined Social/Nonsocial

1.   Index of social/Nonsocial rewards minus costs of use
The total good things from a list of positive drug effects and social outcomes which the using respondent checked as having actually experienced and the non-using respondents checked as what they perceived they would experience e as a result of using the substance minus the total bad things checked (there is an equal number of good and bad possible consequences in the list).

2.   Overall reinforcement balance
Respondents' assessment of whether on balance mostly good things or mostly bad things would or did happen.

3.   Usual effects felt when used
Respondents' report of the effects the substance usually has on them (from no effect, to mostly good, to mostly bad effects).

II.   Winfree, Mays and Vigil-Backstrom (1994)

A.   Differential Association

1.   Peer gang members: About how many of your best friends are gang members?
(1=none or nearly none, 2=less than half, 3=more than half, 4=all or nearly all)

2.   Peers' disapproval: What is the attitude toward gangs of the teenagers whose opinions you value or think are important?
(1=strongly approve, 2=approve, 3=depends, 4=disapprove, 5=strongly disapprove)

3.   Significant adult disapproval: What is the attitude toward gangs of most of the adults whose opinions you value or think are important?

(1=strongly approve, 2=approve, 3=depends, 4=disapprove, 5=strongly disapprove)

B.   Differential Reinforcers:

1.   Peers reactions: What would most of your friends most likely do if they though you were a member of a gang?

(1=positive reaction, 2=neutral reaction, 3=negative reaction)

2.   Parents reactions: What would your parents or guardians most likely do if they though you were a member of a gang?

(1=positive reaction, 2=neutral reaction, 3=negative reaction)

3.   Net effects = sum of the all following items (alpha=.50): Whether or not you are a member of a gang, what good things do you think would happen to you as a member of a gang?

(i. feel successful, ii. be cool, iii. be more like someone else, iv. excitement, v. money: yes=1 and no=0)

      Whether or not you are a member of a gang, what bad things do you think would happen to you as a member of a gang?

(i. feel guilty, ii. get in trouble with the police, iii. get in trouble with my parents, iv. get hurt, v. lose friends: yes=-1 and no=0)

C.   Differential Definitions (alpha = .83)

      Do you approve or disapprove

1.   having friends in gangs

2.   being in a gang yourself

3.   taking part in illegal gang activities like fights

4.   doing whatever the gang leaders tell you to do

(1=disapprove, 2=neither disapprove nor approve, 3=approve)

D.   Pro-gang Attitude

1.   Gang membership: 1=yes, 0=no.

Chapter 8
The Subculture of Violence Theory

The idea that culture contributes to crime is rooted in many sociological theories. Durkheim (1893) considered crime a conflict against collective conscience. Wolfgang's mentor and life-long friend Thorsten Sellin (1896-1994) proposed a concept of culture conflict as early as 1938. He argued that legal definitions are relative, changing over time as a result of changes in conduct norms, which are different from culture to culture. Conflict occurs when following the norms of one's own culture causes a person to break the legislated conduct norms of the dominant culture. Crime is not a result of deviant individuals but of conforming individuals who happen to belonging to cultures with norms that conflict with the dominant ones.

Sutherland elaborates the idea of normative culture conflict and incorporates it into his differential association theory (1947). One of the major causes of criminal behavior is the cultural idea — the definitions favorable to law violation. Shaw and McKay (1942) conceptualize the subcultural transmission of delinquent norms as a consequence of social disorganization and as a cause of the continuity of delinquency over time in certain geographical areas. Strain theorists Cohen (1955) and Cloward and Ohlin (1960) both attribute a role of subculture in the development of status frustration. Cohen's contribution is so important that Wolfgang and Ferracuti (1967: 97) credit him with "the first and most fertile theoretical statements about the meaning of subculture."

In these theories, however, cultural ideas are one of sources, not the only source of violence and criminal behavior. It was Marvin Wolfgang (1924-1998), along with Franco Ferracuti, who explicitly drew on subcultural values in explaining violent behavior. Wolfgang and Ferracuti (1967:385) argued that the "overt use of force or violence ...... is generally viewed as a reflection of basic values that stand apart from the dominant central, or parent culture." That is, the immediate causes of most assaults and homicides are ideas—values, norms, and expectations of behavior, rather than the social conditions. This chapter is therefore devoted to Wolfgang and Ferracuti's theory of subculture of violence.

The Subculture Theory

One of the most cited explanations for interpersonal violence is the subculture of violence, for which Wolfgang and Ferracuti (1967) developed fully in their book *The Subculture of Violence: Toward an Integrated Theory of Crime*. Based on research conducted in inner-city Philadelphia in the mid-1950s (Wolfgang 1958), Wolfgang and Ferracuti

(1967:161) attempt to bring together "psychological and sociological constructs to aid in the explanation of the concentration of violence in specific socio-economic groups and ecological areas." A subculture is "a normative system of some group or groups smaller than the whole society" (1967: 103). Examples of subculture include the Amish, Mormons, delinquents, prison inmates, ethnic groups and social classes. Specifically, Wolfgang and Ferracuti argue that certain segments of society have adopted distinctively violent subcultural values. This value system provides its members with normative support for their violent behavior, thereby increasing the likelihood that hostile impulses will lead to violent action. Subcultures of violence are characterized by social values that are transmitted during socialization and govern behavior in a variety of structurally induced situations. In addition, relying on official data on violent crime, Wolfgang and Ferracuti (1967) speculate that there is a black subculture of violence and a Southern subculture of violence.

Wolfgang and Ferracuti's subculture of violence theory attempts to integrate a wide range of disciplinary approaches to understanding violent behavior. From the sociological perspective, Wolfgang and Farracuti include culture conflict, differential association, and theories on culture, social and personality system. From psychology they choose theories on learning, conditioning, developmental socialization, and differential identification. Finally, they also incorporate findings from research on criminal homicide and other assaultive crimes.

According to Wolfgang and Ferracuti, "not all values, beliefs, or norms in a society have equal status, that some priority allocation is made, that the subcultural variants may partially accept, sometimes, deny, and even construct antithesis of, elements of the central, wider, or dominant values, yet remain within that culture system" (1967:99). Violence results from adherence to a set of values which supports and encourages its expression. The subculture of violence "is only partly different from the parent culture" (1967:100). It cannot be totally different from the culture of which it is a part. The subculture need not display violence as the predominant mode of expression, but a "potent theme of violence" differentiates the subculture from the larger culture. A subculture of violence exists when, in some social situations, "a violent and physically aggressive response is either expected or required" (1967: 159). Those in the subculture of violence learn a willingness to resort to violence and share a favorable attitude toward the use of violence. Members of the subculture are obliged to resort to violence to defend their "honor." An attack on one's physical prowess or sexuality, for example, demands violent retaliation. Learning is facilitated by positive reinforcement of violent behavior and, conversely, imposition of negative sanctions upon failure to respond violently to the appropriate stimuli. Lower-class males that inhabit the locate of a subculture of violence and that are not hesitant to respond to perceived insults with skillfully deployed violence are accorded prestige, while those males that deploy nonviolent means of conflict resolution are scorned and ostracized. Because members of the subculture learn violence as a normal way to manage interpersonal conflict, guilt is obviated. It is said that within the subculture of violence, various stimuli such as a jostle, a slightly derogatory remark, or the appearance of a weapon in the hands of an adversary evoke a combative reaction which will result in violence.

In the 1990s, the subculture of violence received a renewed attention. It has been found to be correlated with gun ownership (Cao et al. 1997) and willingness to shoot (Cao et al. 2002). Observing that the South continues to lead the nation in terms of gun ownership and homicide, Ellison (1991) extends the southern subculture of violence and suggests that this pattern has persisted throughout most of the twentieth century. Individuals socialized in the South learn to approve of violence in a wide range of situations and to view violence as important in enhancing their honor or reputation. Nisbett and Cohen (1996) specify that the culture of honor in the South is related to violence in the South and this culture of honor was developed because of the southern history of herding economy, sensitivity to insults, and uses of warfare, and because of the Scotch-Irish roots.

Measurement of the Key Concepts

Unlike the previous theories where there are various possible relationships between many not well defined key concepts, the test of the subculture of violence theory is relatively simple because the causal mechanism is direct and straightforward as long as the elusive nature of subculture of violence can be ferreted out. Most tests of the theory focus on the twin theses – black subculture of violence and southern subculture of violence.

At the macro-level, a number of studies claiming to have tested the subculture of violence have used the group membership to measure subculture. For example, to test the black subculture of violence or the Southern subculture of violence, variables of percentage blacks in an area and grownup in the south before the age of 16 as a dummy are used as substitutes for the black/southern subculture of violence (Hackney 1969; Hawley and Messner 1989; Messner 1983; Nelsen, Corzine, and Huff-Corzine 1994; Parker 1989; Williams and Flewelling 1988). Gastil (1971) constructs an index of Southernness based on the degree to which the state was initially settled by southerners (see Table 8.1). States of the Confederate South (except Florida) receive a value of 30 in the index; states such as Oklahoma, with populations that initially were overwhelmingly from the South receive a 25; those such as Colorado, with populations about half from the South at the time of settlement, receive a 20. New England states, with very little Southern populations at any time receive a 5. Gastil's study supports the southern subculture of violence in homicide rates. More recently, Nisbett and Cohen (1996) use the same index and are able to duplicate the results even after controlling for poverty index and Gini index in their models.

While these studies have found a relationship between the south and violence and between percentage blacks and violence, it is difficult to tell if subculture of violence among blacks and the Southerners are responsible. Furthermore, Wolfgang and Ferracuti (1967) state clearly in their argument that the subculture of violence is a value system. As a result, macro-level studies that use proxy measures for the black subculture of violence or southern subculture of violence risk mismeasuring the concept, and their results may provide misinformed knowledge about the association between region/race and the subculture of violence.

This chapter looks largely at the studies that employ a direct measure of the subcultural values and beliefs, which represents a more truthful reflection of Wolfgang and Ferracuti's original scheme. Wolfgang and Ferracut (1967) argue that much violent activity among humans is responsive to specific sets of circumstances, that the behavior is learned and shared in a cultural setting, in which violence becomes the expected reaction to certain environmental stimuli. In their own words, "the potential resort or willingness to resort to violence in a variety of situations emphasizes the penetrating and diffusive character of this culture them" and this subculture can be captured through surveys because "The use of violence in a subculture is not necessarily viewed as illicit conduct and the users therefore do not have to deal with feelings of guilt about their aggression" (Wolfgang and Ferracuti 1967: 159-160).

Measures of subculture of violence, by definition, have to rely on multiple indicators that are able to differentiate the nonviolent responses from violent responses. Using attitudinal measures of approval of violence at the individual level are more appropriate than using aggregate group membership in testing the original thesis advanced by Wolfgang and Ferracuti, who suggest that the subculture of violence is a value system. Also excluded from our discussion is the research based on the single item measure of subculture of violence, such as the study by Doerner (1978) or on more general measure of subculture, such as subculture of deviance (Sampson and Bartusch 1998).

Based on a modified version of Ball-Rokeach's (1973) survey items and the insight from Erlanger (1974), Hartnagel (1980) creates two indexes of subculture of violence (see Table 8.1): one based on punching and the other on knifing. The five stimulus situations range from very little provoking to being hit. The intended violent response is either punching or knifing, both fit well with Wolfgang and Ferracuti's subculture of violence. Their findings offer a partial support for the subcultural model. Only a moderate amount of variation in violent behavior is explained.

Tittle et al. (1989) propose the most comprehensive measure of subculture of violence. Their index measure includes four aspects of subculture of violence with six items: two items tap values of respondents, two capture the norms of respondents, one measures belief of respondents and one gets hold of customs of respondents (see Table 8.1). While there is evidence that when the subculture of violence is related to behavior, their study, however, is not a direct test of Wolfgang and Ferracuti's subculture of violence. Future research on violent behavior may explore this measure's utility in testing the linkage of the subculture of violence with actual violent behavior.

Felson et al. (1994), however, suggest a measure of subculture of violence based on three very generalized items (see Table 8.1), in which violent behavior is not specified. Instead, it is asked whether "it is a good thing" for people to tolerate a variety of stimuli. The answer categories range from "very good" to "very bad." The moralist tone in answering these items may provide a clue for many respondents to choose "politically correct" answers. It is, however, a reasonable effort in extending the test of Wolfgang and Ferracuti's subculture of violence among adolescents and in broadening the theory so as to include a subculture of delinquency.

Recently, drawn from the work of Caspi et al. (1994) and Heimer (1997), Baron et al. (2001) assemble a 13-item index of subculture of violence or approval for violence (see Table 8.1). A close look at the items in the index reveals that there are actually two conceptually different latent dimensions within the index: one (Item 1 to Item 9) seems to emphasizes on the justification of violence under various situations and the other (Item 10 to Item 13) appears to tap the inner enjoyment of violence. The index's Cronbach's alpha reliability coefficient is .89. The results of the study shows the subculture of violence makes homeless youths more likely to demand reparation for harm and that the subculture of violence has a direct influence on aggressiveness, which is defined as willingness to persevere and use force to settle a dispute. Without a comparison group, however, it is difficult to determine whether the level of subculture of violence they found among these homeless street youths is higher than that among their counterparts in schools.

A lot of tests of subculture of violence rely on items from General Social Survey. After conducting a careful factor analysis of data, Dixon and Lizotte (1987) deduce two direct addictive index measures of attitudes in their study of the relationship between gun ownership and subculture of violence. They label them defensive attitudes and offensive attitudes separately. They only consider, however, the offensive attitudes as an indicator of subculture of violence (see Table 8.1). The index of defensive attitudes taps approval for violence undertaken to protect children, women and property from an assailant. This measure was later adopted by Cao et al. (1997) and Ellison (1991) in their study of subculture of violence. Built on Brearley's insight of southern subculture, Ellison (1991) agrees that the normative combination of chivalry, grace, and vengeance contribute to the particular willingness of southerners to resort to violence in cases of gross breaches of trust, injuries to family, and threats to the "good name" of women. The defensive index captures this nature of southern subculture of violence. Felson finds in his study evidence that native southerners are disproportionately inclined to condone defensive or retaliatory forms of violence.

For offensive subculture of violence, four items are selected in Dixon and Lizotte's study (1987) in the response to the situations of a protest march, accidentally bumping, using vulgar language against a police officer, and being a suspect of murder (see Table 8.1). The responses range from 0 for no, 1 for unsure answers and 2 for yes answers. An addictive index is formed, but Dixon and Lizotte (1987) did not report their index's reliability coefficient.

Cao et al. (1997), in testing the black subculture of violence, employ the same measure of the defensive attitudes created by Dixon and Lizotte. Following Felson (1991), they consider it as an indicator of defensive subculture of violence. They report that their index's internal consistent reliability is .553. They, however, did not use Dixon and Lizotte's index of offensive subculture of violence, pointing out the internal conceptual divisions in their measure. They found Dixon and Lizotte's four-item-scale of offensive subculture of violence confounded two types of items within the scale. In two of the items (see Table 8.1), the subject was *the generalized others* striking another man while in the other two items the subject was the more specific others—*a policeman*—striking another male civilian. The word "policeman" might cause a reaction that is different from the reaction to the word "man," which might result in the acceptance of violence. The subculture of violence is a rebellion against civil behavior or conventional culture, not necessarily against state power, for which the *police* represent. Instead, Cao et al. (1997) adopt two separate items to analyze the offensive subculture of violence (see Table 8.1). Contrary to the expectations of the black subculture of violence thesis, the results of their analysis indicate that white males are significantly more likely than blacks to express violent tendencies in the defensive situations, and there is no significant difference between white and black males in the two offensive scenarios, *ceteris paribus*. This finding, however, is consistent with early conclusion by Erlarger (1974) who also tests the hypothesis directly that poor white males aged 21-64 are more likely to fight than poor blacks in the same age group.

Shoemaker and Williams (1987) create a Guttman's scale of subculture of violence, utilizing five items out of the seven items in Dixon and Lizotte (see Table 8.1). Their scale emphasizes the increasingly more serious levels of provoking, from a minor provocation of marching in a protest to very serious provocation of breaking into one's house. Guttman's method of scaling is also called scalogram analysis (Guttman 1944). It is designed to ensure that there is only one unique combination of responses for each different scale score. With Likert scaling, there may be more than one way to make a score of 2, but there is only one way to make a score 2 on a Guttman's scale (Bailey 1982). Generally speaking, it thus is more difficult to construct a Guttman's scale than a Likert scale because a Guttman's scale is more likely to be unidimensional (Philips 1976). Shoemaker and Williams' findings indicate that while blacks and American Indians have had more violence experiences (hitting and firearms) than the general population, blacks and Hispanics have had actually lower tolerance of violence than the general population. If their measure of subculture is correct, then this finding is contradictory to Wolfgang and Ferracuti's black subculture of violence.

Summary and Discussion

Wolfgang and Ferracuti's theory of subculture of violence is not intended to explain all crime, or even all violent behavior. Instead, it has a more limited goal: it attempts to explain only assaults and homicides that occur spontaneously or in what is popularly termed the heat of passion. Most violence is of this variety rather than of a premeditated nature or of psychotic origin. It is speculated that spontaneous violence is particularly prevalent among people in the south, blacks, late adolescent to middle-age males in lower-class settings according to the official statistics of their time.

Wolfgang and Ferracuti's efforts represent an early attempt to integrate various theoretical explanations for violence into a single explanatory framework. Although both social learning theory and the theory of subcultural of violence build on value heterogeneity, there are important differences between the two theories. Vold et al. (1998: 189) observe that while social learning theory emphasizes on the *process* of learning and how that process eventually affects behavior, the subculture of violence emphasizes the *context* of what is learned and how that learned value will influence the behavior. The validity of social learning theory only partially relies on finding such a subculture, while the validity of subculture of violence is solely on the identification of such a violent subculture.

The theory, however, has been criticized for three reasons: that it is circular (Nettler 1984a), that it fails to consider the structural sources of the cultural values (Berkowitz 1982), and that weak values free people to engage in violence but that no one values violence itself (Kornhauser 1978). Most extension of the theory tends to separate the two twin theses of black subculture of violence and southern subculture of violence. Nisbett and Cohen (1996) and Ellison (1991), for example, examine southern subculture of violence exclusively while Sampson (1987), Sampson and Bartusch (1997), and Wilson (1996) shift attention toward the structural causes of urban black violence. Great progress has been made in the attempts to capture the subculture of violence. As far as the *general indicator* and *lower level* of subculture of violence are concerned, these measures are quite valid. The relationships between subcultures and violence in these empirical studies, however, have been inconclusive, indicating that these measures may not be good indicators for any *specific subculture* of violence, such as homicide. Although there must be a strong correlation between assaults and homicide, the intention to kill and the intention to beat after all are very different. In that regards, our measures of the subculture of violence has not advanced beyond the time of Wolfgang and Ferracuti when they acknowledged that "basic evidence for the existence of a subculture of violence is till missing or tautological" (1967:312).

Table 8.1 Measures of Subcultural Violence Theory

I. Baron, Kennedy, and Forde (2001)
    Violent Subculture (alpha = .89):
    1. It's all right to beat people up if they started the fight.
    2. It's all right to physically beat up people who call you names.
    3. If people do something to make you really mad, they deserve to be beaten up.
    4. If you don't physically fight back, people will walk all over you.
    5. It is sometimes necessary to get into a fight to uphold your honor.
    6. It is sometimes necessary to get into a fight to put someone in their place.
    7. When someone hurts me, I try to get even.
    8. I am ready to fight when someone takes advantage of me.
    9. Sometimes I hit people who have done something to deserve it.
    10. I get a kick out of really scaring people.
    11. I admit I sometimes enjoy hurting people.
    12. I enjoy a good brawl.
    13. I like to watch a good vicious fight.
    (1=strongly disagree, 2=disagree, 3=agree, 4=strongly agree)

II. Cao, Adams, and Jensen (1997) (General Social Survey)
    Offensive Subculture of Violence:
    1. Would you approve of a man punching a stranger if the stranger was in a protect march showing opposition to the other man's view?
    2. ... if the stranger was drunk and bumped into the man and his wife on the street?
    (1=yes and 0=no)

III. Dixon and Lizotte (1987) (General Social Survey)
    A. Defensive Subculture of Violence:
    1. Would you approve of a man punching a stranger who had hit the man's child after the child accidentally damaged the stranger's car?
    2. ... who was beating up a woman and the man saw it?
    3. ... who had broken into the man's house?

B.   Offensive Subculture of Violence:

1.   Would you approve of a man punching a stranger if the stranger was in a protect march showing opposition to the other man's view?

2.   ... was drunk and bumped into the man and his wife on the street?

3.   Would you approve of a policeman striking an adult male citizen if the mail citizen had said vulgar and obscene things to the policeman?

4.   ... if the male citizen was being questioned as a suspect in a murder case?

(0=no, 1=don't know and not sure, 2=yes)

IV.   Felson, Liska, South, and McNulty (1994)

Is any of the followings "a good thing for people to do?"

1.   Turning the other cheek and forgiving others when they harm you

2.   Replying to anger with gentleness

3.   Being kind to people even if they do thing against one's own belief

(1=very good, 2=good, 3=fairly good, 4=fairly bad, 5=bad, 6=very bad)

V.   Gastil (1971)

Southernness index:

30 = Virginia, West Virginia, Kentucky, Tennessee, Arkansas, North Carolina, South Carolina, Mississippi, Louisiana, Alabama, Georgia;

25 = Florida, Texas, Oklahoma, New Mexico, Arizona;

20 = California, Nevada, Colorado, Kansas, Missouri, Illinois, Indianan, Ohio, Maryland, Hawaii, Alaska;

15 = Washington, Oregon, Idaho, Michigan, Montana, Wyoming, Delaware;

10 = Utah, Nebraska, Iowa, Pennsylvania, New York, New Jersey;

5 = North Dakota, South Dakota, Minnesota, Wisconsin, Vermont, New Hemisphere, Massachusetts, Connecticut, Rhode Island, Maine.

VI.   Hartnagel (1980)

A.   Would you approve of Andy, a teenage boy, punching Bill, another teenage boy if

1.   Andy didn't like Bill?

2.   Andy had been ridiculed and picked on by Bill?

3.   Andy had been challenged by Bill to a fist fight?
4.   Andy had been hit by Bill?
5.   Bill had attached Andy with a knife?
B.   Would you approve of Andy, a teenage boy, knifing Bill, another teenage boy if
1.   Andy didn't like Bill?
2.   Andy had been ridiculed and picked on by Bill?
3.   Andy had been challenged by Bill to a fist fight?
4.   Andy had been hit by Bill?
5.   Bill had attached Andy with a knife?

(2=approval, 1=unsure, 0=disapproval)

VII.   Shoemaker and Williams (1987) (General Social Survey) Violence Tolerance (Guttman scale, coefficient of reproducibility = .927 and coefficient scalability = .600)

1.   Would you approve of a man punching a stranger if the stranger was in a protect march showing opposition to the other man's view?
2.   ... if the stranger was drunk and bumped into the man and his wife on the street?
3.   ... if the stranger had hit the man's child after the child accidentally damaged the stranger's car?
4.   ... if the stranger was beating up a woman and the man saw it?
5.   ... if the stranger had broken into the man's house?

VIII.   Tittle (1989)

1.   How serious is it to physically harm someone on purpose? (beliefs)

(very serious, serious, somewhat serious, not very serious, not serious at all)

2.   How morally wrong is it to physically harm somebody on purpose? (values)

(very wrong, wrong, somewhat wrong, not very wrong, not wrong at all)

3.   There are a lot of things that people would like to do, even though they may not do them, for one reason or another. Again using this card, I'd like you to tell me whether you would like to physically harm someone (value)

(almost always, a lot of the time, once in a while, never)

4.   Please tell me the letter from this card that matches the number of times in the last five years that you have physically harmed someone on purpose? (custom)

(once or twice, three to five, six to ten, eleven to twenty-five, twenty-six to fifty, more than 50 times)

5.   If tomorrow you were to physically harm another person, how much respect would lose among people you know personally if they found out about it? (norms)

(none, almost none, a little bit, quite a bit, a great deal)

6.   Of all the people you know personally, how many of them physically harm others on purpose at lease once a year? (norms)

(all of people, most of the people, about half of the people, a few of the people, none of the people)

Chapter 9
Social Bond Theory

Explicitly or implicitly, the previously discussed criminological theories all concern about the motivation of crime. Control theory, in contrast, proposes that motivation is not important because crime and deviance have natural attraction to people. As a result, the key question to ask is not why people commit a crime, but why people do not commit a crime. Among various versions of control theory (Nye 1958; Reckless 1961; Reiss 1951), Hirschi offers the most popular version of the theory and evidence in support of it. In this chapter, we give particular emphasis on Hirschi's social bond theory, which argues that choice of behavior is considerably affected by the strength of people's bond to conventional role models. When a person's bond to society is broken or weak, he/she is more likely to commit a crime.

Control Theory

The philosophic root of contemporary control theories lies in the work of French sociologist Durkheim. Durkheim (1897/1951) argued that social solidarity was the most important glue in holding us together in society. Social solidarity was maintained by two distinct sets of social functions: those involving integration and those involving regulations. Human nature was a blend of two aspects: the social self and the egoistic self or the primal self. This primal self was incomplete without society and it was full of impulses knowing no natural limits. According to Durkheim, conditions of social solidarity based on highly developed functions of social integration and social regulation allowed the more primal self to become humanized fully. One implication of the theory is that "*unless* such social solidarity is developed and maintained, we may *expect* crime and delinquency" (Lilly et al. 1995: 78, emphasis original).

Therefore, conformity cannot be taken for granted, and nonconformity, such as crime and delinquency, is to be expected when social control is less than completely effective. Moral connections represent a bond with, and hence a bondage to, others. According to Durkheim, the restraint is necessary both for the psychic health of the human being and for social life to ensue. Durkheim's notion of "restraint" is accord with Freud's view that civilization requires "repression" (Nettler 1984). Criminality is a function of individual socialization and the sociopsychological interactions people have with the various organizations, institutions, and processes of society. Many people reside in the most deteriorated areas of the country are law-abiding citizens who compensate for the financial problems by hard work, frugal living, and an eye to the future. Conversely many members of the privileged classes engage in the theft, drug use, and many other crimes.

Albert J. Reiss (1951: 196), one of the early control theorists, argued that "Delinquency results when there is a relative absence of internalized norms and rules governing behavior in conformity with the norms of the social system to which legal penalties are attached, a breakdown in previously established controls, and/or a relative absence of or conflict in social rules or techniques for enforcing such behavior in the social groups or institutions of which the person is a member."

Another early control theorist, Ivan F. Nye (1958), proposed a *family-focused theory of social controls*. He set forth a more systematic version of control theory, making explicit the formulation of the problem as one of explaining conformity rather than nonconformity. Nye stated (1958:5): "It is our position, therefore, that in general behavior prescribed as delinquent or criminal need not be explained in any positive sense, since it usually results in quicker and easier achievement of goals than the normative behavior." Accordingly, the problem of the theorists was not to find an explanation for delinquent or criminal behavior; rather it was to explain why delinquent and criminal behaviors are not more common. Nye identified three main categories of social control that prevent delinquency. First, direct control, by which punishment is imposed or threatened for misconduct and compliance is rewarded by parents. Second, indirect control, by which a youth refrains from delinquency because his or her delinquent act might cause pain and disappointment for parents or others with whom they have close relationships. Third, internal control, by which a youth's conscience or sense of guilt prevents him or her from engaging in delinquent acts.

Walter Reckless' *Containment Theory* (1961) called an individual's ability to resist criminal inducements containments, the most important of which are a positive self-image and "ego strength," which is essentially formed by age 12. Other containments are internal pushes (restlessness, discontent, hostility, rebellion, mental conflict, anxieties and need for immediate gratification), external pressures (relative deprivation, poverty, unemployment, insecurity, minority status, limited opportunities, and inequalities), and external pulls (deviant companions, membership in criminal subcultures or other deviant groups). The good kid has developed an "insulated" self-concept with which to withstand the influences that lead other peers into delinquency.

All of the earlier control theories are superseded by the version proposed by Travis Hirschi in his book *Causes of Delinquency* (1969). One general way of characterizing Hirschi's theory is that "while delinquents are born, nondelinquents, or normative oriented individuals, are made" (Wiatrowski and Anderson 1987: 76). It would be fair to say that Hirschi's version of social control theory has been the dominant theory of criminal and delinquent behavior for the past 30 years. It is the most frequently discussed and tested of all theories in criminology (Stitt and Giacopassi 1992).

Hirschi starts with the basic assumption that we all have the motivation to be delinquent. The argument is not that "delinquents and criminals alone are animals, but that we are all animals, and thus all naturally capable of committing criminal acts" (1969:31). The reason some are not delinquent is due to a person's bonding with conventional elements of society. Building on Nye's alternate theory of delinquency, Hirschi proposes that what needs to be explained is "why don't people do it?" In seeking to answer the question, he formulates a psychosocial version of control theory. He assumes a single set of beliefs in society, which constitutes the conventional moral order. He theorizes that it is an individual's bond to society that makes the difference. Individuals are prevented from engaging in delinquency by four elements of social bond. When the bond is weak, the individual is "free" to engage in delinquency and, given the appropriate motivation, is likely to engage in delinquency.

The first element of the social bond is *attachment*, which refers to the affection and respect that the individual holds toward significant others such as parents, teachers, and peers. Attachment to parents is the most important. Even if a family is shattered by divorce or separation, a child must retain a strong attachment to one or both parents. Individuals with high affection and respect are less likely to engage in delinquency since they do not want to harm or incur the disapproval of people they care about.

The second element of the social bond is *commitment*, which refers to the individual's actual or anticipated investment in conventional activities such as "getting an education, building up a business, or acquiring a reputation for virtue." Individuals who have invested much in conventional activities are less likely to engage in delinquency since they have too much to lose. The lack of commitment to conventional society may foreshadow a condition in which risk-taking behavior, such as delinquency, becomes a reasonable behavior alternative. The third element of the social bond is *involvement*, which refers to the amount of time spent engaged in conventional activities such as reading and doing homework. Individuals who spend much time in such activities have less time for delinquency. Involvement in school, recreation, and family insulates people from the potential lure of criminal behavior.

Finally, the fourth element of the social bond is *belief*, which refers to the individual's commitment to the central value system of the society, such as sharing, sensitivity to the rights of others, and admiration for the legal code. If these beliefs are absent or weakened, individuals are more likely to participate in antisocial or illegal acts. Conversely, individuals who believe they should obey the rules of society are less likely to engage in delinquency.

It is interesting to note that Hirschi's belief and its operationalization are greatly influenced by Sykes and Matza's concept of techniques of neutralization (1957). Hirschi regards these techniques as attempts to answer the question of why a person can believe that an act is morally wrong and still commit it, but he rejects the notion that these techniques allow delinquents to break away from strongly held conventional beliefs. Instead, he proposes that endorsement of the techniques of neutralization simply indicates that conventional beliefs are weakly held by delinquents in the first place because they fail to be strongly enough socialized into the conventional beliefs. Therefore, there is no strongly held prior conventional belief to be neutralized. In other words, the techniques of neutralization do not neutralize and delinquent kids have nothing to neutralize.

Hirschi contends that delinquent kids are detached loners whose bonds to family and friends have been broken or weakened. Delinquents are rationally calculating individuals who seek to satisfy their self-interest at the sacrifice of others, including their friends. They are motivated to commit deviant acts to obtain these interests, unless constrained.

Measurement of the Key Concepts

Hirschi's social bond theory is one of those rare "data-driven" theories. Hirschi is well aware of the importance of theory verification and of the available data that would be able to test his theory. As a result, his four elements of social bond are relatively measurement-friendly and his theory has spawned considerable empirical research. In most of the empirical tests of his theory, however, reconceptualization is fairly common (Kempf 1993).

Hirschi reports empirical support for his own theory with comparison of percentages and birelationships among various variables based on data collected in 1965 in the Richmond, California, Youth Survey. His data include self-report, police and school information for 3,605 boys. In examining the effects of the independent variables, his book presents roughly a hundred tables (Greenberg 1999). In essence, he provides a theoretical framework and simply sets up a benchmark that the following researchers can build upon their own research.

His data later were reanalyzed with more sophisticated techniques of analysis and methods (Costello and Vowell 1999; Greenberg 1999; Matsueda 1982). In Costello and Vowell's reanalysis of the original data (1999), there are five latent elements of social bond (see Table 9.1). These five elements are attachment to parents, virtual supervision, attachment to friends, school bond, and belief. Hirschi's original elements of commitment and involvement are combined in the new element called school bond. These five elements are combined to form one single latent concept – social bond. The reanalysis by Costello and Vowell indicates that while both social bond and friends' delinquency influence delinquency, the effect of the social bond has substantially stronger effect on delinquency than does friends' delinquency.

In a major effort to formulate a revised social bond theory, Wiatrowski et al. (1981) analyze the data from Youth in Transition Study. Although all of the four elements of social bond in Hirschi's theory remain, the content of these elements has been greatly enriched (see Table 9.1). Their attachment index, for example, includes attachment to parents, closeness to parents, attachment to friends, time with friends, both positive and negative school attitudes indexes, academic achievement index, self concept and teacher interests. Their belief measures the conventional morality of honesty and guilt. Their study finds empirical support for their reformulation of the theory. Dating is strongly related to delinquency, indicating that those boys who date are involved to a greater extent with delinquency. Later, Wiatrowski and Anderson (1987), relying on the same data, but better techniques of analysis, constructed eight measures of social control and found that four of them (parental attachment, school attachment, dating and belief) affect delinquency. Agnew (1993) also used these same four measures in his test of social control theory.

Using data from National Youth Survey, Agnew (1991) makes use of the longitudinal design to test social bond theory. Attachment is broken into two parts: attachment to parents and attachment to school (see Table 9.1). Commitment is taped by an adolescent's subjective and objective evaluation of his/her school performance. Involvement is not measured. Following Wiatrowsdi et al.'s interpretation (1981), deviant beliefs are measured as conventional morality of the respondents by asking how wrong it is. Their data provide a limited support for social control theory.

In analyzing longitudinal data from Youth in Transition Project, Matsueda (1989) abstracted an index of belief based on the spirit of Hirschi's social control theory. The index taps a person's conventional morality directly by asking issues of honest, trust, and truthfulness (see Table 9.1). The findings indicate that the effect of belief on deviance is relatively small and dwarfed by the effect of deviance on belief.

In reconceptualization of parental controls to include both direct and indirect controls, Burton et al. (1995) provide a comprehensive test of social control theory. They elaborate social control theory and argue that indirect controls are the constraint on youths that flow from the quality of their affective attachment to parents, and direct controls are the actions that parents consciously take to limit misconduct. Their indirect parental controls are operationalized as an index of four items: their family is the most important thing, juveniles would like to be the type of people their parents are, they have always gotten along well with their parents, and they have a lot of respect for their parents (see Table 9.7). The reliability coefficient for the scale is .78. The direct parental controls are also an index of three items: whether parents would impose sanctions if the respondent did something really wrong or was arrested. The reliability coefficient for the scale is .58. The results indicate that the indirect parental controls for boys and girls are not significant, but direct controls are significant for boys. Teenage boys appear to be susceptible to delinquency in the absence of direct parental efforts to monitor their behavior.

In one of the more comprehensive extension of Hirschi' social bond theory, Marcos, Bahr, and Johnson (1986) refine Hirschi's four elements of the social bond and yield the four similar elements of the social bond: parental attachment, religious attachment, educational attachment, and belief in conventional values (see Table 9.1). They consider their new element of religion attachment as strengthening social control theory. Their educational attachment contains both educational involvement and commitment. Their measure of belief is different in wording from all the previous mentioned measures. The dependent variables of the study are lifetime cigarette use, alcohol use, marijuana use, amphetamines and depressants use, and overall drug use for teenage boys and girls. Their results indicate that the processes leading to involvement with drugs appear to be very similar across drug types and while elements of social bond influence the drug use as predicted, the best single predictor of drug use is association with drug-using friends.

Summary and Discussion

Various versions of control theory, including those of Reiss (1951), Nye (1958), and Reckless (1961), have gathered much empirical support for their basic arguments. Hirschi (1969) is one of those few theorists who not only propose a theory but also present a large body of data in support of the theory. His theory can apply to both middle- and lower-class delinquency. It explains its theoretical constructs adequately so elements of social bond can be measured. Cross-sectional data has been empirically consistent. With limited exceptions, the findings of Hirschi have been replicated by others (Agnew 1991; Costello and Vowell 1999; Greenberg 1999; Hindelang 1973; Junger and Marshall 1997; Krohn and Massey 1980; LaGrange and White 1985; Matsueda 1989; Wiatrowski et al. 1981; Wiatrowski and Anderson 1987). Generally speaking, data indicate that control theory is able to explain from 25% to 50% of the variance in delinquency (Shoemaker 1984).

Akers (2000: 100) maintains that there is really not much difference between social bond theory and other theories in the type of questions about crime and delinquency that each tried to answer. All theories of crime, including control theory, have to answer the same question of why some do and some do not commit crime. Control theory does not try to explain conformity, altruism, meritorious achievement, or pro-social contributions to the welfare of society. Hirschi's book is entitled *Causes of Delinquency*, not causes of conformity. In testing control theory, all studies have used the same dependent variables – delinquency and deviance – as in other criminological theories. Conformity and crime are two sides of the same coin. It makes no meaningful difference which of the two a theory claims to explain because to account for one accounts for the other.

Lack of conceptual clarity is seriously impeding a wider acceptance of social bond theory in the criminological community. While it is true that social bond theory is a "data-driven" theory, it is also true that reconceptualization is just too common in testing the theory. Each researcher proposes their own interpretation of the theory and advances their own measures. Underlying the seemingly consistent support for the theory, there is not much in common regarding to the contents in each measure adopted. Widely accepted measures from the theory have never emerged and the accumulation of empirical studies has failed to contribute to a more valid and more parsimonious theory. Empirical tests of the theory have never resulted in the accumulation of scientific body of knowledge about the theory and the theory has never been systematically revised in light of new empirical evidence.

Wiatrowski and Anderson (1987) argue that the fact that Hirschi's theory is almost always tested with delinquency data and attachment is the most frequently included element (Kempt 1993) indicates that social control theory is, in effect, a theory of socialization. Sampson and Laub's extension of control theory to adults is an exception (1993). They provided the only piece of research that shows adult social bonds – such as employment and cohesive marriages – can redirect offenders into a pathway to conformity well beyond their childhood years. Hirschi's social bond theory attempts to explain how adolescents become bonded to the society and what prevent them from engaging in delinquency. By stressing that personal control comes through social control, the theory locates the burden of control in the social system rather than the individual. It emphasizes prevention through the strengthening of conventional systems rather than through a policy of deterrence relying primarily on fear of getting caught. It insists that regulation of the individual must come through integration into the social order rather than through social isolation or punishment. The theory, however, is largely astructural. None of the structurally important sociological variables appears to be important in the causality of the theory. The popularity of Hirschi's theory may have rested to both its ideological appeal in the unique era of American history in the early 1970s (Greenberg 1999; Lilly at al. 1995), and to the specious empirical evidence that the theory is able to generate.

TABLE 9.1   Measures of Social Bond Theory

I.   Agnew (1991) (National Youth Survey)
- A.   Parental Attachment
  1.   Family that does lots of things together.
  2.   Have parents that you can talk to about almost everything.
  3.   Get along well with your parents.
- B.   School Attachment
  1.   Teachers don't call on me in class even when I raise my hand.
  2.   I often feel like nobody at school cares about me.
  3.   I don't feel as if I really belong in school.
  4.   Even though there are lots of kids around, I often feel lonely at school.
- C.   Commitment
  1.   What is your grade point average?
  2.   Are you doing well even in hard subjects?
  3.   Do you have a high grade point average?
- D.   Deviant Beliefs
  1.   How wrong is it for someone your age to purposely damage or destroy property that doe not belong to him or her?
  2.   ... to steal something worth less than $5?
  3.   ... to hit or threaten to hit someone without any reason?
  4.   ... to steal something worth more than $50?

II.   Burton, Cullen, Evans, Dunaway, Kethineni, and Payne (1995)
- A.   Direct Parental Control (alpha = .78)
  1.   My family is the most important thing in my life.
  2.   I'd like to be the type of people my parents are.
  3.   I have always gotten along well with my parents.
  4.   I have had a lot of respect for my mother and father.
- B.   Indirect Parental Control (alpha = .58)
  1.   My parents would be very disappointed if I do something really wrong.
  2.   My parents would restrict my participation in extracurricular activities at school if I do something really wrong.
  3.   My parents would think less of me if I were arrested.

(1=strongly agree, 2- agree, 3=somewhat agree, 4=somewhat disagree, 5=disagree, 6=strongly disagree)

III. Costello and Vowell (1999)
    A. Attachment to Parents (alpha = .72)
    1. Does your (father, mother) ever explain why he/she feel the way they do?
    2. How often have you talked over your future plans with your (father, mother)?
    3. Do you share your thoughts and feelings with your (father, mother)?
(1=never, 2=sometimes, 3=often)
    4. When you come across things you don't understand, does your (father, mother) help you with them?
    5. When you don't know why your (father, mother) makes a rule, will sh/he explain the reason?
(1=never, 2=sometimes, 3=usually)
    B. Virtual Supervision
    1. Does your (father, mother) know where you are when you are away from home?
    2. Does your (father, mother) know who you are with when you are away from home?
(1=never, 2=sometimes, 3=usually)
    C. School Bonds (alpha = .58)
    1. In general, do you like or dislike school?
(1=dislike school, 2=like and dislike equally, 3=like school)
    2. I try hard in school
(1=strongly disagree, 2=disagree, 3=undecided, 4=agree, 5=strongly agree)
    3. How important is getting good grades to you personally?
(1=completely unimportant, 2=fairly important, 3=somewhat important, 4=very important)
    4. On average, how much time do you spend doing homework outside school?
(1=no homework, 2=less than half an hour a day, 3=half an hour a day, 4=1 hour a day, 5=an hour and a half a day, 6=2 or more hours a day)
    D. Attachment to Friends
    1. Do you respect your best friend's opinions about the important things in life?
    2. Would you like to be the kind of person your best friends are?
(1=not at all, 2=in a few ways, 3=in most ways)
    E. Belief

1. Most things that people call "delinquency" don't really hurt anyone.
2. To get ahead, you have to do some things which are not right.
3. The man who leaves the keys in his car is about as much to blame for its theft as the man who steals it.
4. It is alright to get around the law if you can get away with it.
5. Suckers deserve to be taken advantage of.

(1=strongly disagree, 2=disagree, 3=undecided, 4=agree, 5=strongly agree. All items coded so that high scores reflect belief, reverse coded when items indicate "definitions.")

IV. Marcos, Bahr, and Johnson (1986)
   A. Parental Attachment
   1. Do you remember any special things your family has done together that were lots of fun, such as trips, holidays, or other activities?

(0=No, nothing, 1=very few things, 2=some things, 3=quite a few things, 4=very many things)

   2. When you have problems can you talk to your mother about them?
   3. When you have problems can you talk to your father about them?
   4. In your free time away from home, does your mother or father know where you are?

(0=never, 1=seldom, 2=sometimes, 3=usually, 4=always)

   B. Religious Attachment
   1. How often do you go to church?

(0=never, 1=less than once a month, 2=about once to twice a month, 3=about once a week or more)

   2. How important is religion in your life?

(0=not important, 1=a little important, 2=quite important, 3=very important)

   C. Educational Attachment
   1. Some people like school very much while others don't. How do you feel about going to school?

(0=I don't like school at all, 1=I don't like school very much, 2=I like school some, 3=I like school quite a lot; 4=I like school very much)

   2. How important is it to you to get good grades in school?

(0=not important, 1=a little important, 2=quite important, 3=very important)

3.   About how much time do you spend on school work outside of class each day?

(0=none at all, 1=less than half an hour, 2=about an hour, 3=between 1 and 2 hours, 4=more than 2 hours)

4.   What grades do you receive in school?

(0=D's and F's, 1=mostly D's, 2=C's and D's, 3=mostly C's, 4=B's and C's, 5=mostly B's, 6=A's and B's, 7=mostly A's)

5.   How far do you expect to go in school?

(0=I do not expect to finish high school, 1=I expect to finish high school only, 2=I expect to go to technical, nursing, or business school, 3=I expect some college training, 4=I expect to graduate from a 4-year college, 5=I expect to get an advanced degree after graduating from college)

D.   Conventional Values

1.   It is okay to sneak into a movie or ballgame without paying.

2.   It is okay to steal a bicycle if one can do it without getting caught.

(0=strongly agree, 1= agree, 2=undecided, 3=disagree, 4=strongly disagree)

3.   It is important to pay for all things taken from a store.

4.   It is important to try to follow rules and obey the law.

(0=strongly disagree, 1=disagree, 2=undecided, 3=agree, 4=strongly agree)

V.   Matsueda (1989)

Belief: Is this a good thing for people to do?

1.   Always telling the truth, even though it may hurt oneself or others.

2.   Never cheating, or having anything to do with cheating situations, even for a friend.

3.   Not copying during a test even though others in the class are copying.

(1=Very bad, 2=bad, 3=fairly bad, 4=fairly good, 5=Good, 6=very good)

VI.   Wiatrowski, Griswold, Roberts (1981) (The Youth in Transition Survey)

A.   Attachment

1.   Index to closeness to mother

     a.   How close do you feel to your mother?

     b.   How much do you want to be like the kind of person your mother (or female guardian) is?

2.   Index to closeness to father

a. How close do you feel to your father?

b. How much do you want to be like the kind of person your father (or male guardian) is?

3. Attachment to friends: How important would you say friends are in your life?

4. Time with friends: How important is it to spend time with your friends?

5. Positive school attitudes index

a. I feel satisfied with school because I learn things I want to know.

b. I believe school will help me be a mature adult.

6. Negative school attitudes Index

a. School is very boring for me and I'm not learning what I feel is important.

b. I feel the things I do at school waste my time more than the things I do outside of school.

7. Academic Achievement Index

a. Studying constantly in order to become a well educated person.

b. studying hard to get good grades in school.

8. Self-concept of academic ability: How do you rate yourself in school ability compared with those in your grades at school?

9. Teacher interest: How often do teachers take an interest in my work?

B. Commitment

1. Duncan ranking of aspired occupation

2. Clarity of occupational plans: How likely is it that your plans will work out this way?

3. On-the-job-training: How likely are you to receive on-the-job training?

4. Complete high school: How likely are you to complete high school?

5. Military training: How likely are you to receive job training in the military?

6. Attend college: How likely are you to attend college?

7. Made college plans: Have you made plans to attend college?

8. Made college plans: Have you made plans to go to college?

9. Dating plan:

a. On the average, how many evenings a week during the school year do you usually go out for fun and recreation?

        b.   On the average, how often do you go out on dates?

C.   Involvement

1.   Time on Homework: About how many hours do you spend in an average week on all your homework, including both in and out of school?

2.   Discuss homework with friends: Outside of homework how often do you have discussions with friends about ideas that come up in your courses?

3.   Extra school work: How often are you interested enough to do more reading or other work than the course required?

D.   Belief

1.   Honest index

        a.   Never cheating or having anything to do with cheating situteions even for a friend.

        b.   Helping a close friend get by in a tight situation even though you may have to stretch the truth a bit to do it.

2.   Guilt index

        a.   I do things I feel guilty about afterwards.

        b.   When I do wrong my conscience punishes me.

Chapter 10
Labeling Theory

Despite their many differences in explanations of causes of crime, the theories in the preceding chapters are similar in several ways (Barkan 1997). They try to explain why crime occurs and locates its causes either in individuals or in their social environment. Classical theorists believe in the concept of free will and argue that people are rational beings that decide whether or not to violate the law. The psychoanalysts claim that aberrant behavior is attributable to some traumatic early experience unsatisfactorily resolved. The social structure and social process theorists view the individual as acting with the specific contexts of their environment. These theorists only question the actor's behavior and never challenge the very definition of crime, nor ask who the audience is. In other words, they fail to explain why certain behaviors and people come to be defined as crime and criminals.

Contrary to these emphases, social reaction theorists highlight social and institutional response to crime and criminals. Instead of asking who the criminal is, these theorists ask who the audience is. Moreover, they are not as interested in the allegedly illegal act as they are in the way in which the act is responded to by social control agents. They point out that crime is an artifact of social interaction. The outcome of this interaction is variously interpreted by actors and audiences. Social reaction theorists observe that what is deviant depends on what is negatively reacted to, what is not tolerated in social interaction, or what is sanctioned in social interaction. Proper behavior is learned, not by memorizing abstract norms, but by observing what is tolerated and punished in specific situations. Hence, deviance is defined in terms of social control. Social control, not deviance, should be the focus of study. Social reaction theorists view the individual as a largely passive being that is forced into the role of a criminal by societal definitions or by the reactions of others. I am going to devote two chapters of this book to social reaction perspective. This chapter discusses labeling theory and the next chapter examines social control theory.

Labeling Theory

Labeling theory[1], as a social reaction perspective, focuses its theoretical attention on the process of criminalization and on criminal careerism. It challenges the common sense assumption that when crime happens, the most prudent societal response is the state intervention: either to scare offenders straight, to rehabilitate them, or to incapacitate them (Lilly et al. 1995). Using the interactionist concept of crime and deviance, labeling theorists attempt to show that state intervention can have the unanticipated consequence of deepening the very behavior it is meant to halt.

Labeling theory became popular in the 1960s because the rapid social change of the time. Labeling theorists attempt to shift criminological inquiry from the criminal act to the machinery of social control and social reaction. Instead of asking who is a deviant or a criminal, labeling theory sees it as always a process of interaction between at least two kinds of people: those who commit a deviant/criminal act and those who are watching the act. This chapter discusses labeling theory and the attempts at measuring the key concepts of this theory.

Although less systematic approach using some of the key labeling theory's concepts can be found in the works of sociologists such as Cooley (1902), Mead (1918), and Merton (1957), criminologists in general, trace labeling theory to Frank Tannenbaum's book *Crime and Community* (1938). Tannenbaum suggested that deviant behavior was not so much a product of the deviant's lack of adjustment to society as it was the fact that s/he had adjusted to as a special group. A tag was attached when a child was caught in delinquent activity. This initial interaction constituted "dramatizations of evil" that established enduring deviant behavioral tendencies. Tannenbaum argued that the process of tagging criminals or delinquents might actually drive people deeply into the realm of delinquency and criminality (1938: 19-20).

According to labeling theory, "Deviance, like beauty, is in the eyes of the beholder. There is nothing inherently deviant in any human act, something is deviant only because some people have been successful in labeling it so" (Simmons 1969: 4). Deviance as well as crime does not exist independent of the negative reaction of those who condemn the act (Pfohl 1985). Nothing is intrinsically deviant or criminal. Deviance or crime is defined by the social audience's reaction to people and their behavior, and the subsequent effects of that reaction. It is not defined by the moral content of the illegal act itself. It is not a quality of the act the person commits, but rather a consequence of the application of rules and sanctions to an "offender" (Erickson 1962). Deviant/criminal behavior is the outcome of interactions between actors and reactors. The deviant is one to whom the label has successfully been applied; deviant behavior is behavior that people so label (Becker 1963).

Labeling theorists are most concerned with two effects of labeling: the creation of stigma and its effect on self-image. Labels are believed to produce stigma. The labeled deviant becomes a social outcast who may be prevented from enjoying higher education, well-paying jobs, and other social benefits. Beyond immediate results, the label tends to redefine the whole person. People begin to react to the content of the label and what the label signifies, and not the actual behavior of the person who bears it. This is referred to as retrospective reading, a process in which the

134

past of the labeled person is reviewed and reevaluated to fit his or her current outcast status (Siegel 2001).

One of the well known views on the consequences of becoming labeled is Edwin Lemert's concept of primary and secondary deviance (1951). According to Lemert, primary deviances are initial acts of norm violations or crimes that have very little influence on the actor and can be quickly forgotten. It is non-patterned acts. In contrast, secondary deviance occurs when the actor reorganizes his or her personality around the consequences of the deviant act. It is persistent forms of deviance around which people organize their lives. It is unique in that it is the hardened product of the interaction of deviant behavior on the part of the actor and the labeling responses of reactors. The drug experimenter becomes an addict; the recreational drinker an alcoholic; the joy rider a car thief. As the society begins to recognize and sanction these behaviors, the application of the labels increases or "amplifies," rather than decreases the very act (Wilkins 1964). The offenders feel isolated from the mainstream of society and they become firmly locked within their deviant roles. They may seek out others similarly labeled in order to form deviant subcultures or groups. As a result, deviance amplification effect occurs.

Lemert's concept of secondary deviance expresses the core of labeling theory: Deviance is a process in which one's identity is transformed. Efforts to control the offenders, whether by treatment or punishment, simply help lock them in their deviant roles. Prior to public labeling, deviants' violations of the law are believed to be unorganized, inconsistent, and infrequent. With the societal reaction, the deviance is likely to stabilize into a deviant career. Contrary to Reckless' containment theory, a negative or delinquent conscious self-image follows the act of delinquency rather than precedes delinquency.

Labeling scholars further argue that a lawbreaker's behavior is only one factor and perhaps not the most important factor in determining whether a criminal label is conferred. "The degree to which an act will be treated as deviant depends also on who commits the act and who feels he has been harmed by it" (Becker 1963: 12). In other words, deviant labels are not randomly distributed across the social structure. They are more likely to apply to the powerless, the disadvantaged, and the poor. Schur (1971) would argue that the probability of being labeled is a function of person's race, wealth, gender and social status. Rather than assuming that criminal behavior causes societal reaction, labeling theorists posit that societal reaction causes criminal behavior.

In summary, labeling theory considerably broadens criminologist investigation on the crime-related phenomena and challenges the very definition of crime itself. There are essentially three basic issues with which labeling theory is concerned. First, labeling theory is concerned with the development of new labels and laws. Second, extra legal factors such as one's race, class, gender tend to influence the probability of being labeled. Third, labeling theory is concerned with the effects of deviant label on one's self-image and on one's subsequent behavior because of the negative label.

For the first issue of labeling theory, the label is regarded as a dependent variable. As such, there seems to be ample historical evidence in support of its claims. Becker (1963) investigated how the commissioner of the Treasury Department's Federal Bureau of Narcotics served as a "moral entrepreneur" who led a successful campaign to outlaw marijuana in 1937. Pfohl (1977) described the "discovery of child abuse" in the 1960s and Tierney (1982) examined the creation of the wife beating problem in the mid-1970s. Chambliss (1964) reviewed the history of vagrants. Sinclair focused on the prohibition years. Schneider (1978) carefully discussed the process of transforming deviant drinking into a disease. These studies indicate that it is not simply the extent of harmfulness of a behavior that determined its labeling or de-labeling. After all, drug use, child abuse, and wife battering had long escaped state criminal intervention despite injurious effects while vagrant and drinking were considered crimes in history. The definitions of these behaviors were changed only when the social context was ripe and groups existed that were sufficiently motivated and powerful enough to bring about legal reform.

For the second issue of the differential treatment of less powerful groups, a number of labeling theory studies, using quasi experiment design and/or participant observation designs, illustrate this principle (Chambliss 1973; Heussenstamm 1975; Piliavin and Briar 1964). The best example of quasi-experimental participant observation study of delinquency was conducted by William Chambliss on two small town gangs (1973). In that study, Chambliss demonstrated that social class played a key role of not only attitudes among juveniles, the local citizens, the locations of delinquency, but also whether labels were concurred. Piliavin and Briar (1964) observed that police reactions (outright release, official reprimand, arrest, and confinement) to suspected adolescent offenders were strongly influenced by race, class, and demeanor of the suspect and were not merely a reflection of the evidence pointing to a violation of the law. Heussenstamm's experimental study indicated that police officers were differentially reacting to citizens with a black panther's bumper sticker and without it (1975). Through these and similar studies, labeling theorists reveal that the nature of state criminal intervention is not simply a matter of an objective response to illegal behavior but is shaped intimately by a range of extra-legal characteristics, such as race, class, and gender.

For the third issue of the consequences of deviant label on one's self-image and on one's subsequent behavior, results of empirical research are evasive and the following session is devoted to a more detailed discussion.

Measurement of the Key Concepts

Labeling theorists argue that deviance and crime will increase, not decrease when a person is singled out for a public labeling, whether it is through punishment or rehabilitation. This is referred to as the deviance amplification effect or hypothesis. This hypothesis is perhaps the most complex and most controversial issue in testing the validity of labeling theory because it is in the direct competition with the hypothesis from rational choice/deterrence theory. As a result, considerable attention in the empirical literature has been paid to the consequences of being labeled on one's self-image and behavior. To test this hypothesis of labeling theory, data requirement is higher than the test of other theories. In general, the effects of deviance amplification are best to be tested with longitudinal data. The relationship between a formal delinquency label and consequent delinquency/identity problems has been analyzed through both qualitative and quantitative research designs. This section only discusses the quantitative research.

Early efforts pay more attention to the effect of official labels on subsequent delinquency (Bazemore 1985; Downs et al. 1997; Farrington 1977; Hagan and Palloni 1990; Kaplan and Johnson 1991; Palamara, Cullen and Gersten 1986). Bazemore's analysis of 15 years of longitudinal data did not support labeling theory's claim that changes in self-esteem or delinquent identity are required intervening processes in the relationship between labeling and future offending or reform, which is defined as by the absence of felony or misdemeanor arrests after 18 years old. The measures of labeling theory are presented in Table 10.1. The formal labeling is captured by an index of three items from juvenile court data: seriousness of disposition, the frequency of delinquency, and the number of times processed in courts. School labeling is operationalized by the cumulative high school grade point average (GPA). GPA is considered as an objective index of the organizational image of the student, but such an indicator also reflects the aggregate subjective ratings of teachers that are always a part of the grading process and has the advantage of providing a cumulative summary of the labeling response of several educators. The correlation between the formal labeling and reform is negative as labeling theory would suggest.

With data from Cambridge Study in Delinquent Development, which is a longitudinal survey, not retrospective data, Farrington (1977) conducted a test of labeling theory. With a careful matching of publicly labeled kids and non-delinquency kids in every available characteristics, he found public labeling (measured by criminal convictions) increases subsequent deviant behavior (measured by self-reported delinquency scores). Such matching procedures, however, can control only a limited subset of potentially extraneous variables. Therefore, they can produce problems of sample selection, and they are generally not useful in exploring multivariate causal processes. In a major reanalysis of the same data, Hagan and Palloni (1990) used poisson models and ordinary least squares regressions to estimate the effects of labeling effects in producing delinquency. Three variables from labeling theory are derived: parents' labeling, son's labeling and the interaction between parents' labeling and son's labeling (see Table 10.1). With simultaneously controlling four variables of parents' background, and fourteen variables of son's background and behavior, they are able to show the significant effects of parents' as well as son' labeling on self-reported delinquency at 16-17 years old. In a separate model where the interaction effect of parents' and son's labeling is introduced, the interaction effect is significant.

Downs et al. (1997), built on the previous research by Ray and Downs (1986), examine the labeling theory's hypothesis on drug use. The official labeling is operationalized by two variables: one is an index of using the number of formal services, such as hospitals and police; the other is whether the respondent is in a diversion program or not (see Table 10.1). The two informal labels are how the respondents see themselves and how their parents see them (see Table 10.1). The results indicate that more deviant self-labels at baseline are a significant predictor of greater follow-up drug use, evidence supporting secondary deviance. The formal labeling, both as the index of social services and as being in the diversion programs, also tends to increase the follow-up drug use, again in line with labeling theory's argument. Parental labeling, however, is insignificant.

In extending labeling theory to the Chinese setting, Zhang (2003) tests the hypothesis that official labeling negatively affects self-esteem of the labeled youths. Indeed, his data support the hypothesis, but his study does not further explore whether or not official labeling or self-esteem is related to delinquency.

The effect of unofficial labeling on delinquency is also tested (Adams and Evans 1996; Bartusch et al. 1996; Heimer and Matsueda 1994; Matsueda 1992; Ward and Tittle 1993). Adams and Evan (1996), relying on data from National Youth Survey, create an index of negative label by teachers. This index is consisted of four items (see Table 10.1) and the reliability is .85. In their analysis, it is found that negative label by teachers increases the subsequent delinquency. When the effect of associations with delinquent peers is controlled for, however, the effect of negative labeling by teachers becomes insignificant.

Kaplan and Johnson (1991) in their longitudinal test of the amplification hypothesis from labeling theory measure negative social sanctions with a three-item index: suspended or expelled from school, had anything to do with police, sheriff or juvenile officers, and taken to the office for punishment (see Table 10.1). The self reports may reflect the responses of others to the person's deviance or the self-perceptions of being the object of rejecting or punitive responses by others. It is regarded to be the construct reflecting both phenomena. This negative social response is hypothesized to increase subsequent delinquency. Their elaborated model using LISREL VI confirms the hypothesis of labeling theory. Indeed, negative social sanction has a direct positive effect on deviance and an indirect positive influence on deviance through deviant peer associations.

Matsueda (1992) proposes a theory of delinquency based on a symbolic interactionist view of the self as a reflection of the appraisals of others. He specifically tests labeling theorists' notions of dramatization of evil, deviance amplification and secondary deviance. We focus only on the effects of parents' negative appraisals and self appraisals on the subsequent delinquency. These two measures are two indexes (see Table 10.1). Consistent with a deviance amplification hypothesis, both parental appraisals of a youth as a rule violator and youth-reflected appraisal as a rule violator have a positive effect on delinquency. They increase the subsequent self-reported delinquency. Heimer and Matsueda (1994) and Bartusch et al. (1996) later largely duplicate these effects in their studies.

Finally, relying on retrospective data from college students, Ward and Tittle (1993) test labeling theory against deterrence theory. They use four measures of labeling (see Table 10.1): primary deviance, sanctions, informal labeling, deviant identity. The subsequent deviance is measured by an index of how many times he/she "seriously" considered cheating in the course. Their analysis indicates that future cheating is not related to deterrence effect or informal labeling, but is related to sanctioning and deviant identity. The results partially support labeling theory's claim.

Summary and Discussion

Labeling theory points to the labeling process as a possible reason for continued deviance and as a potential cause of stabilization in deviant/criminal identities. It develops concepts of criminal careers and shows that the deviant label is not applied uniformly. The poor, minority groups and the disadvantaged are more likely to be labeled deviant for a given act than are more advantaged individuals who behave in the same way. Labeling theory also helps us understand deviance from the perspective of the victim of deviant acts. Much analysis of criminal behavior from a symbolic interactionist viewpoint, however, has frequently – and often deliberately – failed to raise the question of which people are most likely to become involved in the sequence of events that lead to crime. Data are not unequivocal in supporting the thesis that deviance is no more than a subjective reaction and that state intervention deepens criminality. Furthermore, labeling theory does not explain the original reason why a person commits a crime, and places too much emphasis on society's role in the labeling process. It is thus also called a "sensitizing theory" (Scheff 1974) because it sensitizes the complex role of state intervention of deviance, and explains why some juvenile offenders do not become adult criminals.

Gibbons (1994: 83) even contends that labeling theory should not be called a theory because it is only "a collection of 'sensitizing' notions or a broad perspective about deviance and criminality rather than an explicit set of concepts and propositions." Most criminologists, however, regard it as a theory. Shoemaker (1996:204), for example, argues that it is appropriate to view labeling theory a theory when the theory is defined as "an attempt to make sense out of observations."

Quantitative analysis on the effect of deviance amplification has measured three aspects of labeling: official/formal labeling, school/teacher labeling, and parental/informal labeling. These tests of labeling theory's causal effects have yielded mixed results. As research by Sampson (1986), by Link et al. (1987) and by Smith and Paternoster (1990) cautions, societal reaction is a complex process and its effects have yet to be understood fully or established empirically.

Many labeling theorists have attempted to revise the theory and abandoned the hypothesis of labeling as deviance-causing. Instead, they have re-emphasized the need to identify how the labeling process itself takes place. The most prominent of the retheorization is proposed by John Braithwaite (1989b) in *Crime, Shame, and Integration*. Braithwaite set out to answer the question, when is a criminal label likely to have the effect of producing a criminal self-concept and future criminal behavior, and when is it likely to have the opposite effect of preventing crime? He claims that disintegrative shaming produces the former and reintegrative shaming produces the latter. His theory offers the hope of re-energizing labeling tradition.

Table 10.1   Measures of Labeling Theory

I.   Adams and Evans (1996) (National Youth Survey)
      Negative label by teachers (alpha = .85)
      1.   How much would your teachers agree you are a bad kid?
      2.   How much would your teachers agree you break rules?
      3.   How much would your teachers agree you get into troubles?
      4.   How much would your teachers agree you do things against the law?
      (1=strongly disagree, 2=disagree, 3=neither agree nor disagree, 4=agree, 5=strongly disagree)

II.   Bazemore (1985)
      A.   Court Labeling Index (alpha = .75):
      1.   Most serious juvenile disposition.
      2.   Number of juvenile offenses.
      3.   Number of times processed.
      B.   School Labeling:
      1.   Cumulative high school grade point average.
      C.   Delinquent Identity Index (alpha = .64):
      1.   Doesn't cause trouble.
      2.   People think I'm delinquent.
      3.   Self analysis – good.
      4.   Self analysis – delinquent.
      D.   Self-Esteem Index (alpha = .65):
      1.   See self as smart.
      2.   Remembered as good student.
      3.   See self studious.
      4.   See self intelligent.

III. Downs, Robertson, and Harrison (1997)
      A.   Formal Labels:
      1.   Please check the following list for any services you have ever used (yes=1 and no=0): a) Social services department, b) various private agencies, c) local mental health programs, d) hospitals, e) the police, f) the juvenile justice system, and G) residential treatment programs (an additive index).
      B.   Informal Labels:
      1.   How do you categorize yourself?
      2.   How do your parents categorize you?

(1=nonuser, 2=experimenter, 3=occuational user, 4=regular user, 5=drug abuser, and 6=addicted to drugs.)
3.   Diversion Program: yes=1 and no=0.

IV.   Hagan and Palloni (1990)
1.   Parents' labeling:
Parent convicted before son was 10 years old (1=convicted as juvenile or adult).
2.   Son's labeling, son convicted at:
14-15(1=convicted), 16-17(1=convicted), 18-19 (1=convicted).
3.   Intergenerational labeling:
Parents' labeling * son's labeling at 14-15

V.   Kaplan and Johnson (1991)
Negative Social Sanctions (alpha = .43):
1.   Suspended or expelled from school.
2.   Had anything to do with police, sheriff, or juvenile officers.
3.   Taken to the office for punishment.

VI.   Matsueda (1992) (National Youth Survey)
A.   Parental Negative Appraisals:
1.   My son/daughter get into trouble.
2.   My son/daughter breaks rules
B.   Reflected Negative Appraisals:
1.   How much would your parents agree you get into trouble?
2.   How much would your friends agree you get into trouble?
3.   How much would your teachers agree you get into trouble?
4.   How much would your parents agree you break rules?
5.   How much would your friends agree you break rules?
6.   How much would your teachers agree you break rules?
(1=strongly disagree, 2=disagree, 3=neither agree nor disagree, 4=agree, 5=strongly disagree)

VII.   Ward and Tittle (1993)
1.   Primary deviance: How many times had you ever cheated on any classroom exam (including high school and community college)?
(Never, once or twice, a few times, a lot of times, many times)
2.   Sanctions: Consider the most memorable time your cheating became known other students in the class. How

sever did you regard the students' reaction to your heating?

(No reaction [missing data], very lenient to very severe [6-point scale])

3.   Labeling: At the beginning of last semester, how do you think most of your friends would have described your cheating ability?

4.   Identity: At the beginning of last semester, how would you have described your ability as a classroom cheater?

("Not a cheater" to "a very skilled cheater" [a 5-point scale])

Chapter 11
Conflict Theory

All theories of the preceding chapters are generally considered as the consensus view of crime. Although labeling theory questions the official definition of crime, it does not go far enough. It only focuses on "nuts, sluts, and perverts" (Liazos 1972) and ignores the sources of the power inequality that affects the making of laws. In contrast, conflict theory advocates a "pluralistic conflict model" of criminal law, arguing that conflict is normal and ubiquitous in society. According to conflict theory, a variety of groups in a society compete for control of the law-making and enforcement machinery in order to protect their vested interests. The criminal justice system is serving the interests of the elite in a society's power structure. Criminal law reflects the will and the customs of the dominant class rather than the normative standards of the public at large. The criminal justice system thus is the controlling mechanism by which compliance is gained (Browning and Cao 1992). Conflict theory discussed in this chapter is best represented in the writings of Vold (1958), Blalock (1967), Turk (1969), Quinney (1970), Chambliss and Seidman (1971), and Blau (1977).

Conflict perspective sometimes is used as an umbrella framework that refers to both conflict theory and radical criminology of all kinds. Although both grow out of a Marxian analysis, there are three major differences between conflict theory and radical theories. First, as Platt (1975) observes, while conflict theorists are often critical of the established order, the lack of a historical and dialectical perspective inevitably set the stage for nihilism or a wishy-washy relativism. Conflict theorists catalogue various inadequacies and injustices present system, but stop short of condemning capitalism or fall back to apologetic relativism. Second, while conflict theory specifies stratification as a criminogenic factor, the radical theories specify the political economy of capitalism as the criminogenic factor. Finally, Bohm (1987:326) adds that "Conflict criminology is basically reformist (i.e., not radical), while radical criminology is revolutionary." The conflict theory discussed in this chapter represents the pluralistic conflict model that rejects the image of the system as tightly controlled by small, powerful elite at the top. Instead, it is characterized as a decentralized, "loosely coupled" system (Hagan 1989; Wright 1993b) into which multiple elites and competing groups interject their influence. Since radical theorists hold Marxist theory as a fact to be illustrated rather than a subject for empirical investigation, they show little concern about measurement of their theories with few exceptions (see Lynch et al. 1994 and He 1999). Consequently, this chapter is not going to examine radical theories.

Conflict Theory of Crime

Conflict theory looks back to Karl Marx (1818-1883), Frederick Engels (1820-1895), Georg Simmel (1858-1918), Max Weber (1864-1920), and Willem Bonger (1876-1940) for inspiration. It begins with the assumption that society is not held together by agreement and consensus on major values but rather is "congeries of groups held together in a dynamic equilibrium of opposing groups interests and efforts" (Vold 1958: 204). Law is a type of external application of formal negative sanctions in the form of punishment for wrongdoing. It is supported by the legitimized and authoritative coercion of the state. It is the system of rules promulgated and enforced by the sovereign political state which exercises authority over a territory and recognizes no higher secular authority. As every normative system induces or coerces activity, the normative system we have defined as "law" uses State power to this end (Chambliss and Seidman 1971).

In his classic *Theoretical Criminology* (1958), George Vold, one early chief proponent of conflict theory, proposed that group conflict explained not only criminal law and justice but criminal behavior as well.

> The whole political process of law making, law breaking, and law enforcement becomes a direct reflection of deep-seated and fundamental conflicts between interest groups and their more general struggles for the control of the police power of the state. Those who produce legislative majorities win control over the police power and dominate the policies that decide who is likely to be involved in violation of the law. (Vold 1958: 208-9)

Citing Simmel, Vold agreed that conflict should not be regarded as abnormal but rather as a fundamental social form characteristic of social life in general. Social order was not presumed to rest entirely upon consensus but in part upon the stability resulting from a balance of power among the various conflicting forces which comprise society. Vold cautioned that while his theory pertained to crime in general, it was most appropriate for explaining crime arising from racial and ethnic clashes.

The view of conflict theory is in sharp contrast with the consensus view of law, which implies that society's members have a standard set of rules and values to guide their daily lives. The existing legal code reflects and codifies these generally agreed upon conduct norms. Crimes are defined as violations of the criminal law and are believed to be behaviors repugnant to all elements of society. From a consensus standpoint, the criminal justice system is not discriminatory but represents the shared

146

values of society. As a result, there is little difference in the way the system treats individuals (Browning and Cao 1992).

Thomas Bernard has maintained Vold's statement of the theory with some extensions and expansion. Quinney (1970), Chambliss and Seidman (1971), and Turk (1969) further developed the conflict approach and placed it at the forefront of criminological theory. They have suggested that crime reflects the needs of those holding social and political power. Some behaviors are socially defined as criminal and these definitions reflect certain interest groups that control the legal system; economically disadvantaged groups are punished more harshly.

Blau (1977) proposes a general macro-level theory of structural conflict. He specifically argues that inequality in a society, defined by the distribution based on a hierarchical ordering like income, is most likely to engender pervasive conflict, which finds expression in a high incidence of criminal violence. Showing a greater concern for structural causes of crime than the cultural causes of crime, he states that, "the structures of objective social positions among which people are distributed exert more fundamental influence on social life than do cultural values and norms" (1977: x). He proposes that persons are motivated by structurally defined constraints imposed by the material conditions of life. That is, great economic inequalities generally foster conflict and violence, but ascriptive inequalities (such race) do so particularly. Pronounced racial inequality in resources implies that there are great riches within view but not within reach of many people destined to live in poverty. Similarly, Chambliss and Seidman (1971: 33) state, "The more economically stratified a society becomes, the more it becomes necessary for the dominant group in society to enforce through coercion the norms of conduct which guarantee their supremacy." Jacobs (1979:923) argues that the greater the economic cleavages the more likely will elites exercise coercive control, and under certain historical conditions, racial cleavage will have similar effects.

Although some empirical studies support the relationship between economic deprivation and crime, there is substantial debate on the underlying mechanism linking the two concepts. Some have argued that violent crimes are committed out of economic necessity: where there is more economic want, crimes rates are higher (Vold and Bernard 1986). Others suggest that in poor areas there emerges distinctive subculture prone to deviant behavior, which drives up the crime rate in these areas (Gastil 1971). Braithwaite (1979) argues that both the poverty and inequality approaches originate in a common notion, that it is lack of wealth and its associated purchasing power that predict greater criminal involvement in general and higher levels of homicide in particular. Extending the Marxian approach and Merton's emphasis on the gap between cultural goals and legally sanctioned ways of attaining these goals, Blau and Blau (1982) attribute the high violent crime rates found in the inner-city to the relative deprivation sensed by people living in these areas. Karl Marx comments (1933: 268-269) that "A house may be large or small; as long as the surrounding houses are equally small it satisfies all social demands for a dwelling. But if a palace rises besides the little house, the little house shrinks into a hut." Blaus (1982) propose that crime rates should increase when both the poor and wealthy live in close proximity to one another within communities. Witnessing wealth and luxury first-hand leads to a state of frustration and anger. The deprived justifiably feel enraged, which in turn leads to expressions of hostility and criminal behavior. Further, Blaus argue that extreme economic inequalities promote violence, and "ascriptive inequalities do so particularly" (p. 119). Ascriptive inequality refers to the inherent inequality one was born into (such as race and gender) and it is impossible to change for the rest of one's life. To Blaus, high violent crime rates found the large urban centers are the price paid for maintaining a racial and economic inequality in the United States. Deprivation has become a relative term as people increasingly have come to realize that crime is not totally endemic to the ghetto, but is also committed by those who live in environments of cultural and economic advantages.

Power is the principal determinant of the outcome of this conflict. The most powerful groups control the legislation process and can pass the law that reflects their values as the legal standards for behavior. The criminal justice system is arranged to protect the interests of the dominant class by imposing the will of the power elite (protection of self and property) on the masses. Law does not represent the "public interest," rather, it represents the interests of those in power. Class, race, sex, age, ethnicity, and other characteristics that denote social positions in society determine who gets apprehended and punished.

In a concerted effort to lay the theoretical foundation for systematic empirical investigation of social process involving unequal power groups in a society, Blalock (1967) specifies a minority threat hypothesis. He attempts to give a precise depiction of the implications of static and changing levels of numerical and resource inequality between groups. The core of Blalock's argument is that as each group struggles toward dominance or to maintain a favored position, its success depends on its level of resources (including its size), its degree of cohesiveness, and the extent to which competing groups are fractionated. Resources – both political and financial – are invoked as needed to prevent competing groups from moving forward. Blalock (1967) notes that the majority's resistance to minority efforts to improve its position should increase exponentially with increases in minority size or resource until the minority group reaches numerical majority or has accumulated sufficient resources to assure its dominance. At that point, such protection efforts slack off dramatically.

148

Minorities are thus frequently perceived as posing a political and economic threat.

Similarly, Turk (1969) proposes a conflict analysis of how power groups achieve authority and legitimacy in society. According to Turk, social order is based in a consensus-coercion balance maintained by the authorities. Any shakeup of a traditional balance will meet with resistance, and in the United States, culturally and racially dissimilar subordinate groups are perceived by authorities as threatening the social order. Scholars following Blalock and Turk have investigated the extent to which mechanisms of the state—especially policing and incarceration – are mobilized to preserve existing power balances.

Although consensus is recognized in conflict theory, law and criminal justice are explained primarily by reference to power and group conflict. Law is both the results of, and a weapon to be used in, group conflict. Conflict theory rejects "pluralism," because they believe it views the political state as nothing more than a fair and neutral arena for the expression and adjudication of competing interests. Crime is no longer defined simply as a violation of law. Instead, crime is defined as a violation of societal rules of behavior as interpreted and expressed by a criminal legal code created by people holding social and political power. Individuals who violate these rules are subject to sanctions by state authority, social stigma, and loss of status.

Measurement of the Key Concepts

Conflict theory takes a macro-level view of crime. Rather than being concerned with the behavior and motives of individuals, its intention is primarily focused on the relationship between the groups that compose society. Conflict theory examines the distribution and use of power in society, and it is largely tested at the macro-level. This chapter examines two key hypotheses derived from conflict theory: inequality hypothesis and threat hypothesis.

The relationship between poverty and crime has long been noticed by criminologists, but the systematic linkages between relative deprivation and crime and racial inequality and crime are raised by Blau (1977) and tested by Blau and Blau (1982). Blau and Blau (1982) use the Gini index as the general measure of inequality and socio-economic inequality in race as the other measure of racial specific inequality (see Table 11.1). The Gini is a commonly used measure of the degree of inequality of income derived from a Lorenz curve (see Figure 1). It ranges from 0.0 to 1.0. A score of 0.0 indicates perfect equality in income in a nation/region while a score of 1.0 perfect inequality. The SES inequality in race is operationalized as the difference in averaging socioeconomic status between whites and nonwhites based on Duncan's SEI score. Blau and Blau test their hypotheses with data from 125 largest standard metropolitan statistical areas. Their results imply that if there is a culture of violence, its roots are pronounced economic inequalities, especially if associated with ascribed position. Blaus conclude that high rates of criminal violence are the price we pay to maintain such a system of racial and economic inequality.

Extending Blau and Blau's thesis in the international scene, Messner (1989) further tests the hypothesis of inequality and crime with data from 52 nation-states circa 1980. He constructs a variable of economic discrimination to capture the spirit of Blau's theme. This measure is taken from *World Handbook of Political and Social Indicators*. Scope is operationalized by the relative size of the population discriminated economically against in each population and intensity is measured by an ordinal scale with scores ranging from 0 to 4. The composite index is the product of "weighted" measure by multiplying the scope and the intensity scores (see Table 11.1). The results indicate that economic discrimination against social groups is positively related to homicide rates despite fairly extensive controls for other theoretically relevant national characteristics. Messner concludes that the structuring of economic inequality on the basis of ascribed characteristics is a particularly important source of lethal violence in contemporary societies. Later, in analyzing data from 154 cities in the United States, Messner and Golden (1992) adopt more refined measures of racial SES inequality and resource deprivation (see Table 11.1) in their model. The results indicate that both racial inequality and resource deprivation independently affect total homicides and race-specific homicides.

In testing the hypothesis that rape is related to inequality, Maume (1989) employs the data of 284 standard metropolitan statistical areas (SMSA) in the U.S in 1980, and substitutes Blaus's measure of racial inequality in status with a measure of racial inequality in income (see Table 11.1). This measure uses mean black family income as the numerator and mean white family income as the denominator. The smaller the number of the product, the greater the income inequality is between races. Although Maume finds a significant effect of racial inequality on rape, this effect is mediated when general opportunity index and racial differences in lifestyle are introduced. Following the similar strategy, but using the robbery rate as the dependent variable, Cao and Maume (1993) get a similar finding from their analysis of 296 SMSA data: the effect of relative deprivation is mediated by the lifestyle index in the equation. The unmeasured concept of relative deprivation is captured by the combination of the Gini index and racial inequality (see Table 11.1). Note that the numerator of racial equality is mean white income in order to be consistent with the Gini index, where the large the number, the greater the inequality. Although there is no direct impact of relative deprivation on robbery, it influences the lifestyle, which in turn exerts a significant effect on robbery.

In a major update of data, Kovandzic et al. (1998) compare three measures of inequality: Gini index, inequality ratio, and quintile 5. The inequality ratio is operationalized with the ratio of the percentage of total U.S. income received by the top 20% of families to the percentage received by the lowest 20% of families. Quintile 5 is captures by the share of income received by the top 20% of families. Poverty is measured by the percentage of the population below the Social Security Administration's poverty line. Data are based on the 190 U.S. cities that had a population of 100,000 or more. Inequality, poverty, and percentage of blacks show consistent effects on both total homicide and disaggregated homicide rates.

The explicit test of the racial group threat hypothesis comes from the study of 170 U.S. cities by Jacobs and O'Brien (1998) in predicting police killings. Policing killing is the total rate of police killings per 100,000 residents in a city over seven years (1980 to 1987). Racial threat is captured by several variables (see Table 11.1): racial inequality, squaring percentage blacks and the percentage black change in population. Squaring the percentage of blacks in a city weights the greatest percent black values more heavily and puts greater emphasis on the largest black populations that should be most threatening. It is found that racial inequality is significant even when the murder rate is controlled. Neither of squaring percentage blacks nor the percentage black change is found to have a direct effect on policing killings. Separate analysis of policing killings of blacks indicates, however, that percentage black squaring, the percentage of black change, racial inequality all are significant predictors. Earlier, Jacobs and Britt (1979) test conflict theory with state data of police-caused homicide rate and find that economic inequality (Gini) and percentage change (new immigrants) in population are both positively related to the police-caused homicide rate while the percentage of black is not. In other words, state with the greatest economic disparities experience the largest number of police killings. Sorensen et al. (1993) show that inequality (Gini) and percentage black are associated with police killings of felons (5 years total) per million residents per year (see Table 11.1). The effects of percentage of poor and inequality are compared in separate models and it is found that inequality is better predictor than percentage poor. As a result, both inequality hypothesis and racial threat hypothesis are supported.

Liska et al. (1985) test a more complete model of conflict theory of crime control against the economic production model of crime control with a sample of cities over 100,000 population. Certainty of punishment for the seven index crimes is used as the dependent variable, which is the ratio of arrests to crimes known to the police. The conflict model includes the Gini index, the percentage of nonwhites, and racial residential segregation, which is measured by the dissimilarity index describing the extent to which the racial composition of city blocks reflects the racial composition of the

151

city as a whole (see Table 11.1). Their results show a mixed support for an inequality effect, but a consistent support for the racial threat effect: more minority population in a city, the more arrests. The effect of racial residential segregation is also consistent with the conflict prediction.

Most other tests of minority group threat hypothesis have used different dependent variables than crime. Crawford et al. (1998) test the racial threat with data on sentencing of habitual offenders. Holmes (2000) tests minority threat with data on civil right violations criminal complaints against the police. Jackson and Carroll (1981), and Jackson (1986, 1989) link racial threat with municipal police expenditures in both large and small cities. Jacobs' (1979) study of the determinants of police strength in SMSAs shows that in 1960, the size of the police force is found to be mainly influenced by economic inequalities and the rate of crime, but by 1970, after a decade of urban social upheaval, the relative size of the black population also exerts a substantial effect on police strength. Liska and Yu (1992) reveal that police use of deadly force is related to percent nonwhite population in a city. Using time-series regression to explain yearly changes in the per capita number of law enforcement personnel in the United States, Jacobs and Helms (1997) provide further evidence of the relationship between economic inequality and police strength although this relationship is historically contingent. McGarrell (1993) finds that percentage of African Americans and violent crime rate are consistent predictors of incarceration rate. Finally, Kane (2003) provides partial support for threat hypothesis in his study of police deployment in precincts of New York. His longitudinal data show a curvilinear relationship between Hispanic populations and police deployment, but no significant relationship between the percentage black population and patterns of police deployment is found.

Summary and Discussion

The tumultuous 1960s gave rise to conflict theory. The utopian belief in a just society had been replaced by the sobering realization that inequality, both economic and racial, was deeply entrenched in the United States of America (Cullen and Agnew 1999e). Conflict theory is interested in understanding the effect of inequality on crime and how the social and criminal justice systems respond differentially to persons suspected of violating the law. Especially, it is interested in the effect of social conditions such as structurally generated deprivation, poverty, and inequality on crime and its control. It is clear that some of the variables examined here can be found in the structurist criminological theories such as social disorganization theory and strain theory (Cullen 1983). Indeed, Groves and Sampson (1987: 205) noticed that "there is already a fair amount of convergence between the two traditions with respect to certain

152

causal variables." Although these two traditions may use the same variables in their causal models, the philosophical foundations of these theories are far apart. Unlike strain and disorganization theories, which encourage the maintenance of social stability, conflict theory is not troubled by the presence of dissent and social change. As a result, the interpretation of the empirical results remains far apart. The percentage of blacks/Hispanics is generally considered an index of heterogeneity in social disorganization theory and a subculture in the theory of subculture of violence, but it is considered a racial threat in conflict theory.

As is clear from the above discussion, there are three most widely used measures in testing conflict theory: the Gini as a general index of inequality, the ratio of racial inequality (in education and/or in income) as ascriptive inequality, and the percentages of blacks and Hispanics as indicators of threat. Although the results are not always consistent (see Stack 1984), among the various measures of income inequality, the Gini is the most widely adopted and arguably the better measure of general income inequality (He, Cao, Wells, and Maguire 2003). The dependent variables in testing conflict theory, however, are quite varied. Furthermore, conflict theory can also be tested at the micro-level to include research on the subjective class (Dunaway et al. 2000) and on the consensus or dissensus in public opinions about what, and how strongly, acts are disapproved (Browning and Cao 1992). If the laws resonate with agreed-upon public morality and values, then there ought to be some consensus in public opinions and some congruence between the legal and social definitions of wrong-doing and consequent penalties. There is a sizable variation in the average opinion for criminal justice ideology, however, and there is a significant difference between races regarding crime and its control (Browning and Cao 1992). In general, the new generation of conflict theorists is more concerned with the causes of criminal and delinquent behavior although the focus has remained largely on the notion of crime as an outcome of definitions imposed as part of the consequences of conflict among various segments of society (Lilly et al. 1995).

Table 11.1   Measures of Conflict Theory

I.   Blau and Blau (1982)
    1.   the Gini index
    2.   SES inequality in race = the difference in averaging socioeconomic status between whites and nonwhites based on Duncan's (1961) SEI scores

II.   Cao and Maume (1993)
    1.   relative deprivation = the Gini index + mean white family income/mean black family income

III.   Jacobs and O'Brien (1998)
    A.   Dependent Variables:
    1.   Total police killing in seven year/city pop*100,00
    2.   Log (1+total blacks killed by the police/black pop*100,00)
    B.   Independent Variables:
    1.   square (percentage blacks)
    2.   square root of percentage of black change from 1970 to 1980
    3.   Black mean family income/white mean family income

IV.   Kovandzic (1998)
    1.   Inequality ratio: percentage of total U.S. income by the top 20% of families/ the percentage received by the lowest 20% of familes
    2.   Quintile 5: the share of income received by the top20% of families

V.   Liska, Chamlin, and Reed (1985)
    1.   Residential segregation = dissimilarity index
    2.   Percentage nonwhites

VI.   Maume (1989)
    1.   Racial inequality in income=mean black family income/mean white family income

VII.   Messner (1989)
    1.   Scope = percentage of the total population that is subject to economic discrimination
    2.   Intensity: 1 = least severe to 4 = most severe

3.   Economic discrimination= scope * intenstiy

VIII.   Messner and Golden (1992)
      A.   Racial Inequality:
      1.   White median family income/black median family income
      2.   White median years of schooling/black median years of schooling (25+)
      3.   Black unemployment rate/white unemployment rate
      B.   Resource Deprivation/Affluence:
      1.   percent poor+kids two parents+median income+Gini+percent black +unemployment rate

IX.   Sorensen, Marquart, and Brock (1993)
      A.   Dependent Variable:
      1.   Annual police killings of felons * 1,000,000 residents/population of a city/ 5 (years)
      B.   Independent Variables:
      1.   the Gini index
      2.   percent poor
      3.   percent black,
      4.   violent crime/ 100,000

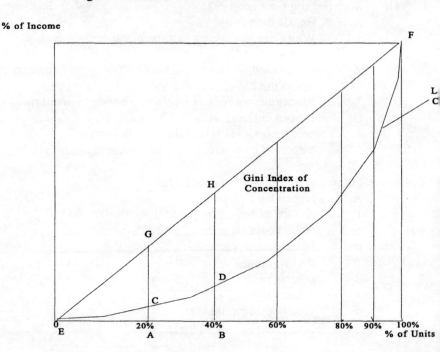

Figure 1 Lorenz Curve and Gini Estimation

The Gini is actually the proportion of the triangular area on a Lorenz diagram that falls between Lorenz curve and the diagonal (EF). The diagonal indicates a perfect equality. The closer the Lorenz curve to the diagonal the less the inequality. The larger the proportion between the diagonal and the Lorenz curve the more the inequality. Our Gini coefficient is estimated by the following formula:

$$\text{Gini} \approx 1 - \Sigma\,(BE - AE)(CA + DB)$$

Theoretically speaking, Gini coefficient ranges from 0 (perfect equality) to 1 (perfect inequality).

156

Chapter 12
Integrative Theories

In the previous chapters, major criminological theories have been discussed and their measures have been presented. In general, these theories have been regarded as unique criminological theories. Since the late 1970s, however, a new trend of theory development – theory integration – has captured the imagination of scholars. A variety of efforts has been made to produce many integrated criminological theories. The current chapter is devoted to an examination of some efforts in this regard. Because of the nature of the discussion, the subtitles are arranged differently from the previous chapters. I will first attempt to review the history of theory construction, then move on to discuss the gains and losses from theory integration, and finally present a few examples of side-by-side integration and end-to-end integration.

Theory Construction

While this is not a place to embark on a sociology of theory construction, it is edifying to briefly discuss the process of theory construction historically. Theory is regarded as the most important and distinctive activity for human beings. It is not surprising that it is also the most time-consuming activity in history (Kaplan 1964). In general, theory construction is based on two seemingly contradictory directions. The first is called theory elaboration and the second is called theory integration. Early in human development, knowledge was limited and a Jack-of-all-trades was possible. Aristotle (B.C. 384-322), according to today's standards, can be considered both as a philosopher and as a scientist. With increased division of labor and expanded specialization of knowledge, more and more specialized theories are needed to provide explanations for specific social phenomena. Theory elaboration thus attempts to build a more comprehensive model on a phenomenon by logical extension of the basic propositions contained in a grand theory. New theory is split off from a grand theory through such elaboration and theoretical fission prospers on theory elaboration. Criminological theories developed before the 1970s could largely be regarded as such. Many sociology-related criminological theories, such as social disorganization theory, anomie theory, and control theory can trace their roots to Emil Durkheim. When more and more theories were developed, however, an outcry for theory reduction was heard and integration through theoretical fusion came into fashion. Since the late 1970s, a variety of theories have been produced as integrated theories

(Braithwaite 1989; Cullen 1994; Elliott et al. 1979; Gottfredson and Hirschi 1990; Katz 1988; Thornberry 1987; Tittle 1995).

On the surface, theoretical integration seems to work in the opposite direction as theory elaboration. According to Liska et al.'s interpretation (1989: 1) of Webster's dictionary definition of integration, "to integrate theories is to formulate relationships among them." Thus, theories can be tested side by side with the intention to increase the explanatory power of the model. They can also be linked in sequence so that variables from one theory may influence variables in another theory, and these variables may singly or together influence the dependent variable – crime or delinquency. In addition, the macro level theory can be integrated with a micro-level theory and different kinds of theories in different academic disciplines can be integrated into one statistical model. Finally, through elaboration, one theory can subsume one or more other theories.

In reality, most theories are developed with a mixture of elaboration and integration. They elaborate one main thesis of a grand theory, with insight from one or more minor theories. For example, depending on which aspect one emphasizes, anomie theory (Merton 1938) can be regarded as a result of theory elaboration or of theory integration. It is Merton's elaboration of Durkheim's theory of anomie. It is also Merton's integration of Durkheim's European theory with the insight of American structural theory. Similarly, Albert Cohen (1955), and Richard Cloward and Lloyd Ohlin's (1960) theories can be regarded as an elaboration of Merton's strain theory as interpreted by Hirschi (1969) and Kornhauser (1978), but they can also be regarded as integrating Sutherland's differential association theory with Merton's anomie theory as Cohen and Cloward and Ohlin themselves perceived it. In Cloward's own words, his theory was to "consolidate two major sociological traditions" (Cloward 1959: 164). Clearly stated, the subculture of violence theory proposed by Marvin Wolfgang and Franco Ferracuti (1967) was an attempt to integrate most of the theoretical work of its day.

The current fascination on theory integration is largely driven by three historical forces. First, it is argued that criminology is an eclectic science, drawing its theories from diverse currents in psychology, sociology, anthropology and law, but this diversity has proved to be an embarrassment of riches (Person and Weiner 1985). The perceived fragmentation within criminology has hindered the growth of criminology and the major benefit for an integration, according to this argument, is that it can provide a reference point for organizing research findings.

Second, the emphasis on theory integration also results from the fact that falsification of theory in social sciences is not perceived as

158

successfully as it is in natural sciences. Before the 1970s, optimism was widely spread that social sciences could follow the paths of natural sciences, and to unlock the secret of human behavior was similar to that of physical behavior. Sir Karl R. Popper (1962) was a dominant figure in the philosophy of science. He proposes that a scientific explanation is in principal falsifiable. Different theories make contradictory hypotheses and research can test these hypotheses to determine which theoretical predictions are consistent with data. Under the influence of Popper, falsification was the domination method of choice for many years. Until 1990, Thomas J. Bernard insisted that it was only through falsification that scientific progress could be made. Falsifiability thus was considered the hallmark of an authentic scientific theory. Since the late 1970s, however, it has become increasingly clear that it is harder to understand human behavior than natural phenomena, and falsification of a social science theory is very difficult (Hanson 2002; Laudan and Leplin 1991; von Hayek 1989).

Third, the widespread use of the variable approach has naturally led to the conclusion that an increased explained power is possible with theoretical integration (Elliott et al. 1979). In this approach, theories are no longer regarded as an integrated whole. Instead, they have been reduced to a number of most representative variables. By putting more of these variables into the same statistical model, the explained variance of criminal behavior will increase. Since the causes of crime and deviance are multiple in nature, having a variety of predictive variables in one integrated statistical model is supposed to reflect the entire range of relevant causes.

These three forces have gradually joined hands and have emerged as a powerful push toward theory integration. Theory construction since the late 1980s has been largely attributed to some kinds of theoretical integration. Many perceived benefits from integration, however, remain empirical, waiting for definitive evaluations. In the next section, the advantages gained from theory integration are discussed together with the disadvantages of it.

Theory Integration

To some extent, integrated theory is a misnomer. There is no theory that is not at least partially influenced or integrated by some extant theory. As the saying goes, there is no theory or hypothesis that is so absurd that someone in the past has somehow or somewhere proposed it. It is not an exaggeration to say that there can be no theory development without some kind of integration. The real issue here is the degree of integration and how we look at things. We can stand on the shoulders of giants or we can hide under the shadow of great masters. Either way, we cannot escape the influence.

Currently there are three main attitudes towards theory integration. First, Barak (1998), Bernard and Snipes (1996), Elliott et al. (1979), and Pearson and Weiner (1985) argue forcefully for the integration of existing criminological theories. Bernard and Snipes (1996) even delivered a death sentence to the Popperian approach of falsification[1]. After being a disciple of Popper's argument for many years (see Bernard 1990), Bernard, together with Snipes took a new stand on the issue. They advocated (1996) the integrative approach and regarded theoretical integration as becoming the only future to the perceived fragmented criminology. They no longer viewed any theories as competitive with each other, but as complementary to each other. Moreover, they considered widespread competitive testing of criminological theories as "a waste of time and money" (1996: 343).

Second, Einstadter and Henry (1995), Gibbons (1994), Hirschi (1979; 1989), Regoli and Hewitt (2003), and Short (1979) either argue against or at least raise serious questions about the propriety of such efforts. Hirschi (1989; 1989) specifically discussed the issue of comparability of the philosophical assumptions behind each theory and declared that separate and equal is better. Similarly, Regoli and Hewitt (2003) saw integration as violating theoretical assumptions that often contradicted each other. Gibbons (1994) was skeptical about the extent of conceptual clarity of such an effort.

Third, Akers (1989) and Cao (2003) take a middle-of-the-road approach. Akers (1989) maintains that if integration is pushed too far, the risk of generating theoretical mush is great; if integration is ignored, important commonalities in seemingly competing theories may be missed. Cao (2003) agrees with Akers, but maintains that theory integration has always been a way of theory building. It is only in recent years, however, that this way of theory construction has been brought into the spotlight of theory construction. He further proposes that although the emphasis on theory elaboration or theory integration may have been asymmetric at one period of time in history, the genuine development of theory is symmetrically dependent on both theory elaboration and theory integration in the long run. There should be, thus, a balanced emphasis on both theoretical elaboration and theoretical integration.

Proponents of theoretical integration hope to achieve three major goals. First, a good scientific theory is supposed to be the one that integrates or unifies empirical findings (Hempel 1966). Braithwaite (1989a) and Tittle (1985) make a similar argument when they advocate a general theory for criminology[2]. Second, many different theories do not necessarily contradict each other. Instead, they focus on different aspects of the same phenomenon. These theories can be combined through theoretical integration into a smaller number of the larger theories (Bernard and Snipes 1996). Third, since each current criminological theory captures only a slice of reality, a combination of theories potentially offers a more complete explanation of crime (Elliott et al. 1979). Freed from unnecessary allegiance to any specific theory, an integrated theory can grab the most powerful variables from a theory and incorporate them into a single model of all factors.

Theoretical integration, however, also has many hurdles to overcome. Something is inevitably lost in the process of theory integration. First, integration assumes that criminological knowledge grows most quickly by trying to bring theories together rather than by having competing perspectives. Most measures of criminological theories, however, do not have the consensus among criminologists that they are actually valid, nor that they are capable of representing the entire theory, nor that the causal order is appropriate. For example, it is generally agreed that delinquent peers are associated with delinquent behavior, but whether peers cause delinquency through exposure to social learning is not settled (Sampson 1999). In contrast, competition between theories has the advantage of forcing theorists to sharpen their arguments and to search for innovative measures, better capturing the concepts in their theories that are more able to account for criminal behavior (Hirschi 1989).

Second, integration can lead to sloppy theorizing in which scholars pick a variable they like from one theory and then a variable from another, but they do not reconcile the philosophic differences behind these variables and thus, the result may be a theoretical mush (Hirschi 1979; Lilly et al. 2002). The philosophical assumptions behind individual theory are very different. For example, differential association theory assumes that one must account for the motivation of delinquent behavior while social control theory explicitly denies that delinquent motivation is necessary. In addition to the comparability of philosophical assumptions, each theory has its own unique images of delinquents/criminals and the process leading to delinquent/criminal lives. By combining two or more theories, the distinctive image created by each theory is lost. The theoretical image of a delinquent from control theory, for example, is one who is not bonded to society and is perceived as an outcast and as mean to his friends. In contrast, the theoretical image of a delinquent from differential association is one who is well absorbed into the subculture of deviance and a "popular" guy among friends. By combining the two theories, the distinct image of delinquents is doomed to disappear.

Third, in the hope of improving explanatory power, theoretical integration diverts attention "from the fundamental purpose of theory construction—the explanation of a particular phenomenon—to a secondary purpose—the reconciliation of differences found in previous theories" (Thornberry 1989: 56). Theories are different and the task of reconciling these differences is tricky. Integrationists are forced to make decisions trampling one theoretical perspective or another and claims of evenhanded treatment of all perspectives are never tenable.

Fourth, while it is normal to reduce a theory into a few testable hypotheses in a model, it is wrong to assume that the theory can *only* be tested with these few hypotheses. Theory is always richer than the few hypotheses would indicate. The empirical reductionism is a necessary evil in doing research, but reducing a theory into one or two most "representative" variables or creating "straw men" is too big an evil. It is worth remembering that variables in statistical models seldom, if ever, can fully represent concepts in a theory, and refutation of a specific statistical model of a theory does not necessarily refute the theory represented by the model (Papandreous 1958).

Furthermore, there is an inherent tension between theorists and researchers. Even if the intention of the original theorist is to create an integrated theory that is all-encompassing, the theory may not escape the fate of being reduced to a few representative variables in the hands of empirical researchers. For example, Gottfredson and Hirschi (1990) aimed to construct a general theory to explain all varieties of criminal behavior and to provide all the social and behavioral correlates of crime. Since they themselves did not provide a concrete example of how to test their theory, their general theory of crime has been reduced and re-labeled as self-control theory (Arneklev et al. 1993; Burton et al. 1998; Deng and Zhang 1998; Longshore et al. 1996; Turner and Piquero 2002; Wood et al. 1993). Once accepted as self-control theory, it has soon been "integrated" into other theories (Kennedy and Forde 1995). For trained empirical researchers, their cutting edge is reductionism – the breaking apart of nature into its natural constituents and testing these constituents one by one (Wilson 1998). Social researchers look for what is new in a theory and then match that newness with what is available in the data that can test the theory. They seldom, if ever, would design comprehensive research to test a theory in its entity (Gibson et al. 2002a).

Finally, the term integration itself has not been well defined and clearly agreed upon. Some use it interchangeably with efforts in developing a general theory (Gottfredson and Hirshi 1990; Pearson and Weiner 1985; Tittle 1985) while others use it more narrowly to indicate efforts increasing the explained variance in the dependent variable (Cao and Deng 1998; Cao and Maume 1993; Elliott et al. 1985; He et al. 2003; Thornberry 1987). Apparently, a more detailed discussion of any of these issues is beyond the scope of this chapter. Consequently, this chapter only examines theory integration from the perspective of empirical analysis: the side-by-side integration and end-to-end integration. These efforts may not result in general theory or theories, and they do not introduce new explanatory variables. Instead, they lean heavily on variables and propositions from various extant theories. As a result, these efforts qualify them as efforts at theory integration.

Examples of Testing Integrated Theories

Since most integrated theories do not introduce new variables, this section is arranged differently from the previous chapters in a sense that the theoretical paths in models are also presented. Two kinds of integration are discussed – side-by-side integration and up-and-down integration. It is important to remember, however, that these efforts are tentative and exploratory.

Side-by-side Integration. It is also called horizontal integration. It is probably the easiest theoretical integration (Liska et al. 1989), and it is useful in explaining criminal acts differing widely in significance (Hirschi 1979). Cao and Deng (1998) conducted one such study, integrating three theories in predicting shoplifting.

Many theories of crime are complementing each other without much theoretical contradictions. Strain theory and differential association theory are two such theories (Cloward and Ohlin 1960; Cohen 1955; Merton 1997a). Both are perceived as to elucidate low-class crime. While strain theory emphasizes the structurally induced strain, differential association theory focuses more on the process of transmitting criminal value and skills. It is argued that combining these two theories may allow each theory to capture its unique area of criminality as well as to increase the explanatory power of the model. In addition to sociological theories, it is argued that Katz's theory of seduction is well suited to explain the thrill part involved with shoplifting and that it compensates sociological theories' lack of concern for the foreground variables[3]. Consequently, an integrated model is proposed where variables from three theories are regressed on shoplifting (see Table 12.1). The detailed descriptions of measures of strain theory and of differential association theory appear in Chapters 6 and 7 respectively. Indeed, the results show that these three theories work well statistically: putting them together did not falsify any of the three theories. Instead the integrated model explains significantly more variance in shoplifting than any one of the single theory.

End-to-end Integration. It is also called sequential integration. It refers to conceptualizing a dependent variable in one theory as an independent variable in another, and independent variable in one theory as a dependent variable in other, or both. The most cited integrated model by Elliott et al. (1979; 1985) belongs to this type of integration at the micro-level. Elliott et al. (1985) combine three leading sociological theories of delinquency – strain theory, social control theory, and differential association/social learning theory – into one statistical model (see Figure 12.1). Three layers of causal linkages are described: (1) social disorganization theory, strain theory, and socialization theory are associated with weak conventional bonding; (2) weak conventional bonding increases the likelihood of association with delinquent peers; and (3) association with delinquent friends increases the likelihood of delinquency. Longitudinal data from the National Youth Surveys are used to test the proposed causal model and the tempo order among variables was controlled. The integration of these theories is done with some modification and extension of the original theories. The results support the proposed causal linkages in the model and indicate that the explanatory power of the integrated model is highly relative to the multivariate tests of pure explanatory models. The model accounted for 52-58 percent of the variance in delinquency.

Similarly, Thornberry (1987) proposes an interactional theoretical model largely consisting of an end-to-end integration of micro-level variables although he describes how certain macro-level variables may affect the micro-level variables in his model. Thornberry et al. (1994) test their modified version of interactional model with data from the Rochester Youth Development Study. The tested model is not limited to either a social control or a social learning perspective. Rather, it incorporates elements of both into a broader body of explanatory principles. It goes beyond them by taking into consideration developmental process and bidirectional causal structures (See Figure 12.2). The reciprocal relationships make his model more complicated than is commonly portrayed. Thornberry et al. (1994) argue, however, that most variables have reciprocal causal effects on one another. Delinquency itself is involved in this pattern of reciprocal causation. In addition, the model controls both the lagged and instantaneous reciprocal efforts for each of the dyadic relationships. The results suggest that associating with delinquent peers increases delinquency via the reinforcing environment of the peer network. Engaging in delinquency then leads to increases in association with delinquent peers and delinquent beliefs exert lagged effects on peers and behavior, which tend to "harden" the formation of delinquent beliefs.

At the macro level, Cao and Maume (1993) conducts a study of end-to-end integration of the three macro-level theories in predicting metropolitan robbery rates: urbanization theory, lifestyle/routine activity theory, and relative deprivation theory (see Figure 12.3). The urbanization theory is represented by the index combining percentage of urban population and the population size of a metropolitan area. It is used as the exogenous variable influencing the relative deprivation index, lifestyle index, and the robbery rates. The relative deprivation theory is captured by an index consisting of two variables: the Gini index and the ratio of average white income over average of black income. This relative deprivation, in turn, affects both the lifestyle index and the robbery rates. The lifestyle/routine activity index is composed of percent homes without a car, percent homes with one or more persons per room, percent renters, percent divorced or separated, and percent using public transportation (see Chapter 3 for a more detailed description). Finally, the lifestyle index predicts the robbery rates of standard metropolitan statistical areas. The results of their analysis show, however, there is no direct influence from the relative deprivation index to the robbery rates while all other paths are significantly related as hypothesized.

I have not examined the up-and-down integration because the complex nature of the endeavor and a host of other unresolved issues (see Liska et al. [1989] for a detailed discussion). In general, the aim of the up-and-down integration is to subsume one or more theories and to result in a new theory. For example, using this method of integration, Akers (1989) tried to subsume Sutherland's social differential association theory within his own social learning theory. More recently, he further attempted to subsume social bonding theory and strain theory (1989), but his efforts were not well accepted and were accused of theoretical hegemony.

Summary and Discussion

Faced with the increased number of criminological theories, criminologists seem to have to choose whether they intend to reduce the number of theories through falsification or through integration. In reality, criminologists don't have to choose between the two. There are overwhelmingly positive benefits from theoretical diversity. It is through controversy that judgment develops. In the absence of absolute rules for good practice, judgment is crucial. It is also through diversity that new developments arise. Although falsification in a pure Popperian sense has foundered, it is premature to abandon falsification altogether in our research. Both theoretical elaboration and integration are needed in any efforts of future theory construction. Integration should not be regarded as an alternative to falsification. Instead, it should be considered a supplement to falsification. In this chapter, I have examined the merits and problems associated with theoretical integration and presented several examples of side-by-side integration and end-to-end integration. It is concluded that it is premature to regard theory integration as the only solution for the future theorizing (see the next chapter) and criminologists need to first create more standardized measures for each theory before serious efforts can be put into more theory integration.

In examining different types of theoretical integration, Akers (1989) particularly recommended conceptual integration, by which concepts from one theory are shown to overlap in meaning with concepts from another theory. He argued that belief in social bonding theory "is very close to" the concept of definitions in social differential association theory. While the purpose of such integration is debatable (Liska et al. 1989), Akers did raise an important point because interest in a criminological concept waxes and wanes over years. Before the 1990s, concepts such as social disorganization (Bursik 1988), willingness to intervene (Hackler et al. 1974), territorial functioning (Taylor 1988), and informal social control (Greenberg and Rohe 1986) were more popular, but since the 1990s, concepts such as informal collective security (Cao et al. 1996) or confidence in neighbors (Cao et al. 1997), and social integration and collective efficacy (Gibson et al. 2002b; Sampson et al. 1997) have come to dominate the literature. In measurement terms, these concepts are highly correlated. Instead of generating more and more of these murky concepts, empirical criminologists should seriously focus on one or two of these concepts and begin to design a common measuring instrument so that future researchers can stand on the shoulders of present researchers. Therefore, conceptual integration appears to be an area that future research may further explore. It is possible that conceptual integration, as a step-stone, may lead to propositional integration, which may eventually lead to broader theoretical integration.

Notes

1.   This is, of course, my interpretation of Bernard and Snipes (1996). Here is the original statement of Bernard and Snipes (1996: 303): "competitive testing, in which two theories are tested against each other with the expectation of falsifying one or the other, is *almost always inappropriate* at the theoretical level" (emphasis added).

2.   Merton (1968c) considered a general theory for sociology to be premature. He stated that sociology was not ready for the formulation of a general theory "broad enough to encompass the vast ranges of precisely observed details of social behavior, organization, and change and fruitful enough to direct the attention of research workers to a flow of problems for empirical research" (p. 45). Instead, he urged sociologists to construct less imposing but better grounded theories of the middle range in order to forge a closer connection between theory and research. Within criminology, Braithwaite (1989a: 129) seems to agree with Merton when he says that "there may be little hope for a single general theory of crime" while Gibbons (1994: 196-97) argues that "the more moderate goal of developing 'a family of theories' makes the greatest sense for the criminological enterprise." In describing a general evolution history of nature science, Kuhn (1970) observes that social sciences are still in the pre-paradigm period, where competing theories coexist, but the transition to maturity need not be associated with the acquisition of a paradigm. One dominant paradigm is not always a blessing. It may often become entrenched, resisting any substantial change, and delay the arrival of a new paradigm that would emerge eventually and supplant the old one through revolution.

3.   It is interesting to note that Shoham and Seis (1993: 127) regard Katz's theory as "an excellent combination of both existential and phenomenological approaches to the study of crime."

Table 12.1   An Example of Side-by-side Integration

I. Cao and Deng (1998)
 A. Strain Theory:
  1. Immediate goals (alpha = .71):
  2. Blocked opportunity (alpha = .75):
  3. Perceived solution: "Shoplifting could offer an easy and quick solution to my needs." (0=no and 1=yes).
 B. Differential Association Theory
  1. Definition favorable to criminality (alpha = .81)
  2. Deviant association (alpha = .68)
 C. Seduction Theory (alpha = .76)
  1. It is exciting to shoplift;
  2. Sometimes I find it exciting to do things for which I might get in trouble;
  3. Sometimes I feel it is exciting to get around the law.
  (strongly agree, somewhat agree, slightly agree, slightly disagree, somewhat disagree strongly disagree)

Figure 12.1   The Integrated Model *

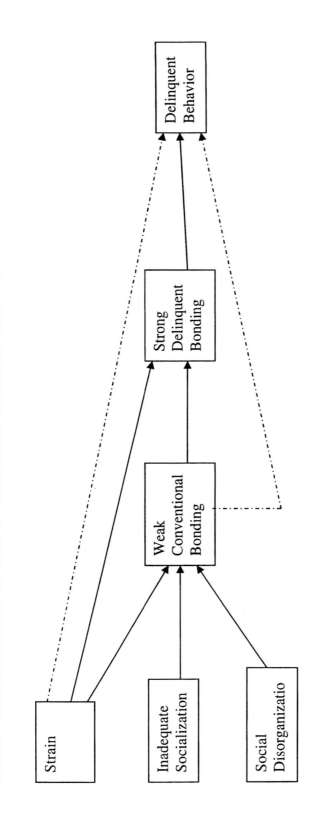

* The figure is adopted from Elliott et al. (1985: 66).

169

Figure 12.2 Theoretical Model of Causal Relationships among Delinquent Peers, Peer Reactions, Delinquent Beliefs, and Delinquent Behavior *

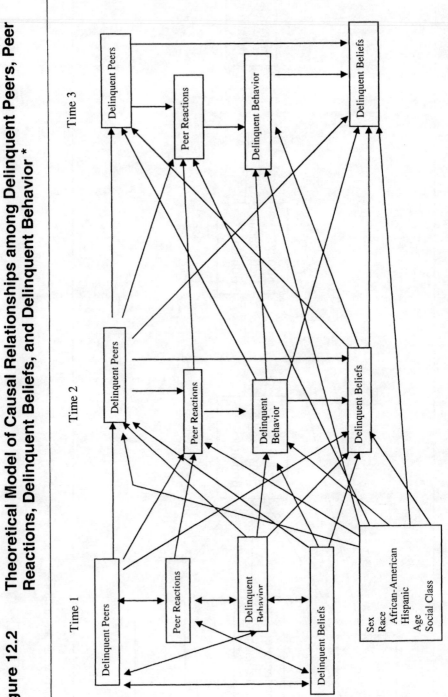

* The figure is adopted from Thornberry et al. (1994: 52).

Figure 12.3 A Comprehensive Model of Robbery *

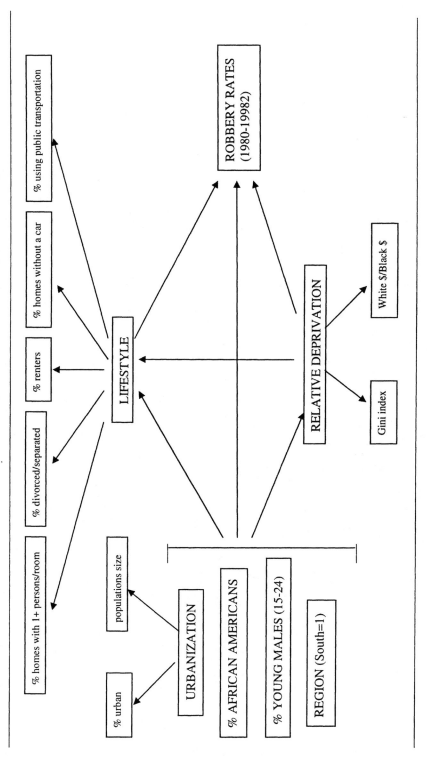

* The figure is adopted from Cao and Maume (1993: 16).

171

Chapter 13
The Future of Criminological Theories

Current textbooks have devoted systematic attention to the substance of a theory or qualitative validation. I take a different approach in this book and focus on measuring instruments for major criminological theories. The measurement issue is strategically located in all quantitative research, and thus it deserves more attention from researchers in the process of building up criminology as a science. Measurement falls at the center of the two greatest methodological divides in research. First, it allows us to dissect the contention between those who believe it sensible to treat social events in a quantitative manner versus those who assume the meaning of human action is open only to qualitative appreciation. Second, measurement marks a traditional split line between those studies that are thought of as basically conceptual and theoretical versus those that are deemed to be empirical (Pawson 1989).

Taking measures of major criminological theories to be the focus of methodological scrutiny allows us to sharpen our ideas about the task, as well as the criticisms, of empirical criminology, thus further separating our work from speculation, hearsay, intuition, or superstition. The real obstacle to criminology as a science is not technical, but conceptual. Measurement is not only simply a matter of assigning numbers to observation, but also of conceptualizing these numbers. The conclusion to be drawn from this book is that scientific criminology must face the challenges posed by measurement. Criminologists must begin moving toward more explicit and clearer conceptualization of the key concepts in each theory – one that results in appropriate operationalization of the concepts and one that is accepted by the majority of researchers, instead of inventing a new measure for each and every new project.

The Existing Problems in

Testing Criminological Theories

In the previous ten chapters, I have covered the most widely used and unique measures of thirteen major criminological theories and have examined the efforts at integrating many of these theories. With few exceptions for the macro-level theories, most key concepts in the major criminological theories are not well-defined and/or do not have their corresponding measuring instruments commonly accepted by the criminological community. Consequently, several theoretically important issues emerge from this endeavor. First, there is not much effort toward standardization of measurement in some theory. Second, at the other end of the extreme, there is a tendency to reify the concepts of a theory and to ban any new interpretation and new measures into the empirical field. Third, theory is seldom considered as a whole, but as separable pieces and in disconnected hypotheses. These problems have prevented criminology from achieving a higher status in social sciences. I will discuss these problems in more detail in the following. Since the problems of methodology in criminology transcend all those found in any social sciences, my comments may be applicable to a broader social scientific community.

First, at one extreme, there is not much effort toward standardization of measurement in some theory. This is true even for the theories whose authors themselves are empirically oriented. Hirschi's social bond theory is one such example. It is one of the most tested theories, but in most empirical tests of this theory, reconceptualization is a normal exercise. Seldom, if ever, are the key concepts in the theory measured in the same way. Extensions and new measures are common in testing the theory. After a careful evaluation of tests of the theory, Kempt (1993: 153) concludes that "there was no single element that appeared in every study." As a result, no progress has been made in the sense of accumulating verified knowledge about this theory. Gibbs (1985:48) is also partially right when he claims "that Hirschi's theory is not systematically testable." I think, however, that this is not an unrepairable problem of the theory. The clearer definition of the concepts could be derived from social bond theory, and their operationalizations could gradually move toward more standardization.

Second, at the other extreme, there is a tendency to reify the extant theory and its limited measures. Merton's anomie theory is one such example. The difficult task of measuring anomie has been discussed repeatedly in many books for all these years, but new attempts to test the original theory at either micro or macro levels are constantly rejected. The interpretation of anomie theory is enshrined (Cullen and Wright 1997). There seems to be an elite of empirical researchers who consistently block any reinterpretations of the theory that are different from their own. For the reified theory, data in support of a theory are easier to publish than evidence against the theory. Cole (1975: 213) notes that Merton's paradigm has succeeded in fulfilling a "major latent function" to a theory's growth: providing puzzles for scientists to work on ...." I would argue, however, that it is time to consider providing a solution to the puzzle by giving a measure of anomie, even though it may not be perfect. Merton (1968a: 478) maintains that "A premature insistence on precision at all costs may sterilize imaginative hypotheses."

Third, in testing a theory or conducting a research, criminologists usually take the variable approach (Blumer 1956). There is a conspicuous absence of rules, limitations, and prohibitions to govern the choice of variables in theory testing. If one of the variables in the data can reveal something interesting or something new, the researcher will go ahead and conduct the research. The goal of such efforts is, of course, to publish their results. Pressure of publication overshadows more important scientific concerns. Considering that knowledge is cumulative and that techniques of analysis develop quickly, this lackadaisical approach is deemed acceptable in many cases. After all, with rapid development of technology, and the relative slow involvement of theory, the variable approach does have a function to serve in academia[1]. It is totally wrong, however, if all the research is of this kind. As Merton (1968a: 467, emphasis in original) comments, "There is, in short, a clear and decisive difference between *knowing how to test* a battery of hypotheses and *knowing the theory* from which to derive hypotheses to be tested. It is my impression that current criminological training is more largely designed to make students understand the first than the second." The validity of a theory's empirical status needs more comprehensive research instead of the piecemeal approach. As discussed in the previous chapter, the variable approach is one of the three driving forces for the fad of theory integration.

The Implication of these Problems to

Theory Construction

The above-mentioned problems have resulted in frustration among many criminologists and accumulated into a crisis in the development of criminological theory. Many mainstream criminologists who consider themselves social scientists have also voiced their dissatisfaction with the current status of criminological theory. Cullen and Wright (1997: 185) state that criminological theories "have been stunted in their growth." Gibbs (1985: 49) declares that "positivism has been the whipping boy in criminology for over fifteen years." Gottfredson and Hirschi (1990: xiii) express their unhappiness "with the ability of academic criminology to provide believable explanations of criminal behavior." Sampson (1999:447) maintains "that previous research almost never offers a critical test of competing hypotheses." Leavitt (1999: 390-91) concludes "a large share of past and present criminological theorizing more closely resembles art work rather than science." Bernard (1990) laments that criminology is failing to make scientific progress. Gibbons (1994) argues that much of the time, criminologists literally do not know what they are talking about, due to the fuzzy and murky nature of the discursive theorizing that characterizes criminology. Braithwaite (1989a: 133) proclaims that "the present state of criminology is one of abject failure in its own terms."

At the beginning of Chapter 1, I listed three problems facing criminologists today. The first issue of the fragmentation of criminology is partially discussed in Chapter 12. The second issue of discursive theorizing and the third problem of measurement standardization are both highly relevant to be discussed further here. Many criminological theories need to begin anew from the precise definitions of its key concepts, thus establishing a basis for judging the quality of one's measures, and enabling others to evaluate the meaning of one's research findings. This process of formulating and clarifying concepts is linked to both theory testing and theory construction. The beginning researcher would be well advised, therefore, to rely on existing theoretical definitions in the criminological literature. This should help tie his or her research to existing theory and to the broader scientific enterprise of developing a general body of knowledge.

The poignant performance of criminological theory is related to the lack of standardization of measures in each theory and the lack of interplay between empirical research and theory construction. The lack of commonly accepted measures in criminological theory has seriously hampered the progress of the development of scientific criminology as a discipline. Two of the seminal purposes of standardization in measurement are for comparability and for accumulation of knowledge. During the past few centuries, standardized quantitative measurement has been extended into all natural sciences, often with impressive results. It is time for criminologists to consider the issue of standardization. Standardization – qualitative as well as quantitative – is clearly a very effective epistemic strategy for comparison (Ziman 2000). Without measurement comparability, a shared body of knowledge will never cumulate in the empirical literature. It is not an exaggeration to say that without measurement comparability there will be no progress in social sciences, including criminology. Therefore, comparability of measures is a basic issue for scientific criminology, and there is much for criminologists to do in this area.

The lack of interplay between empirical research and theoretical construction has seriously endangered the general well-being of criminology. The development of any scientific theory depends on the hypothetico-deductive procedure (see Chapters 1 and 2 for a more detailed discussion). Braithwaite (1989a) argues that a failure to attempt reconstruction of a theory after testing is a failure to nurture explanation. Merton (1968a: 476) criticizes the "bifurcation of theory and empirical research" and advocates the interaction between theory and research. In discussing the development of criminological theory, Cullen and Agnew (1999a) hold that criminological theories are dynamic, not static. Gibbons (1994:7) insists that theory and research are "inter-related parts of the process of inquiry." Tittle (1985) points out that there is a malfunctioning interplay between theory and research. Theory grows as initial formulations are modified in light of empirical evidence. There should be flexible reciprocation between theory and research so that the theory can constantly revise and grow.

Despite requirements of science and in spite of the above-mentioned compelling arguments from leading criminologists, current theories and their tests are still unidirectional. That is, researchers test the theories, but few theorists modify their theories in response to the empirical reality. Anomie theory is much the same today as it was when first formulated, despite decades of empirical research. Because of its rejection to mutate, Tittle (1985: 114) regards anomie theory as "one of many failed general theories." On the other hand, because of the fuzzy nature of its major concepts, social bond theory is considered a boon to those who are engaged in empirical tests of the theory to the point that there are criminologists who spend their entire careers testing just that theory.

Both the lack of standardized measures of a theory and the lack of interplay between empirical research and theory building inhibit a healthy development of criminology. Perhaps, our worst crime is our specious activities about what really involves in a scientific project; our easy satisfaction with the amount of research we have produced; and our smug assumption that whatever we are doing statistically is science. Criminology, as a fledgling discipline in public universities, must realize its claim that it is a science so that it will eventually make its way to the ivy league universities in the United States and to more university curricula all over the world. Kaplan (1968) asserts that building scientific theory is a cumulative process between theory and measurement instruments. The ultimate test of the validity of criminological theories will consist in the invention of widely accepted measuring devices. Criminologists, however, have handicapped theoretical work by adopting inconsistent measures of key concepts, by separating empirical research from theory building, and by tolerating specious practices in research.

Solutions

The concern for measurement is the primary *raison d'etre* to claim criminology as a social science. Progress in science is largely dependent on the measurement used (Pedhzure and Schmelkin 1991). Measurement is the Achilles' heel of criminology's claim as a social science. Akers (2000) and Gibbs (1990) argue that the primary criterion for judging a theory is its verification or refutation by empirical research. In principle, this statement is correct. In reality, criminologists must first resolve the issue of standardization of measures before much ado of evaluation of a theory's empirical status. As discussed in Chapter 2, a variable in a hypothesis can only provide imperfect representation of a concept, and throughout this book, it is clear that a theory can be interpreted in different ways to derive dissimilar hypotheses.

It is time for empirical criminologists to get down to brass tacks and seriously face the challenge. For natural sciences, there is not only an agreement about the importance of measurement, but also about the specific measurement. This is far from being the case in social sciences, including criminology. Yet in criminology, there has been little or no systematic effort stipulating how to measure the key concepts in each theory in order to test the theory more conclusively. Currently, because more than one indicators of the same concept exist, critics will never be able to agree on whether a piece of research has falsified the measure used in the particular statistical model or whether that study has actually falsified the hypothesis of a theory. The efforts put into this research on measurement of the major criminological theories represent a recognition of this crucial role. Too many signs indicate that researchers treat measurement issues less seriously. To treat the social world as though it comes in monadic, discrete, singular lumps omits consideration for the role of theory and conceptualization in the perceptual distinctions we make or as though it is something sacred and untouchable.

I propose three solutions to deal with the three problems discussed above. First, when a concept has more than a dozen ways of operationalization, efforts toward standardization are called for. Second, when there is not much attempt to reinterpret a classic theory, the liberation of the paradigm becomes essential. These two extremes represent the dynamic tension in science between forming a scientific community with a unified standard while keeping the system open to new ideas, and thus to possible theoretical change. As Kuhn (1978: 227) contends, "the successful scientist must simultaneously display the characteristics of the traditionalist and of the iconoclast." Third, comprehensive test of a theory instead of the piecemeal approach is needed in our research design. The variable approach will never be *quid pro quo* for a comprehensive theory-sensitive research design.

Beyond these three points, I also advance a more speculative suggestion for theory construction. Currently, the frustration in theory competition has led many criminologists to try theory integration since the late 1970s (see Messner at al. 1989). Bernard and Snipe (1996) even

178

declared the death of the Popperian approach of falsification. It is critical to reconfirm the merit of falsification here: Pressures at competition between theories tend to force researchers toward internal consistency and conceptual clarity. Falsification cannot be regarded as the only pathway to a more scientific theory, but it remains one pathway. Merton, although not a committed Popperian, argues as late as 1997 that "theories that cannot be falsified have little worth" (1997b: ix).

Presently, theoretical integration seems to have become the only future to the fragmentation of criminology. A cursory glance at current criminological textbooks on the market, however, reveals the fashion of theoretical integration, which may result in a host of problems (see the previous chapter for a more detailed discussion). In general, researchers have not attempted to merge the explanatory principles in a way that satisfies the criminological community. Moreover, although the empirical reductionism is a necessary evil in doing research, reducing a theory into one or two most "representative" variables or creating a caricature of a theory is too big an evil for many criminologists. It is important to remember the limitation of empirical research: Variables seldom, if ever, can represent concepts perfectly in a theory (see Chapter 2 for a more detailed discussion). Furthermore, variables cannot be treated as discrete items. They must be understood as "part of a system regulated by some *generative mechanism*" (Pawson 1989: 324, emphasis original).

An alternative approach is proposed by Gibbs (1985), Gibbons (1994), and Leavitt (1999). These scholars advocate developing formal theories that resemble those described by philosophers of science. I agree partially. Almost all existing criminological theories would flunk their stringent criteria as a scientific theory. I think that the new theory should follow the principles of neopositivism, but the more pressing need in criminology is to realize the full potential of many existing criminological theories by providing precise definitions for concepts and by developing agreed-upon measuring instruments for these concepts. After all, one purpose of theory is to provide puzzles to be resolved.

At the beginning of Chapter 2, I argue that if criminologists pay more attention to measurement of theories, falsification of hypotheses from a theory may be more plausible in the near future and the pressure of reducing the number of theories through integration may be eased. Few extant criminological theories appear to have been exploited to their full potential yet. There may be an embarrassment of riches in criminological theories, but there is also a poverty of agreed-upon measures for key theoretical concepts.

It does not require a guru to see that it is easier to offer a theoretical solution to a problem than a feasible solution. Consequently, I am going to discuss two barriers to conducting better research. First and foremost, the chief impediment to a more scientific criminology is the researcher him/herself. It is perhaps edifying to cite more well-known cases, but almost every criminologist, including myself, is not immune from the observation. Merton apparently knew the significance of the interactive role between research and theory. He published a widely cited essay on the bearing of empirical research on theory (1968b), but he never bothered to change his own theory. His inaction is more understandable because he was a grand theorist and his training in the 1930s might not have equipped him with necessary statistical skills.

What is more perplexing is Hirschi's case. Hirschi (1969) also acknowledges the need for empirical tests to build on one another to achieve theoretical development. During the first twenty years of its existence, however, Hirschi never attempted to revise his social bond theory in light of empirical evidence. Then in 1990, he joined hands with Gottfredson to propose a completely different theory – a general theory of crime, or more popularly known as self-control theory[2].

The second obstruction to better research is the mounting pressure for publication that permeates academia and is ubiquitous within criminology. Criminologists need to stop periodically and think about what we are doing. Confucius (551-479 B.C.), the Chinese philosopher and educator, argued that learning without thinking was bewilderment. How practical is it to "stop and think"? The computer revolution has made it possible to carry out tedious large-scale calculations that were not possible several decades ago (Blalock 1989). This has resulted in the increased borrowing of quantitative approaches developed in other disciplines in the study of criminological issues. In addition, large data sets are also now much more available than before[3]. With assistance of computers, availability of secondary data has greatly expedited our research. The pressure for publication has made many of us a perpetual motion machine. Computers, however, have made us lazy theoretically and theory-sensitive research designs have not emerged in recent years (Sampson 1999). Systematic pressures have driven criminologists toward the piecemeal research. Extant criminological research is strong on the statistical modeling of weak data and on quantitative approaches borrowed from other disciplines, but there is the cavalier indifference to the quality, validity, theoretical meaning of data, and to the issue of measuring instruments of the key concepts in each theory. Blalock (1982: 9) warned two decades ago that "unless very careful attention is paid to one's theoretical assumptions and conceptual apparatus, no array of statistical techniques will suffice. Nor can a series of *ad hoc* empirical studies produce truly cumulative knowledge except in the sense of producing dated and situation-specific findings."

The inconsistency between what one knows and what one practices and the consequence of "publish or perish" reality are two primary invincible obstructions toward doing better research. Both phenomena have been with us for a long time and neither of them is likely to disappear any time in the future. Few scholars are willing to openly recognize their own limitations. Regardless of how successful a criminologist is, the pressure of publication is still with him/her. Paradoxically, Merton's discussion of the anomia of success is quite applicable to criminologists who choose variable approach in order to publish one more article over better designs or more comprehensive approach: "What appeared from below as the end of the road becomes, in the actual experience, only another way station" (1964: 221). Where is the stopping-point where criminologists can conduct their research more rigorously and where concerns over quality take precedence over concerns over publication? It seems almost hopeless, at least in the near future, that criminologists will do much differently from what has prevailed in the field.

What Have I Achieved?

This book is an attempt to improve the consciousness of criminologists about the measuring devices for the major criminological theories. It intends to bridge the theorizing and their measures so that they will become interrelated parts of scientific theory construction. It also aims to provide a guideline for students of criminology and criminal justice to engage in their own research. It hopes to help establish in some small way criminological theory as the basis of a scientific discipline *sui generis* without perverting the intent or content of each criminological theory. Throughout the book, I have tried to restrain myself from commenting on the results of testing hypotheses of a particular theory. Instead, I have focused on describing the unique measures of key concepts in each theory and on conceptualization of these measures.

The criticisms and lament about the current status of criminology should not be interpreted as the hopeless of scientific method or scientific criminology. It is not the intention of this book to sap the confidence of those in scientific criminology. On the contrary, this book intends to strengthen the very foundation of scientific inquiry in doing criminological research. As I argue in Chapter 1, scientific methodology deserves a privileged place in criminology and criminal justice. In order to maintain this position, we must understand and recognize our weaknesses. Socrates (470-399 B. C.), the Greek philosopher, boasted that his superiority lay in his awareness of his own ignorance. By apprising the readers of some fundamental problems and difficulties in conducting research, I hope to provide readers with a sober point of departure in any future endeavor. The problem with the current status of criminology, as Cullen and Sundt (2003: 357) observe, "is that it is insufficiently scientific."

It should be noted that the current failure of scientific criminology has led some criminologists to call for abandoning the search for causes of crime (Fattah 1997; Henry and Milovanovic 1996). Henry and Milovanovic (1996: 153), for example, argue that the search for causes of crime "simply elaborates the distinctions that maintain crime as a separate reality, while failing to address how it is that crime is a part of human agency and society." This call is unwarranted. The current failure of criminological theory is linked to the negligence of a concerted effort to produce comparable and agreed-upon measures to solve the intellectual puzzles handed to us by theoretical giants. It is not the failure of scientific theory itself. Criminologists cannot balk at providing valid theory, nor can they gain anything by retreating from doing better research.

Although constitutive criminology advocated by Henry and Milovanovic (1996) is beyond postmodernism, it continues to share many characteristics of postmodernism despite being affirmative in nature. Post-modernist critiques of positivist empiricism in social sciences collapse into nihilism, anarchism, subjectivism, and defeatism. They stand opposite to positivism, whose nature is both skeptical and optimistic. Ever since its emergence as a social science, criminology has been preoccupied with the search for the causes of crime. Although the study of etiology of the crime is not all that criminologists do, it is undeniably the core of criminology. In the mind of a social scientist, observation without a theory is chaotic and wasteful while a theory without the support of observation is speculative (see Chapter 1). Scientific criminological theory liberated from subjective anarchism and from blinkered defeatism has a potential whose days have not arrived yet.

In a larger sense, the current work is a piecemeal approach to the study of theory testing too. The purpose of this book is to help newcomers grasp the past measures of criminological theories and the problems associated with current empirical research. I have focused on the measurement of specific concepts in theories, but I have not examined in any detail the large constraints of social theory, nor have I touched the broader issue of theoretical causal intricacies, nor have I discussed the interpretation of research results from empirical studies. Theories could be arranged in very different ways, and results of testing could be interpreted using different lenses. Other important issues of theory testing are how the dependent variable is measured and the relationship between the survey language and the natural language. The measures of key concepts are reported, but little discussion of measuring the significance and representativeness of data (probability, sampling, and problems in polling) or of measuring relationships between variables in a theory (association and correlation) are attempted.

Moreover, many new criminological theories are not covered in this book. For example, reintegrative shaming theory by Braithwaite (1989b), social support theory by Cullen (1994), self-control theory by Gottfredson and Hirschi (1990), seduction theory by Katz (1988), institutional-anomie theory by Messner and Rosenfeld (1994), life-course theory by Sampson and Laub (1993), and control balance theory by Tittle (1995) are not yet included because their existence is relatively recent and because tests of these theories are relatively few. I hope that with the passage of time, these theories will be included.

Measuring things quantitatively is demanding. Creating widely accepted measuring devices is more so. Kaplan was amused by his colleague's sally: "if you can measure it, that ain't it!" (1968: 601). While it is true that all measures in social sciences are subjective to a degree, it is also true that by definition, a measure is a basis for comparison. A measure can never be purely subjective, since it involves communal agreement on what entities should be regarded as "standard" (Ziman 2000). Gibbons (1990: ix) contends that theoretical flabbiness (which means a theory with implicit propositions with fuzzy concepts) is "the most serious problem which criminologists must confront." I believe that criminologists must pay immediate and concerted attention to the problems of conceptualization and measurement, which have far too long been neglected. No matter how profound the theoretical insight, how sophisticated the research design, and how elegant the analytic techniques, nothing can compensate for poor measures.

Concluding Remarks

Regrettably, I have to leave this book with the same uncertainty about the future of criminological theories that existed before I began to write it. George Berkeley (1685-1753) wonders why "the illiterate bulk of mankind that walk the high-road of plain, common sense, and are governed by the dictates of Nature, [are] for the most part easy and undisturbed. To them, nothing that is familiar appears unaccountable or difficult to comprehend" (1998 [1710]: 89). Those who devote their time to *verstehen*, however, fail to gain from their pursuit a "greater calm and serenity of mind." What they get, unfortunately, is still more confusion. No sooner did I part from the hunch to reflect on the measurement of criminological theories, than a thousand scruples sprang up in my mind concerning those things that before I seemed fully to comprehend. Endeavoring to deal with them, I have been drawn insensibly into uncouth paradoxes, difficulties, and inconsistencies, which multiply and grow as I advance, till at length, having wandered through many intricate mazes, I find myself just where I was, or which is worse, sit down in a forlorn hope.

Instead of settling too comfortably in the abyss of despair, let me end this book by offering a more palatable outlook for current and future criminologists: Part of the nature of science is puzzle-solving (Kuhn 1970). As Popper (1968: 53) puts it, "the game of science, is in principle, without end." I hope that all criminologists will, at least, relish the new target provided by this work and will endeavor to design better measures to solve the intellectual puzzles. This is a challenging invitation for the newcomers, for being a positivist means to be optimistic: the eternal search for the ever-elusive causes of crime is difficult, but ultimately rewarding.

Notes

1.   Vold et al. (1998: 315) argue that the variable approach has a proper role in the scientific process because it allows "criminology to increase the explanatory power of its theories and to identify practical policy implications of theories that ultimately might reduce crime."

2.   In their general theory of crime, Hirschi and Gottfredson in effect argue that any relationship between social bonds and crime is spurious. They are the consequences of self-control (Evans et al. 1997).

3.   The Inter-University Consortium for Political and Social Research and the National Archive of Criminal Justice Data are two of the best sources with secondary data sets. The quality of data sets, however, varies quite a bit. Readers are advised to be cautious in using some of these data sets. Concerning the data gathering, there seems to be a further division in labor among scholars: those who specialize in getting grants and those are anxious in analyzing these "ready" data. The latter would be ineluctably disappointed because those who get data are more interested in money than in relevant variables or in the quality of data a serious scholar is looking for.

References

Adams, Mike S. and T. David Evans
1996   Teacher disapproval, delinquent peers, and self reported delinquency: A longitudinal test of labeling theory. *The Urban Review* 28: 199-211.

Adler, Freda, Gerhard O.W. Mueller, and William S. Laufer
1995   *Criminology*. Boston: McGraw Hill.

Agnew, Robert
1984   Goal Achievement and Delinquency. *Sociology and Social Research* 68: 435-451.
1986   The techniques of neutralization: An analysis of predisposing and situational factors. *Criminal Justice and Behavior* 13: 81-97.
1991   A longitudinal test of social control theory and delinquency. *Journal of Research in Crime and Delinquency* 28: 126-156.
1992   Foundation for a general strain theory of crime and delinquency. *Criminology* 30: 47-87.
1993   Why do they do it? An examination of the intervening mechanisms between "social control" variables and delinquency. *Journal of Research in Crime and Delinquency* 30: 245-266.
1994a   The Techniques of Neutralization and Violence. *Criminology* 32: 555-560.
1994b   Delinquency and the desire for money. *Justice Quarterly* 11: 411-427.
1999   A general strain theory of community differences in crime rates. *Journal of Research in Crime and Delinquency* 36: 123-155.

Agnew, Robert, Francis T. Cullen, Verlmer S. Burton Jr., T. David Evans, and R. Gregory Dunaway
1996   A new test of classic strain theory. *Justice Quarterly* 13: 681-704.

Agnew, Robert and Helene Raskin White
1992   An empirical test of general strain theory. *Criminology* 30: 475-499.

Akers, Ronald L.
1973   *Deviant Behavior: A Social Learning Approach*. Belmont CA: Wadsworth.
1989   A social behaviorist's perspective on integration of theories of crime and deviance. Pp. 23-36 in *Theoretical Integration in the Study of Deviance and Crime*, edited by S. F. Messner, M. D. Krohn, and A. E. Liska. Albany, NY: SUNY Press.
1992   Linking sociology and its specialties: The case of criminology. *Social Forces* (September): 1-16.
1997   *Criminological Theories: Introduction and Evaluation*. Los Angeles: Roxbury.
1998   *Social Learning and Social Structure: A General Theory of Criminal and Deviance*. Boston: Northeastern University Press.
2000   *Criminological Theories: Introduction, Evaluation, and Application*. Los Angeles: Roxbury.

Akers, Ronald L. and John K. Cochran
1985   Adolescent marijuana use: A test of three theories of deviant behavior. *Deviant Behavior* 6: 323-346.

Akers, Ronald L., Marvin D. Krohn, Lonn Lanza-Kaduce, and Marcia Radosevich

1979   Social learning and deviant behavior: A specific test of general theory. *American Sociological Review* 44: 636-655.

Akers, Ronald L., Anthony J. La Greca, John Cochran, and Christine Sellers
1989   Social learning theory and alcohol behavior among the elderly. *The Sociological Quarterly* 30: 625-638.

Allen, Mary and Wendy M. Yen
1979   *Introduction to Measurement Theory*. Monterey, CA: Brooks/Cole Publishing Company.

American Psychiatric Association Task Force on DSM-IV
2000   *Diagnostic and Statistical Manual of Mental Disorders*. 4th edition. Washington, DC: American Psychiatric Association.

Anderson, Tammy L. and Richard R. Bennett
1996   Development, gender, and crime: The scope of the routine activities approach. *Justice Quarterly* 13:31-56.

Arneklev, Bruce, J., Harold G. Grasmick, Charles R. Tittle, and Robert J. Bursik, Jr.
1993   Low self-control and imprudent behavior. *Journal of Quantitative Criminology* 9: 225-247.

Austin, Roy L.
1977   Commitment, neutralization, and delinquency. Pp. 121-137 in *Juvenile Delinquency: Little Brother Grows Up*, edited by T. N. Ferdinand. Beverly Hills, CA: Sage.

Bailey, Kenneth D.
1982   *Methods of Social Research*. 2nd edition. New York: The Free Press.

Ball, Richard A.
1966   An empirical exploration of neutralization theory. *Criminologica* 4: 22-32.

Ball-Rokeach, Sandra J.
1973   Values and violence: A test of the subculture of violence thesis. *American Sociological Review* 38:736-749.

Bandura, Albert
1977   *Social Learning Theory*. Englewood Cliffs, NJ: Prentice Hall.

Barak, Gregg
1998   *Integrating Criminologies*. Boston, MA: Allyn and Bacon.

Barkan, Steven E.
1997   *Criminology: A Sociological Understanding*. Upper Saddle River, NJ: Prentice Hall.

Baron, Stephen W., Leslie W. Kennedy, and David R. Forde
2001   Male street youths' conflict: The role of background, subcultural and situational factors. *Justice Quarterly* 18: 759-790.

Bartusch, Dawn Jeglum and Ross L. Matsueda

1996 Gender, reflected appraisal, and labeling: A cross-group test of an interactionist theory of delinquency. *Social Forces* 75: 145-176.

Bazemore, Gordon
1985 Delinquency reform and the labeling perspective. *Criminal Justice and Behavior* 12: 131-169.

Beccaria, Cesare
1776[1963] *On Crimes and Punishments* (H. Paolucci, trans.). New York: Macmillan.

Becker, Howard S.
1963 *Outsiders: Studies in the Sociology of Deviance.* New York: Free Press.

Beirne, Piers
1993 *Inventing Criminology: Essays on the Rise of "homo Criminalis."* Albany, NY: SUNY Press.

Beirne, Piers and James Messerschmidt
1991 *Criminology.* New York: Harcourt Brace Jovanovich.

Bentham, Jeremy
1789 *An Introduction to the Principles of Morals and Legislation.* London: Pickering.

Berkeley, George
1710 *A Treatise Concerning the Principles of Human Knowledge.* New York: Oxford University Press (reprinted in 1998).

Berkowitz, Leonard
1982 Violence and rule-following behavior. In *Aggression and Violence*, edited by P. Marsh and A. Campbell. Oxford: Basil Blackwell.

Bernard, Thomas J.
1987 Testing structural strain theories. *Journal of Research in Crime and Delinquency* 24: 262-280.
1989 Forward to the Fourth Edition. Pp. vvi-xi in *Theoretical Criminology* by G. B. Vold, T. J. Bernard, and J. B. Snipes. New York: Oxford University Press.
1990 Twenty years of testing theories: What have we leaned and why? *Journal of Research in Crime and Delinquency* 27: 325-347.
1995 Merton versus Hirschi: Who is faithful to Durkheim's heritage? Pp. 81-90 in *The Legacy of Anomie Theory*, edited by F. Adler and W. S. Laufer. New Brunswick: Transaction Publishers.
1998 Forward to the Fourth Edition. Pp. vvi-xi in *Theoretical Criminology* by G. B. Vold, T. J. Bernard, and J. B. Snipes. New York: Oxford University Press.

Bernard, Thomas J. and Jeffrey B. Snipes
1996 Theoretical integration in criminology. Pp. 301-348 in *Crime and Justice: A Review of Research*, edited by Michael Tonry. Chicago: University of Chicago Press.

Bernburg, Jon Gunnar and Thorolfur Thorlindsson
2001 Routine activities in social context. *Justice Quarterly* 18: 543-567.

Bianchi, Herman
1956   *Position and Subject-matter of Criminology: Inquiry Concerning Theoretical Criminology*. Amsterdam: North Holland Publishing.

Binder, A.
1988   Criminology: Discipline or an interdiscipline? *Issues in Integrative Studies* 5: 41-67.

Blalock, Hubert M., Jr.
1967   *Towards a Theory of Minority Group Relations*. Capricorn Books.
1982   *Conceptualization and Measurement in the Social Sciences*. Beverly Hills, Sage.
1989   The real and unrealized contributions of quantitative sociology. *American Sociological Review* 54: 447-460.

Blau, Peter M.
1977   *Inequality and Heterogeneity*. New York: Macmillan.

Blau, Peter M. and Judith R. Blau
1982   The cost of inequality: Metropolitan structure and violent crime. *American Sociological Review* 47:114-129.

Blumberg, Abraham S.
1981   Crime and the Social Order. In *Currently Perspectives on Criminal Behavior*, 2nd edition, edited by A. S. Blumberg. New York: Alfred A. Knopf.

Blumer, Herbert
1956   Sociological analysis and the "variable." *American Sociological Review* 21:633-660.

Bohm, Robert M.
1987   Comment on "Traditional contributions to radical criminology" by Groves and Sampson. *Journal of Research in Crime and Delinquency* 24: 324-331.
2001   *A Primer on Crime and Delinquency Theory*. 2nd Edition. Belmont, CA: Wadsworth.

Bohrnstedt, George W. and David Knoke
1988   *Statistics for Social Data Analysis*. Itasca, IL: F. E. Peacock Publishers, Inc.

Borgatta, Edgar F. and George W. Bohrnstedt
1981   Levels of measurement: Once over again. Pp. 23-37 in *Social Measurement: Current Issues*, edited by G. W. Bohrnstedt and E. F. Borgatta. Newbury Park, CA: Sage.

Braithwaite, John.
1989a   The state of criminology: Theoretical decay or renaissance. *Australian and New Zealand Journal of Criminology* (September): 129-135.
1989b   *Crime, Shame, and Reintegration*. Cambridge, UK: Cambridge University Press.

Brantingham, Paul J. and Brantigham, Patricia L. (eds.)

1981   *Environmental Criminology.* Beverly Hills, CA: Sage.

Brodbeck, May
1968   Theory construction. Pp. 457-463 in *Readings in the Philosophy of the Social Sciences*, edited by M. Brodbeck. New York: Macmillan.

Brown, Stephen E., Finn-Aage Esbensen, and Gilbert Geis
1991   *Criminology: Explaining Crime and its Context.* Cincinnati: Anderson.

Browning, Sandra Lee and Liqun Cao
1992   The impact of race on criminal justice ideology. *Justice Quarterly* 9: 685-701.

Buffalo, M. D. and Joseph W. Rodgers
1971   Behavioral norms, moral norms, and attachment: Problems of deviance and conformity. *Social Problems* 19: 101-113.

Burgess, Robert L. and Ronald L. Akers
1966   A differential association-reinforcement theory of criminal behavior. *Social Problems* 14: 128-147.

Bursik, Robert J., Jr.
1986   Ecological stability and the dynamics of delinquency. Pp. 35-66 in *Communities and Crime*, edited by A. J. Reiss, Jr., and M. Tonry. Chicago: University Chicago Press.
1988   Social disorganization and theories of crime and delinquency: Problems and prospects. *Criminology* 26: 519-551.

Bursik, Robert J., Jr. and Jim Webb.
1982   Community change and patterns of delinquency. *American Journal of Sociology* 88: 24-42.

Burton, Velmer S., Jr. and Francis T. Cullen
1992   The empirical status of strain theory. *Journal of Crime and Justice* XV (No.2): 1-30.

Burton, Velmer S., Jr., Francis T. Cullen, T. David Evans, Leanne Fiftal Alarid, and R. Gregory Dunaway
1998   Gender, self-control, and crime. *Journal of Research in Crime and Delinquency* 35: 123-147.

Burton, Velmer S., Jr., Francis T. Cullen, T. David Evans, and R. Gregory Dunaway
1994   Reconsidering strain theory: Operationalization, rival theories, and adult criminality. *Journal of Quantitative Criminology* 10: 213-239.

Burton, Velmer S., Francis T. Cullen, T. David Evans, R. Gregory Dunaway, Sesha R. Kethineni, and Gary L. Payne
1995   The impact of parental controls on delinquency. *Journal of Criminal Justice* 23: 111-126.

Cao, Liqun
2003   Reflections on integration and elaboration in theory construction. *Crime and Criminal Justice International* 1: 125-147.

1999 A test of anomie theory with cross-national data. Paper presented at 1999 Annual Meeting of American Society of Criminology, Toronto, Canada.

Cao, Liqun, Anthony Adams, and Vickie J. Jensen
1997 A test of the black subculture of violence: A research note. *Criminology* 35: 367-379.

Cao, Liqun, Francis T. Cullen, Shannon M. Barton, and Kristie R. Blevins
2002 Willingness to shoot: Public attitudes toward defensive gun use. *American Journal of Criminal Justice* 27: 85-109.

Cao, Liqun, Francis T. Cullen, and Bruce G. Link
1997 The social determinants of gun ownership: Self-protection in an urban environment. *Criminology* 35: 629-657.

Cao, Liqun and Xiaogang Deng
1998 Shoplifting: A test of an integrated model of strain, differential association, and seduction theories. *Sociology of Crime, Law, and Deviance* 1: 65-83.

Cao, Liqun, James Frank, and Francis T. Cullen
1996 Race, community context, and confidence in the police. *American Journal of Police* 15: 3-22.

Cao, Liqun and David J. Maume, Jr.
1993 Urbanization, inequality, lifestyle, and robbery: A comprehensive model. *Sociological Focus* 26: 11-26.

Caspi, Avshalom, Terrie E. Moffitt, Phil A. Silva, Magda Stouthamer-Loeber, Robert F. Krueger, and Pamela S. Schmutte
1994 Are Some People Crime-Prone? Replications of the Personality-Crime Relationship across Countries, Genders, Races, and methods. *Criminology* 32: 163-195.

Cernkovich, Stephen A.
1978 Evaluating two models of delinquency causation: Structural Theory and Control Theory. *Criminology* 16: 335-352.

Cernkovich, Stephen A. and Peggy C. Giordano
1979 Delinquency, Opportunity, and Gender. *Journal of Criminal Law and Criminology* 70: 145-151.

Chamlin, Mitchell B. and John K. Cochran
1995 Assessing Messner and Rosenfeld's institutional anomie theory: A partial test. *Criminology* 33: 411-429.

Chambliss, William J.
1964 A sociological analysis of the law of vagrancy. *Social Problems* 12: 46-47.
1973 The saints and the roughnecks. *Society* 11: 24-31.

Chambliss, William J. and Robert B. Seidman
1971 *Law, Order, and Power*. Reading, MA: Addison-Wesley.

Clarke, Ronald V.

1980   Situational crime prevention: Theory and practice. *British Journal of Criminology* 20: 136-147.

Clarke, Ronald V. and Derek B. Cornish, edited
1983   *Crime Control in Britain: A Review of Policy and Research.* Albany: SUNY Press.

Clarke, Ronald V. and Marcus Felson, edited
1993   *Routine Activity And Rational Choice.* New Brunswick: Transaction Publishers.

Cloward, Richard A.
1959   Illegitimate means, anomie, and deviant behavior. *American Sociological Review* 24: 164-176.

Cloward, Richard A. and Lloyd E. Ohlin
1960   *Delinquency and Opportunity: A Theory of Delinquent Gangs.* New York: Free Press.

Confucius
1971   *Confucian Analects: The Great Learning and the Doctrine of the Mean* (James Legge trans.). New York: Dover Publications.

Cohen, Albert K.
1955   *Delinquent Boys: The Culture of the Gang.* New York: The Free Press.
1959   The study of social disorganization and deviant behavior. Pp. 461-484 in *Sociology Today*, edited by R. K. Merton, L. Broom, and L. S. Cottrell. New York: Harper & Row.
1965   The sociology of the deviant act: Anomie theory and beyond. *American Sociological Review* 30: 5-14.

Cohen, Lawrence E. and Marcus Felson
1979   Social change and crime rate trends: A routine activity approach. *American Sociological Review* 44: 588-608.

Cole, Stephen
1975   The growth of scientific knowledge: Theories of deviance as a case study. Pp. 175-220 in *The Idea of Social Structure: Papers on Honor of Robert K. Merton*, edited by L. A. Coser. New York: Harcourt Brace Jovanovich.

Cooley, Charles
1902   *Human Nature and the Social Order.* New York: C. Scribner's Sons.

Cornish, Derek B. and Ronald V. Clarke, eds.
1986   *The Reasoning Criminal: Rational Choice Perspectives on Offending.* New York: Springer-Verlag.

Costello, Barbara J. and Paul R. Vowell
1999   Testing control theory and differential association: A reanalysis of the Richmond Youth Project data. *Criminology* 37: 815-842.

Cote, Suzette

2002   Introduction. Pp. xiii-xxiv in *Criminological Theories: Bridging the Pate to the Future*, edited by Suzette Cote. Thousand Oaks, CA: Sage.

Crawford, Charles, Ted Chiricos, and Gary Kleck
1998   Race, racial threat, and sentencing of habitual offenders. *Criminology* 36: 481-511.

Cressey, Donald R.
1960   The theory of differential association: An introduction. *Social Problems* 8: 2-6.

Cullen, Francis T.
1983   *Rethinking Crime and Deviance Theory: The emergence of a Structuring Tradition*. Totowa, NJ: Rowman & Allanheld.
1988   Were Cloward and Ohlin strain theorists?: Delinquency and opportunity revisited. *Journal of Research in Crime and Delinquency* 25: 214-41.
1994   Social support as an organizing concept for criminology: Presidential address to the Academy of Criminal Justice Sciences. *Justice Quarterly* 11:527-559.

Cullen, Francis T. and Robert Agnew
1999a   Preface. Pp. vi-vii in *Criminological Theory: Past to Present* edited by F. T. Cullen and R. Agnew. Los Angeles: Roxbury.
1999b   Biological and Psychological Theories of Crime. Pp. 1-6 in *Criminological Theory Past to Present: Essential Readings*, edited by F. T. Cullen and R. Agnew. Los Angeles: Roxbury.
1999c   Anomie/strain theories of crime. Pp. 117-122 in *Criminological Theory Past to Present: Essential Readings*, edited by F. T. Cullen and R. Agnew. Los Angeles: Roxbury.
1999d   Learning to be a criminal: Differential association, subcultural, and social learning theories. Pp. 77-81 in *Criminological Theory Past to Present: Essential Readings*, edited by F. T. Cullen and R. Agnew. Los Angeles: Roxbury.
1999e   Critical Criminology: Power, Inequality, and Crime. Pp. 295-301 in *Criminological Theory Past to Present: Essential Readings*, edited by F. T. Cullen and R. Agnew. Los Angeles: Roxbury.

Cullen, Francis T. and Jody L. Sundt
2003   Reaffirming evidence-based corrections. *Criminology & Public Policy* 2: 353-358.

Cullen, Francis T. and John Paul Wright
1997   Liberating the anomie-strain paradigm: Implications from social-support theory. Pp. 187-206 in *The Future of Anomie Theory*, edited by N. Passas and R. Agnew. Boston: Northeastern University Press.

Curran, Daniel J. and Claire M. Renzetti
1994   *Theories of Crime*. Boston: Allyn and Bacon.

Charles Darwin
1996 [1859]   *Origin of Species*. New York : Oxford University Press
1997 [1871]   *Descent of Man*. Amherst, New York: Prometheus Books.

DeFlur, Melvin and Richard Quinney

1966   A reformulation of Sutherland's differential association theory and a strategy for empirical verification. *Journal of Research in Crime and Delinquency* 2:1-22.

deGroot, Adrianus D.
1969   *Methodology: Foundations of Inference and Research in the Behavioral Sciences.* The Hague: Mouton.

Deng, Xiaogang and Lening Zhang
1998   Correlates of self-control: An empirical test of self-control theory. *Journal of Crime and Justice* 21: 89-103.

DiCristina, Bruce
1995   *Method in Criminology: A Philosophical Primer.* New York: Harrow and Heston.

Dillman, Don A.
1978   *Mail and Telephone Surveys: The Total Design Method.* New York: John Wiley and Sons.

Dixon, Jo, and Alan J. Lizotte
1987   Gun ownership and the southern subculture of violence. *American Journal of Sociology* 93:383-405.

Doerner, William G.
1978   The index of southernness revisited: The influence of where from upon whodunnit. *Criminology* 16:47-65.

Downs, William R., Joan F. Robertson, Larry R. Harrison
1997   Control theory, labeling theory, and the delivery of services for drug abuse to adolescents. *Adolescence* 32: 1-24.

Dunaway, Gregory, Francis T. Cullen, Velmer S. Burton, Jr., and T. David Evans
2000   The myth of social class and crime revisited: An examination of class and adult criminality. *Criminology* 38: 589-632.

Durkheim, Emile
1893   *The Division of Labor in Society* (G. Simpson, trans. 1933). New York: Macmillan.
1895   *The Rules of Sociological Method* (S. A. Solovay & J. H. Mueller, trans. 1938). Chicago: University of Chicago Press.
1897   *Suicide: A Study in Sociology* (J. A. Spaulding & G. Simpson, trans. 1951). Glencoe, IL: Free Press.

Edwards, Willie J.
1992   Predicting juvenile delinquency: A review of correlates and a confirmation by recent research based on an integrated theoretical model. *Justice Quarterly* 9: 553-583.

Einstadter, Werner and Stuart Henry
1995   *Criminological Theory: An Analysis of Its Underlying Assumptions.* New York: Harcourt Brace.

195

Elliott, Delbert S.
1985 The assumption that theories can be combined with increased explanatory power: Theoretical integrations. Pp. 123-149 in *Theoretical Methods in Criminology*, edited by R. F Meier. Beverly Hills, CA: Sage.

Elliott, Delbert S., Suzanne S. Ageton and Rachelle J. Canter
1979 An integrated theoretical perspective on delinquent behavior. *Journal of Research in Crime and Delinquency* 16: 3-27.

Elliott, Delbert S., David Huizinga, and Suzanne S. Ageton
1985 *Explaining Delinquency and Drug Use*. Beverly Hills, CA: Sage.

Ellis, Lee and Anthony Walsh
1997 Gene-based evolutionary theories in criminology. *Criminology* 35: 229-276.

Ellison, Christopher G.
1991 An eye for an eye? A note on the southern subculture of violence thesis. *Social Forces* 69:1223-1239.

Erickson, Kai
1962 Notes on the Sociology of Deviance. *Social Problems* 9: 394-414.

Erlanger, Howard S.
1974 The empirical status of the sub-cultures of violence thesis. *Social Problems* 22:280-292.

Evan, T. David, Francis T. Cullen, Velmer S. Burton, Jr., R. Gregory Dunaway, and Michael L. Benson
1997 The social consequences of self-control: Testing the general theory of crime. *Criminology* 35: 475-500.

Farnworth, Margaret and Michael J. Lieber
1989 Strain Theory Revisited: Economic Goals, Educational Means, and Delinquency. *American Sociological Review* 54:259-279.

Farrington, David P.
1977 The effects of public labeling. *British Journal of Criminology* 17: 112-125.

Fattah, Ezzat A.
1997 *Criminology: Past, Present and Future: A Critical Overview*. New York: Macmillan.

Felson, Richard B., Allen E. Liska, Scott J. South, and Thomas L. McNulty
1994 The subculture of violence and delinquency: Individual vs. school context effects. *Social Forces* 73:155-173.

Fishbein, Diana H.
1990 Biological Perspectives in Criminology. *Criminology* 28: 27-72.

Fitzgerald, Jack D. and Steven M. Cox
1975 *Unraveling Social Science*. Chicago: Rand McNally College Publishing Company.

Foucault, Michel
1977   *Discipline and Punish: The Birth of the Prison* (Translated by Alan Sheridan). New York: Vintage Books.

Fowles, Richard and Mary Merva
1996   Wage inequality and criminal activity: An extreme bounds analysis for the United States, 1975-1990. *Criminology* 34: 163-182.

Garland, David
1985   *Punishment and Welfare: A History of Penal Strategies*. Adershot, Hants.: Gower.

Gastil, Raymond D.
1971   Homicide and a regional culture of violence. *American Sociological Review* 36: 412-427.

Gibbons, Don C.
1994   *Talking about Crime and Criminals: Problems and Issues in Theory Development in Criminology*. Englewood Cliffs, NJ: Prentice Hall.

Gibbs, Jack P.
1975   *Crime, Punishment, and Deterrence*. New York: Elsevier
1985   The methodology of theory construction in criminology. Pp. 23-50 in *Theoretical Methods in Criminology*, edited by R. F. Meier. Beverly Hills, CA: Sage.
1987   An incorrigible positivist. *The Criminologist* 4 (No. 4): 1, 3 and 4.
1990   The notion of a theory in sociology. *National Journal of Sociology* 4: 129-158.

Gibson, Chris, Jihong Zhao, and Nicholas P. Lovrich
2002a   Sociological measurement confusion, paradigmatic imperfection, and etiological Nirvana: Striking a pragmatic balance in pursuing science. *Justice Quarterly* 19: 793-808.

Gibson, Chris L., Jihong Zhao, Nicholas P. Lovrich, and Michael J. Gaffney
2002b   Social integration, individual perceptions of collective efficacy, and fear of crime in three cities. *Justice Quarterly* 19: 537-564.

Glaser, Daniel
1956   Criminality theories and behavioral images. *American Journal of Sociology* 61: 433-444.

Goring, Charles B.
1972 [1913]   *English Convict*. Montclair, NJ: Patterson Smith.

Gottfredson, Michael and Travis Hirschi
1990   *A General Theory of Crime*. Stanford, CA: Stanford University Press.

Gottfredson, Denise C., Richard J. McNeil, III, and Bary Gottfredson
1991   Social area influences on delinquency: A multilevel analysis. *Journal of Research in Crime and Delinquency* 28: 197-226.

Greenberg, David F.
1999   The weak strength of social control theory. *Crime and Delinquency* 45: 66-81.

Greenberg, Stephanie W. and William M. Rohe
1986   Informal social control and crime prevention in modern urban neighborhoods. Pp. 79-121 in *Urban Neighborhoods: Research and Policy*, edited by R. B. Taylor. New York: Praeger.,

Groves, W. Byron and Robert J. Sampson
1987   Traditional contributions to radical criminology. *Journal of Research in Crime and Delinquency* 24: 181-214.

Guerry, A. M.
1833   *Essai sur las Statistique Morale de la France*. Paris: Crochard.

Gurwitsch, Aron
1974   *Phenomenology and the Theory of Science*. Evanston, IL: Northwestern University Press.

Guttman, Louis
1944   A basis for scaling qualitative data. *American Sociological Review* 9:139-150.

Hackler, James
1985   Criminology. In *Canadian Encyclopedia*. Edmonton: Hurtig Publications.

Hackler, James C., Kwai-Yiu Ho and Carol Urquhart-Ross
1974   The willingness to intervene: Differing community characteristics. *Social Problems* 21: 328-344.

Hackney, Sheldon
1969   Southern violence. Pp. 479-500 in *Violence in America*, edited by H. D. Graham and T. R. Gurr. New York: Signet Books.

Hage, Jerald and Barbara Foley Meeker
1988   *Social Causality*. Boston: Unwin Hyman.

Hagan, John
1989   *Structural Criminology*. Cambridge: Polity Press.

Hagan, John and Alberto Palloni
1990   The social reproduction of a criminal class in working-class London, circa 1950-1980. *American journal of Sociology* 96: 265-299.

Hamlin, John
1988   The misplaced concept of rational choice in neutralization theory. *Criminology* 26: 425-438.

Hanson, N. Russell
2002   Seeing and seeing as. Pp. 321-339 in *Philosophy of Science*, edited by Y. Balashov and A. Rosenberg. New York: Routledge.

Harries, Keith D.
1990   *Serious violence: Patterns of homicide and assault in America*. Springfield, IL: Charles C. Thomas.

Hartnagel, Timothy F.
1980   Subculture of violence: Further evidence. *Pacific Sociological Review* 23:217-242.

Hathaway, Starke R. and Paul E. Meehl
1951   *An Atlas for the Clinical Use of the MMPI.* Minneapolis: University of Minnesota Press.

Hawley, F. Frederick and Steven F. Messner
1989   The southern violence construct: A review of arguments, evidence, and the normative context. *Justice Quarterly* 6: 481-511

He, Ni
1999   *Reinventing the Wheel: Marx, Durkheim and Comparative Criminology.* Lanham, MD: Austin & Winfield, Publishers.

He, Ni, Liqun Cao, William Wells, and Edward R. Maguire
2003   Forces of production and direction: A test of an expanded model of suicide and homicide. *Homicide Studies* 7: 36-57.

Heimer, Karen
1997   Socioeconomic status, subcultural definitions, and violent delinquency. *Social Forces* 75: 799-833.

Heimer, Karen and Ross Matsueda
1994   Role-taking, role commitment, and delinquency: A theory of differential social control. *American Sociological Review* 59: 365-390.

Heitgerd, Janet L. and Robert J. Bursik, Jr.
1987   Extracommunity dynamics and the ecology of delinquency. *American Journal of Sociology* 92: 775-787.

Hempel, Carl
1966   *Philosophy of Natural Science.* Englewood Cliffs, NJ: Prentice-Hall.

Henry, Stuart and Dragan Milovanovic
1996   *Constitutive Criminology: Beyond Postmodernism.* Thousand Oaks: Sage.

Heussenstamm, F. K.
1975   Bumper stickers and the cops. Pp. 251-55 in *Examining Deviance Experimentally: Selected Readings*, edited by D. J. Steffensmeier and R. M. Terry. Port Washington, NY: Alfred.

Hilbert, Richard A.
1989   Durkheim and Merton on anomie: An unexplored contrast and its derivatives. *Social Problems* 36: 242-250.

Hindelang, Michael J.
1970   The commitment of delinquents to their misdeeds: Do delinquents drift? *Social Problems* 17: 502-509.
1973   Causes of delinquency: A partial replication and extension. *Social Problems* 20: 471-487.
1974   Moral evaluation of illegal behaviors. *Social Problems* 21: 370-385.

Hindelang, Michael J., Michael R. Gottfredson, and James Garofalo
1978   *Victims of Personal Crime*. Cambridge, MA: Ballinger.

Hirschi, Travis
1969   *Causes of Delinquency*. Berkeley: University of California Press.
1979   Separate and unequal is better. *Journal of Research in Crime and Delinquency*
        16: 34-38.
1989   Exploring alternatives to integrated theory. Pp. 37-49 in *Theoretical Integration*
        in the Study of Deviance and Crime, edited by S. F. Messner, M. D. Krohn, and
        A. E. Liska. Albany, NY: SUNY Press.

Holman, John E. and James F. Quinn
1992   *Criminology: Applying Theory*. St. Paul: West Publishing Company.

Holmes, Malcolm D.
2000   Minority threat and police brutality: Determinants' of civil rights criminal
        complaints in U.S. municipalities. *Criminology* 38: 343-367.

Hume, David
1748 [1955]   *An Inquiry Concerning Human Understanding*. New York: Bobbs-
                   Merrill.

Jackson, Pamela I.
1986   Black visibility, city size and social control. *Sociological Quarterly* 27: 185-
        203.
1989   *Minority Group Threat, Crime, and Policing*. New York: Praeger.

Jackson, Pamela I. and Leo Carroll.
1981   Race and war on crime: The sociopolitical determinants of municipal police
        expenditures. *American Sociological Review* 46: 290-305.

Jackson, Elton, Charles R. Tittle, and Mary Jean Burke
1986   Offense-specific models of the differential association process. *Social*
        Problems 33: 335-356.

Jacobs, David
1979   Inequality and police strength: Conflict theory and coercive control in
        metropolitan area. *American Sociological Review* 44: 913-925

Jacobs, David and David Britt
1979   Inequality and police use of deadly force: An empirical assessment of a conflict
        hypothesis. *Social Problems* 26: 403-412.

Jacobs, David and Ronald E. Helms
1997   Testing coercive explanations for order: The determinants of law enforcement
        strength over time. *Social Forces* 75: 1361-1392.

Jacobs, David and Robert M. O'Brien
1998   The determinants of deadly force: A structural analysis of police violence.
        American Journal of Sociology 103: 837-862.

Jeffery, C. Ray

1965 Criminal behavior and learning theory. *Journal of Criminal Law, Criminology and Police Science* 56: 294-300.

1990 *Criminology: An Interdisciplinary Approach.* Englewood Cliffs, NJ: Prentice Hall.

Jensen, Gary F. and David Brownfield
1986 Gender, lifestyle, and victimization: Beyond routine activity. *Violence and Victims* 2: 85-99.

Jensen, Gary F., Maynard L. Erickson, and Jack P. Gibbs
1978 Perceived risk of punishment and self-reported delinquency. *Social Forces* 57: 57-78.

Johnson, Richard E., Anastasios C. Marcos, and Stephen J. Bahr
1987 The role of peers in the complex etiology of adolescent drug use. *Criminology* 25: 323-339.

Junger, Marianne and Ineke Haen Marshall
1997 The interethnic generalizability of social control theory: An empirical test. *Journal of Research in Crime and Delinquency* 34: 79-112.

Kane, Robert J.
2003 Social control in the metropolis: A community-level examination of the minority group-threat hypothesis. *Justice Quarterly* 20: 265-295.

Kaplan, Abraham
1964 *The Conduct of Inquiry.* San Francisco: Chandler Publishing Company.
1968 Measurement in behavioral science. Pp. 601-608 in *Readings in the Philosophy of the Social Sciences*, edited by M. Brodbeck. New York: Macmillan.

Kaplan, Howard B. and Robert J. Johnson
1991 Negative social sanctions and juvenile delinquency: Effects of labeling in a model of deviant behavior. *Social Science Quarterly* 72: 98-122.

Katz, Jack
1988 *Seduction of Crime: Moral and Sensual Attraction in Doing Evil.* New York: Basic Books.

Kempf, Kimberly L.
1993 The empirical status of Hirschi's control theory. Pp. 143-185 in *Advances in Criminological Theory*, edited by F. Adler and W. S. Laufer. New Brunswick, NJ: Transaction.

Kennedy, Leslie W. and David R. Forde
1995 *Self-control, Risky Lifestyles, Routine Conflict and Crime: A Respecification of the General Theory of Crime.* Edmonton: University of Alberta, Center for Criminological Research.

Klepper, Steven and Daniel Nagin
1989 The deterrence effect of perceived certainty and severity of punishment revisited. *Criminology* 27: 721-746.

Knepper, Paul

2001   *Explaining Criminal Conduct: Theories and Systems in Criminology*. Durham, NC: Carolina Academic Press.

Kornhauser, Ruth R.
1978   *Social Sources of Delinquency*. Chicago: University of Chicago Press.

Kovandzic, Tomislav V., Lynne M Vieraitis, and Mark R. Yeisley
1998   The structural covariates of urban homicide: Reassessing the impact of income inequality and poverty in the post-Reagan era. *Criminology* 36: 569-599.

Krohn, Marvin D. and James L. Massey
1980   Social control and delinquency behavior: An examination of the elements of the social bond. *Sociological Quarterly* 21: 529-543

Kuhn, Thomas S.
1970   *The Structure of Scientific Revolutions*. Chicago: The University of Chicago Press.
1978   *The Essential Tension*. Chicago: University of Chicago Press.

Labovitz, Sanford
1970   The assignment of numbers to rank order categories. *American Sociological Review* 35: 515-24.

LaGrange, Randy L. and Helene Raskin White
1985   Age differences in delinquency: A test of theory. *Criminology* 23: 19-45.

Lander, Bernard
1954   *Towards an Understanding of Juvenile Delinquency*. New York: Columbia University Press.

Laudan, Larry and Jarrett Leplin
1991   Empirical equivalence and undetermination. *Journal of Philosophy* 88: 449-472.

Leavitt, Glen
1999   Criminological theory as an art form: Implications for criminal justice policy. *Crime and Delinquency* 45 (3): 389-399.

Lemert, Edwin M.
1951   *Social Pathology*. New York: McGraw-Hill

Lewis, Dan A. and Greta Salem
1986   *Fear of Crime: Incivility and the Production of a Social Problem*. New Brunswick, NJ: Transaction.

Liazos, Alexander
1972   The poverty of the sociology of deviance: Nuts, sluts, and perverts. *Social Problems* 20: 103-120.

Lilly, J. Robert, Francis T. Cullen, and Richard A. Ball
1995   *Criminological Theory: Context and Consequences*. Thousand Oaks, CA: Sage.

Liska, Allen E., Mitchell B. Chamlin, and Mark D. Reed

1985 Testing the economic production and conflict models of crime control. *Social Forces* 64: 119-138

Liska, Allen E., Marvin D. Krohn and Steven E. Messner
1989 Strategies and requisites for theoretical integration in the study of crime and deviance. Pp. 1-20 in *Theoretical Integration in the Study of Deviance and Crime*, edited by S. F. Messner, M. D. Krohn, and A. E. Liska. Albany, NY: SUNY Press.

Liska, Allen E. and Jiang Yu
1992 Specifying and testing the threat hypothesis: Police use of deadly force. Pp. 53-68 in *Social Threat and Social Control*, edited by A. E. Liska. Albany, NY: SUNY Press.

Link, Bruce G., Francis T. Cullen, Elmer Struening, Patrick E. Shrout, and Bruce P. Dohrenwend
1989 A modified labeling theory approach to mental disorders: An empirical assessment. *American Sociological Review* 54: 400-423.

Logan, Charles
1977 Statistical artifacts in deterrence research. Pp. 64-83, in *Quantitative Studies in Criminology*, edited by Charles Wellford. Beverly Hills, CA: Sage.

Lombroso, Cesare
1876 *L'uomo delinquente (Criminal Man)*. Milan: Hoepli.

Longshore, Douglas, Susan Turner, and Judith A. Stein
1996 Self-control in a criminal sample: An examination of construct validity. *Criminology* 34: 209-228.

Lutz, Gene M.
1983 *Understanding Social Statistics*. New York: Macmillan.

Lynch, Michael J., Byron W. Groves and Alan Lizotte
1994 The rate of surplus value and crime: A theoretical and empirical examination of Marxian economic theory and criminology. *Crime, Law and Social Change* 21: 15-48.

Marcos, Anastasios C., Stephen J. Bahr, and Richard E. Johnson
1986 Test of a bonding/association theory of adolescent drug use. *Social Forces* 65: 135-161.

Markowitz, Fred E., Paul E. Bellair, Allen E. Liska, and Jianhong Liu
2001 Extending social disorganization theory: Modeling the relationships between cohesion, disorder, and fear. *Criminology* 39: 293-320.

Martin, Randy, Robert J. Mutchnick, and W. Timothy Austin
1990 *Criminological Thought: Pioneers Past and Present*. New York: Macmillan.

Martinson, Robert
1974 What works? Questions and answers about prison reform. *Public Interest* 35: 22-54.

Marx, Karl
1982 [1847]   *The Poverty of Philosophy*. New York: International Publishers.
1933   Wage labor capital. In *Selected Works*. Vol. I. New York: International
           Publishers.

Matsueda, Ross L.
1982   Testing control theory and differential association: A causal modeling
           approach. *American Sociological Review* 47: 489-504.
1988   The current state of differential association theory. *Crime and Delinquency* 34:
           277-306.
1989   The dynamics of moral beliefs and minor deviance. *Social Forces* 68: 428-457.
1992   Reflected appraisals, parental labeling, and delinquency: Specifying a symbolic
           interactionist theory. *American Journal of Sociology* 97: 1577-1611.

Matsueda, Ross L. and Karen Heimer
1987   Race, family structure, and delinquency: A test of and differential association
           and social control theories. *American Sociological Review* 52: 826-840.

Matza, David
1964   *Delinquency and Drift*. New York: Wiley.

Maume, David, Jr.
1989   Inequality and metropolitan rape rates: A routine activity approach. *Justice
           Quarterly* 6: 513-527.

Mawby, Rob and Sandra Walklate
1994   *Critical Victimology: International Perspectives*. London: Sage.

Mazerolle, Paul and Jeff Maahs
2000   General Strain and delinquency: An alternative examination of conditioning
           influences. *Justice Quarterly* 17: 753-778.

McCarthy, Bill
1996   The attitudes and actions of others: Tutelage and Sutherland's theory of
           differential association. *British Journal of Criminology* 36: 135-147.

McClosky, Herbert and John H. Schaar
1965   Psychological dimensions of anomy. *American Sociological Review* 30: 14-40.

McGarrell, Edmund F.
1993   Institutional theory and the stability of a conflict model of the incarceration rate.
           Justice Quarterly 10: 7-28.

Mead, George Herbert
1918   The Psychology of punitive justice. *American Journal of Sociology* 23: 577-
           602.

Menard, Scott
1995   A developmental test of Mertonian anomie theory. *Journal of Research in
           Crime and delinquency* 32: 136-174.
1997   A developmental test of Cloward's differential-opportunity theory. Pp. 142-186
           in *The Future of Anomie Theory*, edited by N. Passas and R. Agnew. Boston:
           Northeastern University Press.

Merton, Robert
1938   Social structure and anomie. *American Sociological Review* 3: 672-682.
1957   *Social Theory and Social Structure*. Glencoe, IL: Free Press.
1964   Anomie, anomia, and social interaction: Contexts of deviant behavior. Pp. 213-242 in *Anomie and Deviant Behavior: A Discussion and Critique*, edited by M. B. Clinard. New York: Free Press.
1968a   The bearing of sociological theory on empirical research. Pp. 465-481 in *Readings in the Philosophy of the Social Sciences*, edited by May Brodbeck. London: The Macmillan Company.
1968b   The bearing of empirical research on sociological theory. Pp. 481-496 in *Readings in the Philosophy of the Social Sciences*, edited by M. Brodbeck. London: Macmillan.
1968c   *Social Theory and Social Structure*. New York: The Free Press.
1997a   On the evolving synthesis of differential association and anomie theory. *Criminology* 35: 517-525.
1997b   Forward. Pp. ix-xii in *The Future of Anomie Theory*, edited by N. Passas and R. Agnew. Boston: Northeastern University Press.

Messner, Steven F.
1983   Regional and racial effects on the urban homicide rate: The subculture of violence revisited. *American Journal of Sociology* 88:997-1007.
1988   Merton's "Social Structure and Anomie": The road not taken. *Deviant Behavior* 9: 33-53.
1989   Economic discrimination and societal homicide rates: Further evidence on the cost of inequality. *American Sociological Review* 54: 597-611.

Messner, Steven and Judith Blau
1987   Routine leisure activities and rates of crime: A macro-level analysis. *Social Forces* 65:1035-1052.

Messner, Steven F. and Reid M. Golden
1992   Racial inequality and racially disaggregated homicide rates: An assessment of alternative theoretical explanations. *Criminology* 30: 421-445.

Messner, Steven F., Marvin D. Krohn, and Allen E. Liska
1989   Prospects for synthetic theory: A consideration of macro-level criminological activity. Pp. 161-178 in *Theoretical Integration in the Study of Deviance and Crime*, edited by S. F. Messner, M. D. Krohn, and A. E. Liska. Albany, NY: SUNY Press.

Messner, Steven F. and Richard Rosenfeld
1994   *Crime and the American Dream*. Belmont, CA: Wadsworth.
1997   Political restraint of the market and levels of criminal homicide: A cross-national application of institutional-anomie theory. *Social Forces* 75: 1393-1416.

Miethe, Terance D. and Robert Meier
1994   *Crime, and Its Social Context: Toward an Integrated Theory of Offenders, Victims, and Situations*. Albany, NY: SUNY Press.

Miller, Susan L. and Lee Ann Iovanni

1994   Determinants of perceived risk of formal sanction for courtship violence. *Justice Quarterly* 11: 281-312.

Minor, W. William
1981   Techniques of neutralization: A reconceptualization and empirical examination. *Journal of Research in Crime and Delinquency* 18: 295-318.
1984   Neutralization as a hardening process: Considerations in the modeling of change. *Social Forces* 62: 995-1019.

Montesquieu, Charles de Secondat, Baron de
1748   *The Spirit of Laws*, translated by T. Nugent in 1873. Cincinnati, Clarke.

Morris, Albert
1975   The American Society of Criminology: A history, 1941-1974. *Criminology* 13:123-167.

Nagin, Daniel S. and Raymond Paternoster
1994   Personal capital and social control: The deterrence implications of a theory of individual differences in criminal offending. *Criminology* 32: 581-606.

Nelsen, Candice, Jay Corzine, and Lin Huff-Corzine
1994   The violent west reexamined: A research note on regional homicide rates. *Criminology* 32: 149-161.

Nettler, Gwynne
1984a   *Killing One Another*. Cincinnati: Anderson.
1984b   *Explaining Crime*. 3rd edition. New York: McGraw-Hill.

Nisbett, Richard E. and Dov Cohen
1996   *Culture of Honor: The Psychology of Violence in the South*. Boulder: CO: Westview Press.

Nunnally, Jum C.
1978   *Psychometric Theory*. New York: McGraw-Hill.

Nye, Ivan F.
1958   *Family Relationships and Delinquent Behavior*. New York: Wiley.

O'Brien, Robert
1985   *Crime and Victimization Data*. Beverly Hills, CA: Sage.

Osgood, D. Wayne and Jeff M. Chambers
2000   Social disorganization outside the metropolis: An analysis of rural youth violence. *Criminology* 38: 81-115.

Osgood, D. Wayne, Janet K. Wilson, Patrick M. O'Malley, Jerald G. Bachman, and Lloyd D. Johnston
1996   Routine activities and individual deviant behavior. *American Sociological Review* 61: 635-655.

Palamara, Frances, Francis T. Cullen, and Joanne C. Gersten

1986   The effects of police and mental health intervention on juvenile deviance: Specifying contingencies in the impact of formal reaction. *Journal of Health and Social Behavior* 27: 90-106

Papandreous, Andreas George
1958   *Economics as a Science*. Philadelphia: Lippincott.

Park, Robert E. K., Earnest W. Burgess, and Roderick D. McKenzie
1928   *The City*. Chicago: University of Chicago Press.

Parker, Robert Nash
1989   Poverty, subculture of violence, and type of homicide. *Social Forces* 67:983-1007.

Passas, Nikos
1995   Continuities in the anomie tradition. Pp. 91-112 in *The Legacy of Anomie Theory*, edited by F. Adler and W. S. Laufer. New Brunswich, NJ: Transaction Publishers.

Paternoster, Raymond, Linda E. Saltzman, Gordon P. Waldo, and Theodore G. Chiricos
1983   Perceived risk and social control: Do sanctions really deter? *Law and Society Review* 17: 457-480.

Pawson, Ray
1989   *A Measure for Measures: A Manifesto for Empirical Sociology*. New York: Routledge.

Pearson, Frank S. and Neil Alan Weiner
1985   Toward an integration of criminological theories. *The Journal of Criminal Law and Criminology* 76: 116-150.

Pedhazur, Elazar J. and Liora Pedhazur Schmelkin
1991   *Measurement, Design, and Analysis: An Integrated Approach*. Hillsdele, NJ: Lawrence Erlbaum Associates, Publishers.

Pfohl, Stephen J.
1977   The "discovery of child abuse." *Social Problems* 24: 310-323.
1985   *Images of Deviance & Social Control: A Sociological History*. New York: McGraw-Hill.

Philips, Bernard S.
1976   *Social Research: Strategy and Tactics*, 3rd edition. New York: Macmillan.

Piliavin, Irving and Scott Briar
1964   Police encounters with juveniles. *American Journal of Sociology* 70: 206-214.

Plant, James, S.
1937   *Personality and the Cultural Pattern*. London: Oxford University Press.

Platt, Anthony M.
1975   Prospects for a radical criminology in the U.S.A. Pp.95-112 in *Critical Criminology*, edited by I. Taylor, P. Walton, and J Young. London: Routledge & Kegan.

Popper, Karl R.
1945   *The Open Society and its Enemies*. London: Routledge.
1962   *Conjectures and Refutations: The Growth of Scientific Knowledge*. New York: Basic Books.
1968 [1935]   *The Logic of Scientific Discovery*. New York: Harper & Row.
1972   *Objective Knowledge: An Evolutionary Approach*. Oxford: Clarendon Press.

Quetelet, L. Adolphe
1831   *Research on the Propensity for Crime at Different Ages*. Translated by Sawyer Sylvester (1984). Cincinnati: Anderson.
1835   *Physique Sociale: Ou, Essai sur le Developpement des Faculties de L'Homme*. 2 Vols. Brussels: Muquardt.
1842   *A Treatise on Man*. Translated by R. Knox and T. Smibert. Edinburgh: Chambers.

Quinney, Richard
1970   *The Social Reality of Crime*. Boston: Little, Brown.

Radzinowicz, Leon
1966   *Ideology and Crime*. London: Heinemann.

Rafter, Nicole Hahn
1992   Criminal Anthropology in the United States. *Criminology* 30: 525-545.
1997   Psychopathy and the evolution of criminological knowledge. *Theoretical Criminology* 1: 235-259.

Ray, Melvin C. and William R. Downs
1986   An empirical test of labeling theory using longitudinal data. *Journal of Research in Crime and Delinquency* 23: 169-194.

Reckless, Walter C.
1961   A new theory of delinquency and crime. *Federal Probation* 25: 42-46.

Regoli, Robert M. and Eric D. Poole
1978   The commitment of delinquents to their misdeeds: A re-examination. *Journal of Criminal Justice* 6: 261-268.

Reiss, Albert J., Jr.
1951   Delinquency as the failure of personal and social controls. *American Sociological Review* 16: 196-207.

Ridley, Brian K.
2001   *On Science*. London: Routledge.

Rock, Paul
1997   Foreword. Pp. xi-xii in *Criminology: Past, Present and Future* by E. A. Fattah. New York: St. Martin's Press, Inc.

Rogers, Joseph W. and M.D. Buffalo
1974   Neutralization techniques: Toward a simplified measurement scale. *Pacific Sociological Review* 17: 313-331.

Rose, Dina R. and Todd R. Clear
1998   Incarceration, social capital, and crime: Implications for social disorganization theory. *Criminology* 36: 441-479.

Ross, Lawrence H.
1982   *Deterring the Drinking Driver: Legal Policy and Social Control.* Lexington, MA: Lexington Books.

Rousseau, Jean-Jacques
1767   *The Social Contract*, translated by W. Kendall in 1954. Chicago : H. Regnery,

Rowe, David C.
2002   *Biology and Crime.* Los Angeles, CA: Roxbury.

Sacco, Vincent F. and Leslie W. Kennedy
1996   *The Criminal Event: An Introduction to Criminology.* Belmont, CA: Wadsworth.

Sainsbury, Peter
1956   *Suicide in London.* New York: Basic Books.

Sampson, Robert J.
1986   Effects of socioeconomic context on official reaction to juvenile delinquency. *American Sociological Review* 51: 876-885.
1987   Urban black violence: The effect of male joblessness and family disruption. *American Journal of Sociology* 93:348-382.
1999   Techniques of research neutralization. *Theoretical Criminology* 3: 438-450.

Sampson, Robert J. and Dawn Jeglum Bartusch
1998   Legal cynicism and (subcultural?) tolerance of deviance: The neighborhood context of racial differences. *Law & Society Review* 32: 777-804.

Sampson, Robert J. and W. Byron Groves
1989   Community structure and crime: Testing social-disorganization theory. *American Journal of Sociology* 94: 774-802.

Sampson, Robert J. and John H. Laub
1993   *Crime in the Making: Pathways and Turning Points Through Life.* Cambridge, MA: Harvard University Press.

Sampson, Robert J., Stephen W. Raudenbush, and Felton Earls
1997   Neighborhoods and violent crime: A multilevel study of collective efficacy. *Science* 277 (August 15): 918-924.

Schmid, Calvin S.
1928   *Suicides in Seattle, 1914 to 1928.* Seattle: University of Washington Press.

Scheff, Thomas J.
1974   The labeling theory of mental illness. *American Sociological Review* 39: 444-452.

Schneider, Joseph
1978   Deviant drinking as disease: Alcoholism as a social accomplishment. *Social Problems* 25: 361-372.

Schur, Edwin M.
1971   *Labeling Deviant Behavior.* Yew York: Harper and Row.

Schwartz, Martin D., Walter S. DeKeseredy, David Tait, and Shahid Alvi
2001   Male peer support and a feminist routine activities theory. *Justice Quarterly* 18: 623-649.

Seeman, Melvin
1959   On the meaning of alienation. *American Sociological Review* 24: 783-791.

Segrave, Jeffrey O. and Douglas N. Halstad
1983   Evaluating Structural and Control Models of Delinquency Causation: A Replication. *Youth and Society* 14: 437-456.

Sellin, Thorsten
1938   *Culture Conflict and Crime.* New York: Social Science Research Council.

Shaw, Clifford R. and Henry D. McKay
1942   *Juvenile Delinquency in Urban Areas.* Chicago: University of Chicago Press.

Sheley, Joseph F.
2000   *Criminology: A Contemporary Handbook.* 3rd edition. Belmont, CA: Wadsworth.

Sherman, Lawrence W., Patrick R. Gartin, and Michael D. Buerger
1989.   Hot spots of predatory crime: Routine activities and the criminology of place. *Criminology* 27: 27-55.

Shoemaker, Donald J.
1984   *Theories of Delinquency: An Examination of Explanations of Delinquent Behavior.* New York: Oxford University Press.
1996   *Theories of Delinquency: An Examination of Explanations of Delinquent Behavior.* 3rd edition. New York: Oxford University Press.

Shoemaker, Donald J. and J. Sherwood Williams
1987   The subculture of violence and ethnicity. *Journal of Criminal Justice* 15: 461-472

Shoham, S. Giora and Mark C. Seis
1993   *A Primer in the Psychology of Crime.* New York: Harrow and Heston Publishers.

Short, James F.
1979   On the etiology of delinquent behavior. *Journal of Research in Crime and Delinquency* 16: 28-33.

Short, James F. Jr, Ramon Rivera, and Ray A. Tennyson
1965   Perceived opportunities, gang membership, and delinquency. *American Sociological Review* 30: 56-67.

Siegel, Larry
2001   *Criminology.* 7th edition. Belmont, CA: Wadsworth.

Simcha-Fagan, Ora and Joseph E. Schwartz
1986   Neighborhood and delinquency: An assessment of contextual effects. *Criminology* 24: 667-704.

Simmons, Jerry L.
1969   *Deviants.* San Francisco: Boyd & Franser.

Sinclair, Andrew
1964   *Era of Excess: A Social History of the Prohibition Movement.* New York: Harper & Row.

Singleton, Royce A. Jr. and Bruce C. Straits
1999   *Approaches to Social Research.* 3rd edition. New York: Oxford University Press.

Skogan, Wesley G.
1987   *Disorder and Community Decline.* Evanston, Ill.: Center for Urban Affairs and Policy Research, Northwest University.

Smith, Douglas A. and Raymond Paternoster
1990   Formal processing and future delinquency: Deviance amplification as selection artifact. *Law and Society Review* 24: 1109-1131.

Sorensen, Jonathan R., James W. Marquart, and Deon E. Brock
1993   Factors related to killings of felons by police officers: A test of the community violence and conflict hypotheses. *Justice Quarterly* 10: 417-440.

Srole, Leo J.
1956   Social integration and certain corollaries: An exploratory study. *American Sociological Review* 21: 709-716.

Stack, Steven
1984   The effect of income inequality on property crime: A cross-national analysis of relative deprivation theory. *Criminology* 22: 229-257.

Stahura, John M. and John J. Sloan
1988   Urban stratification of places, routine activities, and suburban crime rates. *Social Forces* 66: 1102-1118

Stevens, Stanley S.
1968   Measurement, statistics, and the schemapiric view. *Science* 161: 849-856.
1975   *Psychophysics: Introduction to its Perceptual, Neural, and Social Prospects.* New York: Wiley.

Stitt, B. Grant and David J. Giacopassi
1992   Trends in the connectivity of theory and research in criminology. *The Criminologist* 17:1, 3-6.

Sutherland, Edwin H.
1939   *Principles of Criminology.* 3rd edition. Philadelphia: Lippincott.
1947   *Principles of Criminology.* 4th edition. Philadelphia: Lippincott.

211

Sykes, Gresham M.
1956   *Crime and Society*. New York: Random House.

Sykes, Gresham M. and Francis T. Cullen
1992   *Criminology*. 2nd edition. New York: Harcourt Brace Jovanovich.

Sykes, Gresham M. and David Matza
1957   Techniques of neutralization: A theory of delinquency. *American Sociological Review* 22: 664-670.

Tannenbaum, Frank
1938   *Crime and the Community*. Boston: Ginn.

Tarde, Gabriel
1903 [1890].   *G. Tarde's Laws of Imitation*. Translated by E. Parsons. New York: Henry Holt.

Taylor, Ralph B.
1988   *Human Territorial Functioning*. Cambridge, Cambridge University Press.

Thornberry, Terrence P.
1987   Toward an interactional theory of delinquency. *Criminology* 25: 863-92.
1989   Reflections on the advantages and disadvantages of theoretical integration. Pp. 51-50 in *Theoretical Integration in the Study of Deviance and Crime*, edited by S. F. Messner, M. D. Krohn, and A. E. Liska. Albany, NY: SUNY Press.

Thornberry, Terrence, P., Alan J. Lizotte, Marvin D. Krohn, Margaret Farnworth, and Sung Joon Jang
1994   Delinquent peers, beliefs, and delinquent behavior: A longitudinal test of interactional theory. *Criminology* 32: 47-83.

Thurman, Quint C.
1984   Deviance and the neutralization of moral commitment: An empirical analysis. *Deviant Behavior* 5: 291-304.
1991   Taxpayer noncompliance and general prevention: An expansion of the deterrence model. *Public Finance* XXXXVI: 289-298.

Tierney, Kathleen J.
1982   The battered women movement and the creation of the wife beating problem. *Social Problems* 29: 207-220.

Tittle, Charles R.
1980   *Sanctions and Social Deviance*. New York: Praeger.
1985   The assumption that general theories are not possible. Pp. 93-121 in *Theoretical Methods in Criminology*, edited by R. F. Meier, Beverly Hills: Sage.
1989   Urbanness and unconventional behavior: A partial test of Claude Fischer's subcultural theory. *Criminology* 27: 273-306.
1995   *Control Balance: Toward a General Theory of Deviance*. Boulder, CO: Westview Press.
2000   *Social Deviance and Crime: An Organizational and Theoretical Approach*. Los Angeles: Roxbury.

Tittle, Charles R., Mary Jean Burke, and Elton Jackson
1986   Modeling Sutherland's theory of differential association: Toward an empirical clarification. *Social Forces* 65: 405-432.

Triplett, Ruth and Roger Jarjoura
1994   Theoretical and empirical specification of a model of informal labeling. *Journal of Quantitative Criminology* 10: 241-276.

Turk, Austin T.
1969   *Criminality and the Legal Order.* Chicago: Rand-McNally.

Turner, Michael G. and Alex R. Piquero
2002   The stability of self-control. *Journal of Criminal Justice* 30: 457-471.

Unnithan, N. Prabha, Lin Huff-Corzine, Jay Corzine, and Hugh P. Whitt
1994   *The Currents of Lethal Violence.* Albany, NY: SUNY Press.

Van den Haag, Ernest.
1991   *Punishing Criminals: Concerning A Very Old and Painful Question.* Lanham, MD: University Press of America.

Veysey, Bonita M. and Steven F. Messner
1999   Further testing of social disorganization theory: An elaboration of Sampson and Groves's "community structure and crime." *Journal of Research in Crime and Delinquency* 36: 156-174.

Vold, George B.
1958   *Theoretical Criminology.* New York: Oxford University Press.

Vold, George B. and Thomas J. Bernard
1986   *Theoretical Criminology.* New York: Oxford University Press.

Vold, George, B., Thomas J. Bernard, and Jeffrey B. Snipes
1998   *Theoretical Criminology.* 4th edition. New York: Oxford University Press.

von Hayek, Friedrich August
1989   The pretence of knowledge. *The American Economic Review* 79: 3-7.

Wallace, Walter
1971   *The Logic of Science in Sociology.* Chicago: Aldine/Atherton.

Ward, David A. and Charles R. Tittle
1993   Deterrence or labeling: The effects of informal sanctions. *Deviant Behavior* 14: 43-64

Warner, Barbara D.
2003   The role of attenuated culture in social disorganization theory. *Criminology* 41: 73-97.

Warner, Barbara D. and Glenn L. Pierce
1993   Reexamining social disorganization theory using calls to the police as a measure of crime. *Criminology* 31: 493-518.

Warr, Mark and Mark Stafford
1991   The influence of delinquent peers: What they think and what they do? *Criminology* 29: 851-866.

Wasserman, David and Robert Wachbroit, eds.
2001   *Genetics and Criminal Behavior*. Cambridge, UK: Cambridge University Press.

Weber, Max
1968   "Objectivity" in social science. Pp. 85-97 in *Readings in the Philosophy of the Social Sciences*, edited by M. Brodbeck. New York: Macmillan

Whorf, Benjamin L.
1956   *Language, Thought, and Reality*. New York: Wiley.

Whyte, Willim F.
1943   *Street Corner Society: The Social Structure of an Italian Slum*. Chicago: University of Chicago Press.

Wiatrowski, Michael D. and Kristine L. Anderson
1987   The Dimensionality of the Social Bond. *Journal of Quantitative Criminology* 25: 715-740.

Wiatrowski, Michael D., David B. Griswold, and Mary K. Roberts
1981   Social control Theory and Delinquency. *American Sociological Review* 46: 525-541.

Williams, Kirk R. and Robert L. Flewelling
1988   The social production of criminal homicide: A comparative study of disaggregated rates in American cities. *American Sociological Review* 53: 421-431.

Williams, Frank and Marilyn D. McShane
1999   *Criminological Theory*. 3rd edition. Upper Saddle River, NJ: Prentice-Hall.

Wilkins, Leslie
1964   *Social Deviance: Social Policy, Action, and Research*. Englewood Cliffs, NJ: Prentice Hall.

Wilson, Edward O.
1998   *Consilience*. New York: Knopf.

Wilson, Thomas P.
1971   Critique of ordinal variables. *Social Forces* 49: 432-444.

Wilson, William J.
1996   *When Work Disappears: The World of the New Urban Poor*. New York: Random House.

Winfree, L. Thomas, Jr. and Howard Abadinsky
1996   *Understanding Crime: Theory and Practice*. Chicago: Nelson-Hall Publishers.

Winfree, L. Thomas, Jr., G. Larry Mays, and Teresa Vigil-Backstrom

1994 Youth gangs and incarcerated delinquents: Exploring the ties between gang membership, delinquency, and social learning theory. *Justice Quarterly* 11: 229-256.

Wolfgang, Marvin E.
1958 *Patterns of Criminal Homicide*. Philadelphia: University of Pennsylvania Press.
1973 Cesare Lombroso (1835-1909). Pp. 232-291 in *Pioneers in Criminology*, edited by H. Mannheim. Montclair, NJ: Patterson Smith.

Wolfgang, Marvin E. and Franco Ferracuti
1967 *The Subculture of Violence: Towards an Integrated Theory in Criminology*. New York: Tavistock.

Wood, Peter B., Betty Pfefferbaum, and Bruce J. Arneklev
1993 Risk-taking and self-control: Social psychological correlates of delinquency. *Journal of Crime and Justice* 16: 111-130.

Wooldrege, John D, Francis T. Cullen, and Edward J. Latessa
1992 Victimization in the workplace: A test of routine activities theory. *Justice Quarterly* 9: 325-335.

Wright, Richard A.
1993a *In Defense of Prisons*. Westport, CT: Greenwood Press.
1993b A socially sensitive criminal justice system. Pp. 141-160 in *Open Institutions: The Hope for Democracy*, edited by J. W. Murphy and D. L. Peck. Westport, CN: Greenwood Press.

Yocholson, Samuel and Stanton E. Samenow
1976 *Criminal Personality*. New York: Jason Aronson.

Zhang, Jinpan, Zhong Lin, Yong Zhu, et al. edited.
1995 *History of Law in China* (in Chinese). Beijing: Law Publisher.

Zhang, Lening
2003 Official offense status and self-esteem among Chinese youths. *Journal of Criminal Justice* 31: 99-105.

Ziman, John
2000 *Real Science: What it is, and what it means*. New York: Cambridge University Press.

Zimring, Franklin and Gordon Hawkins
1973 *Deterrence*. Chicago: University of Chicago Press.

Name Index

Subject Index